Fictions of Financialization

T0281871

'Incisive, politically engaged, and theoretically sophisticated, *Fictions of Financialization* is a major critical contribution to debates on financialization. Bernards sets the record straight and makes a powerful case for recentring the exploitation of labour and nature in analyses of the powers of finance in contemporary capitalism. A must-read for anyone concerned with the prospects of a liveable and sustainable future for all on this planet.'
—Ilias Alami, author of *Money Power and Financial Capital in Emerging Markets*

'Nick Bernards provides a comprehensive critique of the financialization discourse, offering vital insights about finance's relationship to production, the state, colonialism, and nature. This is an urgently important intervention on the financial dimensions of capitalist social domination.'
—Jack Copley, author of *Governing Financialization: The Tangled Politics of Financial Liberalization in Britain*

'Bernards' powerful critique of the dogmatic fiction that the power of finance is crowding out "real" capital is a much-needed intervention into the financialization literature and the misconception that definancialization or the democratization of finance are viable pathways for an anti-capitalist future.'
—Angela Wigger, Associate Professor Global Political Economy, Radboud University

'Whoever wants to critique global finance must directly confront capitalism first! With an accessible yet academically rigorous style, Bernards shows that the dizzying complexity of modern financial markets must be grounded in capitalism's ecocidal and crisis-prone motion. He compellingly shows the limits of reformist calls to democratize finance by means of policy, challenging the comforting notion that the "excesses" of global finance can be curbed through effective state action.'
—Alexis Moraitis, Lecturer in International Political Economy, University of Lancaster

Fictions of Financialization

Rethinking Speculation, Exploitation and Twenty-First-Century Capitalism

Nick Bernards

PLUTO  PRESS

First published 2025 by Pluto Press
New Wing, Somerset House, Strand, London WC2R 1LA
and Pluto Press, Inc.
1930 Village Center Circle, 3-834, Las Vegas, NV 89134

www.plutobooks.com

British Library Cataloguing in Publication Data
A catalogue record for this book is available from the British Library

ISBN 978 0 7453 4889 6 Paperback
ISBN 978 0 7453 4891 9 PDF
ISBN 978 0 7453 4890 2 EPUB

This book is printed on paper suitable for recycling and made from fully
managed and sustained forest sources. Logging, pulping and manufacturing
processes are expected to conform to the environmental standards of the
country of origin.

Typeset by Stanford DTP Services, Northampton, England

Simultaneously printed in the United Kingdom and United States of America

Contents

Acknowledgements

I've spent a long time thinking about this book, and a relatively short space of time writing it. As a result, I've built up many slightly diffuse and abstract debts, and relatively few concrete ones. The latter are easy enough to tally up, I hope I can do justice to the former here too.

I am grateful to my students and colleagues at the University of Warwick, who are wonderful to work with, increasingly despite the way the university is managed. I'm fortunate to have had the stability and freedom to pursue forms of research and writing, like that reflected in this book, which are increasingly devalued in the marketized, managerial university. I'm very grateful to have found a niche which has allowed me to write a book like this. I am, relatedly, grateful to comrades in the UCU at Warwick and elsewhere, whom I surely have to thank for the fact that that sliver of space still exists. I'm luckier still to be able to teach about things that are closely connected to those research and writing interests, and to be challenged and inspired by many very bright students. This goes especially for the brilliant PhD students I've had the opportunity to work with during the time I've spent on this book – (alphabetically) Fraser Amos, Ben Hetherington and Laura Quinteros – from whom I've learned volumes.

The ideas here are mine – good ones and otherwise. But, as is normal with these things, I wouldn't have come around to many of them without colleagues' generous engagement with these arguments in various forms. Inevitably, this will be an incomplete list, but particular thanks to (alphabetically) Ilias Alami, Ali Bhagat, Malcolm Campbell-Verduyn, Chris Clarke, Jack Copley, Bridget Kenny, Kai Koddenbrock, Tony Porter, and Susanne Soederberg. Special thanks to Ilias in particular for reading and commenting on a full draft of the manuscript.

This is the second book that I've published with Pluto Press in the last few years. They have been a joy to work with throughout.

I owe particular thanks to Jakob Horstman for his careful editorial work and close reading, yet again. Thanks are also due to three anonymous reviewers for valuable feedback on this project at proposal stage.

I promised Shannon that I would put her name in the acknowledgements this time. Hi Shannon!

On the topic of diffuse debts: It's hard to sum up how much of this and everything, really, that I owe to Laura and Max, together and separately. I truly can't imagine having done this without a supportive partner and friend. It is also proven more helpful than I might have expected to have a small child who just wants to play football with me around. There is no better cure for being overly preoccupied with some obscure point about value theory. I love you both.

Introduction

It has always been a fantasy of mine that a boatload of 25 brokers would be shipwrecked and struggle to an island from which there could be no rescue. Faced with developing an economy that would maximize their consumption and pleasure, would they, I wonder, assign 20 of their number to produce food, clothing, shelter, etc., while setting five to endlessly trading options on the future output of the 20?

– Warren Buffett, 'How to tame the casino society', *Washington Post*, 4 December 1986

You'll find an odd kind of consensus if you look at the pages of the US business press and Marxist journals from the middle of the 1980s. Warren Buffett, in the passage quoted in the epigraph, expresses its core essence fairly clearly. Against the backdrop of Reagan-era financial deregulation, coupled with steep cuts to corporate taxes, the US financial sector was booming. Meanwhile, seemingly as a result of the latter, manufacturing and non-financial sectors continued to stagnate. Financiers were getting filthy rich, without (as Buffett implies) contributing very much to society or the economy, and as a result capitalism in general was in a fragile, uneasy state.

The leveraged buyout (LBO), the archetypical financial money-making scheme of the decade, seemed to exemplify all of this. In an LBO, investors borrow money and use the proceeds to gain a controlling interest in a firm. The assets of the firm being acquired are often used as part of the collateral for the loan – or, the 'real' firm is made to bear the cost of its own acquisition by financiers. Investors then often proceed to strip the acquired firm for parts, cutting costs to the bare minimum by selling off equipment and factories, laying off workers, tearing up supplier contracts. At best, investors in leveraged buyouts aim to spin the company off into smaller and more specialized units that can be sold off as separate companies. At worst, they simply aim to load as much of the debt associated with the purchase onto the company itself and appropriate as much cash flow as possible to themselves through dividends and other payments. Then, when they become unmanageable, leveraged buyers seek to discharge the debts on the company's balance sheet through a fire sale of remaining assets in bankruptcy. In either case, LBOs have the distinct flavour of financial engineering directly undermining otherwise productive firms, for the benefit of financiers alone.

The growing prevalence of LBOs in the early 1980s caused considerable consternation among financial pundits, regulators, and at least some bankers themselves. LBOs were a point of conflict between Paul Volcker, the Chairman of the Federal Reserve Board, and the libertarians in the Reagan administration. Volcker worried about the hazards that LBOs posed for financial stability: 'We spend our days issuing debt and retiring equity, both in record volumes, and then we spend our evenings raising each other's eyebrows with gossip about signs of stress in the financial system.'[1] The LBO craze also helped cement a shift in popular perceptions of banking and finance. The cultural archetype of the greedy investment banker not coincidentally dates to this period – flashy new-money lifestyle, hyper-masculine, morally flexible (if not overtly sociopathic) – maybe most enduringly encapsulated in the character of Gordon Gecko in Oliver Stone's 1987 *Wall Street* (in which LBOs feature prominently as a plot point), or investment-banker-cum-serial killer Patrick Bateman in Bret Easton Ellis' 1991 novel *American Psycho*.

Borrowing a metaphor from J.M. Keynes – a popular one at the time amongst financial and economic commentators – Buffett was one of many contemporaries to describe the rise of a 'casino economy'.[2] The year prior to Buffett's commentary, *Business Week* magazine had run a cover story titled 'The casino society'. Similar to Buffett, the author of the piece, Anthony Bianco, worried that 'More and more of what transpires on the trading floors of Wall and Lasalle Streets has no direct connection to the factory floors of Main Street.'[3] In his *General Theory of Employment, Interest and Money*, Keynes had differentiated 'speculation' (forecasting changes in prices, or 'the psychology of the market') from 'enterprise' (forecasting the long-run productive yield of assets). Keynes argued that 'when the capital development of a country becomes the by-product of the activities of a casino, the job is likely to be ill-done'.[4] If capital accumulation and investment were dominated by speculation for its own sake, it would likely hamper growth and economic development.

Making a very similar distinction, Buffett argued that the financial markets of the 1980s had taken on a new form increasingly distant from a useful role in allocating investment to the productive economy – a tendency epitomized for Buffett, once again, by the ever-present figure of the LBO. Finance instead seemed focused on squeezing money out of productive enterprises and driving the ever-faster turnover in financial assets. Hence, the desert-island fantasy quoted above: What social or economic good, really, were traders and brokers and corporate raiders doing? He has a point in implying that the answer is: little to none. But Buffett – who was and is, of course, himself a billionaire, and one whose profits have come in large part through financial markets at that – was not particularly interested in abolishing the capitalist financial system, let alone capitalism generally. He argued instead that there should be a 100 per cent tax on profits derived from sales of financial instruments that the owner had held for less than a year, arguing that this would lead to 'the substantial brain power and energy now applied to the making of investment decisions that will produce the greatest rewards in a few minutes, days or weeks' being 'instantly reoriented to decisions promising the greatest long-term rewards'.[5] Or, taxes should encourage what Keynes called 'enterprise' and discourage speculation.

Buffett and Bianco were far from the only commentators to invoke the metaphor of the 'casino' to describe financial markets in the 1980s, following the radical experiments in financial deregulation pursued by the Thatcher and Reagan governments. This is about the same time as Susan Strange's classic *Casino Capitalism* was first published.[6] Strange had quite a bit more of substance to say about why the financial boom was taking place than did, say, Buffett or Bianco. She skilfully highlighted the ways that the 'non-decisions' of US and UK authorities had led, in ways they often hadn't predicted, to the formation of a runaway financial system increasingly beyond their control. The 'casino' metaphor had a good deal of purchase on the political left as well. A manifesto on democratic planning, organized under the auspices of the Campaign for Labour Party Democracy in the late 1980s and written by Nicholas Costello, Jonathan Michie, and Seumas Milne, for instance, took the title *Beyond the Casino Economy*. They posed the growing power of the City as both a chief source of British economic malaise and a major obstacle to democratic planning:

> The feverish speculative activity that was unleashed in the financial and securities markets by deregulation and financial globalization in the 1980s has created the most sophisticated and 'efficient' markets in the world, but it has done nothing for the construction of a modern and competitive industrial base in Britain and it has certainly increased instability in the world economy.[7]

In short, commentators in the business press, academia, and on the left in the latter parts of the 1980s shared a growing sense of an imbalance between 'productive' and 'speculative' economies, and that the financial casino running amok lay at the root of persistent stagnation and instability in the heartlands of global capitalism.

But, with a few partial exceptions like Strange, the 'casino' metaphor lent itself more to condemnations of the greed and moral degradation of modern-day finance than it did to understanding what was happening and how to change it. Harry Magdoff and Paul Sweezy had published a series of essays on finance and 1980s capitalism in the Marxist journal *Monthly Review*.[8] Reacting to Bianco's *BusinessWeek* piece specifically, Magdoff and Sweezy rightly noted that these discussions of the financial 'casino' generally lacked any systematic diagnosis of why the financial boom was happening, leaving authors with 'little to contribute beyond dark hints and ominous warnings of unknown perils that lie ahead'.[9] They largely agreed with the descriptive characterization of the shifts underway in Bianco's piece and elsewhere, but thought this financial boom reflected structural shifts afoot in the very nature of capitalist growth regimes. We'll return to Magdoff and Sweezy in greater detail in Chapter 3, but suffice for the moment to say that they saw a quasi-permanent shift in the locus of accumulation in core capitalist economies away from stagnating productive sectors marred by monopoly capitalism, and towards profits obtained in virtually limitless speculative financial markets.

I begin with a digression about the mid-1980s because much about these debates is strikingly familiar to the prevailing discourse in the present – the pervasive unease about the state of global capitalism, the sense that the financial casino is running amok at the expense of the 'real' economy, and the ubiquity of 'dark hints and ominous warnings' (the latter ever-darker and more ominous as we creep further into climate breakdown). This is perhaps no surprise. Looking backwards we can see the 'casino' debates as the first threads of what has come to be a central and pressing debate about finance and the restructuring of global capitalism.

It's hard to disagree that finance is a pervasive part of twenty-first-century capitalism. The share of the financial sector in the North American and European core economies of the capitalist world system has only grown since this motley coalition of authors started worrying about the dominance of the 'casino'. Financial crises have become more frequent and more severe – the 2008 Global Financial Crisis being perhaps the most obvious example, but far from the only one. Global financial flows exercise tightening discipline over peripheral states. There is a growing literature on relations of 'international financial subordination' emphasizing the hierarchical power relations exercised in and through the uneven development of the global financial system, expressed in the form of differential constraints on access to resources, exposure to financial volatility, and ongoing extraction of value disproportionately penalizing actors in peripheral economies.[10] The grip that the hierarchical structure of global finance exerts on peripheral people and states is perhaps exemplified above all by a renewed round of debt crises across the global south in the aftermath of the Covid-19 pandemic.[11] Meanwhile, people and households in the global north and global south alike are faced with deepening levels of indebtedness.[12] Those lucky enough to still have a pension to rely on are likely to find their retirements intimately tied to the rise and fall of the stock market. Indeed, as Bruno Bonizzi and Annina Kaltenbrunner show persuasively, financial subordination and pension privatization have become increasingly closely entangled, as asset managers searching for higher yields have increasingly sought out so-called 'emerging-market' assets, exacerbating financial instability in the periphery in the process.[13] Relatedly, the portfolios of the largest asset managers – companies like BlackRock and Vanguard – have ballooned to tens of trillions of dollars. They are accompanied by a growing array of more specialized asset managers, which find themselves in control of an ever-wider swathe of our daily lives, running from water, energy, and transport infrastructures to low-income rental housing.[14] The rise of finance has taken place alongside the rise of precarious livelihoods globally, seemingly deep-rooted stagnation in the core economies, a widening gap between the poles of fabulous wealth and grinding deprivation, and the acceleration of climate breakdown.

Yet, despite this (or perhaps because of it), financial tools are also increasingly posed as solutions to the crises and contradictions of neoliberal capitalism. Leading states and international organizations propound financial responses to problems ranging from the climate crisis to biodiversity loss to global poverty to crumbling roads and patchy electric grids. Proposals have circulated in recent years for solving the world's problems by converting everything from girls' education, roads, forests, carbon emissions, wildlife, poor peoples' incomes, and shifting weather patterns into financial assets.[15] Access to credit, savings, payments and insurance services for the poorest remains at the forefront of global development agendas despite decades of failures either to reduce poverty, or often even to expand access to formal finance.[16] The World Bank and Gates Foundation, among others, increasingly promote the use of digital financial services to deliver social assistance payments, effectively rendering social protection systems into mechanisms for pushing more and more people to use digital financial services.[17] The results have ranged from lethal crises of overindebtedness to the violent displacement of peasant and indigenous communities in processes of 'green grabbing' to make way for carbon credit projects,[18] to a litany of projects that have simply failed to attract investment of any kind.[19] Finance looms large in various radical and progressive responses to the social and ecological crises we face too, albeit in slightly different ways. Expanding public financing, rolling back and confronting private financial markets, and establishing democratic control over finance figure as increasingly prominent responses to the climate crisis and widening inequalities.[20]

The task of understanding the place and power of finance in twenty-first-century capitalism is therefore urgent – if anything, even more so now than it was in the 1980s. The power of finance capital confronts us as an important obstacle to building just, ecologically viable economies and societies. Yet the very fact that 'casino economy' debates echo so clearly in the present is a sign that the analytical apparatus that we're bringing to bear on these problems has important limits. We remain much more readily able to condemn financial speculation than to understand where, why, and how it is happening. We need the tools to critique financial solutions, to grasp the contradictions of financial accumulation, and to situate finance capital in relation to the ongoing restructuring of the 'real' economies of production and reproduction. We badly need to understand the sources, and the limits, of that power.

This book contributes towards this vital set of tasks in two ways. First, it develops an extended critique of the concept of 'financialization', which has become the dominant way of framing and interpreting the dispersed developments traced above. Originating out of the strange amalgam of Marxist political economy and business commentary that tracked the rise of finance primarily in the US and Britain in the late 1980s, the term 'financialization' was first used in a book by Kevin Phillips (a former adviser to President Richard Nixon) in 1993.[21] It was taken up in Giovanni Arrighi's monumental world-historical discussion of the 'long twentieth century' the following year,[22] and diffused through debates primarily among sociologists and heterodox economists in the 1990s and 2000s, before booming into wider use within and beyond the academy after the 2008 Global Financial Crisis. The concept has become increasingly widespread in media and activist debates in recent years. 'Financialization' is now invoked in venues as disparate as *Forbes*, *The Atlantic*, the *Guardian* alongside dozens of recent pieces in popular leftist outlets *Jacobin* and *Tribune*.[23] It is used by Marxist and other radical writers,[24] as well as by leading figures in establishment Economics.[25] It has also crept into policy

7

debates, particularly through venues like the United Nations Commission on Trade and Development, which have historically been more hospitable to broadly heterodox economic ideas.[26] In short, ideas about the financialization of the economy and of daily life are increasingly part of the common sense about the failures of present-day capitalism across a wide swathe of progressive and radical thought, in the academy and in wider public debate.

Amidst all this stretching and twisting, and despite the obvious political and analytic differences between Marxists and mainstream economists, invocations of 'financialization' mostly retain a core story. In its broad strokes, it's not far off the one Magdoff and Sweezy laid out 35-odd years ago. It runs something like the following: After the collapse of Keynesian economic models in the 1970s, contemporary capitalism has been restructured into a form uniquely dominated by finance. Capitalist profits in this context are increasingly generated through financial channels, coming at the expense of jobs and production in the 'real' economy. This has kicked off a search for speculative profits which has led to the subjection of ever-wider areas of social life and of the natural world to the domination of finance. Profit-making in this context is increasingly speculative, and thus divorced both from the needs of productive economies and from social and ecological reproduction.

This book calls this narrative into question. It makes a case against the growing dominance of this 'financialization' story in our understandings of the crises of contemporary capitalism, and for a perspective rooted in a different reading of Marxist debates. Parts of the financialization narrative no doubt ring true. Since the 1970s, a growing share of capitalist profits has indeed been recorded in the financial sector (though this has taken place to a lesser extent and plateaued more in recent years than is often implied). The scope of speculative trading has boomed in that time. Novel financial instruments and new kinds of financial institutions are still rapidly mushrooming. And people are deeper in debt in many places. The financialization story offers an intuitively appealing diagnosis tying together many of these phenomena with what might be called the 'financial solutionism' still dominant in global discussions about climate mitigation and adaptation, alongside development, education, biodiversity, water, housing and almost countless other things. But invoking 'financialization' ultimately obscures more than it reveals about how these developments are tied together and how the social power of finance in particular and capital in general operate. Far too often, it leads us to overstate the novelty of contemporary financial developments. 'Financialization' serves as a shortcut, a way of attributing disparate social phenomena to the growing power of finance capital. In this way, it offers up a ready-made way of critiquing myriad changes in the way that finance capital and the wider economy operate, allowing authors to more or less uncritically assimilate them as instances of a wider process. In Stefan Ouma's apt phrase, 'Frequently, "financialization" has been turned into an abstract force *sui generis*, morphing from *explanandum* into *explanans*.'[27]

In so doing, invocations of 'financialization' can lead to truncated and politically limited critiques of contemporary capitalism. Far too often talking in terms of financialization implies that the solutions lie in 'confronting finance', rolling back and reining in the financial sector, or 'democratizing' finance, building a better financial system more subject to public control. Financialization stories invite the fantasy that the route to just and sustainable economies and societies will open up if we can get finance capital out of the picture. This risks glossing over the exploitative and unsustainable nature of capitalism, full stop. Stories about financialization in this way can inadvertently make it harder for us to connect up the transformation of finance over recent decades with the shifting terrain of global capitalism more widely. While we can credit the financialization debate with often raising a vital set of questions about the contemporary transformations of capitalism and the place of finance in it, the concept of 'financialization' itself closes down the range of meaningful answers to these questions. Talking in terms of financialization is thus ultimately a dead-end if we want to understand the nature of contemporary capitalism.

This book is not the first critique of financialization debates, by any means. Brett Christophers has questioned the conceptual and empirical foundations of financialization debates in a number of different ways.[28] He points to problems ranging from conceptual ambiguities, to methodological nationalism in analyses of the growing share of profits accrued by the financial sector, to a need to position 'financialization' within a wider process of 'rentieriza-tion'. Susanne Soederberg's discussion of 'debtfarism' engages the state-backed promotion of indebtedness while explicitly critiqu-ing analyses of these processes in terms of financialization.[29] Kai Koddenbrock and colleagues argue that problems of finance and development in the global south need to be understood through a long historical optic more sensitive to relations of imperialism than the framework of financialization permits. The 'divorce' of financial operations from the needs of the productive economy, they show, is a long-run product of colonial histories rather than any recent process of 'financialization'.[30] Beverly Best argues com-pellingly that the rise of finance represents a qualitative shift in the superficial form of appearance of capitalist social relations, rather than a deep historical rupture in the form of capitalist domination, or a meaningful separation of financial circulation from produc-tion.[31] In different ways, other authors have also raised important questions about the practical limits to the growth of the finan-cial sector. Johnna Montgomerie and Daniela Tepe-Belfrage, for instance, show how household-level entanglements of debts with patterns of social reproduction pose limits on processes of finan-cialization.[32] Debts, they note, ultimately need to be 'cared' for, and macro-level patterns of financial accumulation are thus contingent both on the continued availability of income with which to make payments, and on whether or not caring for debts is consistently prioritized over caring for other needs.

I build on these critiques in the first place simply by developing an extended critical engagement with the concept and associated debates. Conceptual critiques of financialization are not really the main object of most of the preceding pieces.[33] The concept and narrative of financialization is a central part of our critical nar-ratives about an ever-wider cross-section of the global political economy. As such it deserves to be reconstructed, contextualized, and critiqued in extended form.

Equally, I build on existing critiques of financialization through the second main aim of this book, which is to lay some ground-work for an alternative way of approaching the power of finance without losing sight of the wider contradictions of capitalist accu-mulation. The value of the financialization debate is in raising the question of how to place finance in global capitalism. This is still a vital question that needs to be engaged, if from a different angle. This book develops an alternative approach by engaging with a range of Marxist thought on money, finance, and forms of exploitation. It may seem superficially rather unproductive to engage with Marx on these issues. Contemporary Marxian perspectives, in various guises, have often been at the forefront of 'financialization' debates, so Marxist perspectives are certainly not inherently immune to 'financialization' narratives. Marx's own writing on money and finance is equally not without problems. His specific notes on finance, credit, and the banking systems, mostly collected in Vol. 3 of *Capital*, are often suggestive, insightful, and prescient, but nonetheless incomplete and sometimes inconsistent.[34] Marx also offers a number of insights on money that can appear almost painfully dated. The most glaring example here is probably that, when Marx talks about money, he talks a lot about gold. This latter tendency has led a number of critics to dismiss Marx as a 'commodity' theorist of money insufficiently removed from either his own era or the classical political economists he sought to critique. Geoffrey Ingham argues in this vein that 'Marx failed to consider money as abstract value'.[35] Andrew Leyshon and Nigel Thrift, while taking a somewhat more sympathetic position, likewise note of Marx's writing on money that: 'The rise of the state and state money, the growth of credit, the decline of gold and the greater role of the financial system in the world economy, the explosion in fictitious capital through a system of virtual money – all these, and many other events, have changed the landscape of money' in the time since Marx wrote.[36]

However, to argue that Marx failed to consider the 'abstract' character of monetary value, or overemphasized the 'commodity' character of money, is to ignore his relatively distinct understanding of commodities themselves.[37] Yes, he talks a good deal about gold, but specifically because of the social role that it fulfilled in the monetary system at the time in which he wrote. Indeed, Marx is explicit in arguing that the value of gold was determined by its use as money, not the other way around.[38] In Marx's approach, monetary relations reflect processes through which the social relations bound up in capitalist production and reproduction are both 'alienated' – rendered subject to impersonal compulsions beyond the direct control of particular people – and 'fetishized' – obscured by the ways that they are mediated by material things. This is, as I argue in greater detail below, a very useful starting place for thinking about the links between the relations of production and financial circuits. I thus share with the handful of recent Marxian critiques of the literature on 'financialization',[39] and indeed with a longer tradition of Marxist theory on finance,[40] an insistence on the centrality of the social relations implicit in money under capitalism to any theory of financial markets.

Building on these analyses, I start from the premise that risk and speculation are core to the operation of capital. Capital, understood in Marx's terms as 'value in process', is at its core a recurring bet that abstract values can be realized through the exploitation of concrete labour and nature in a specific place and time. It is this fact of being perpetually circulated in a speculative search for returns that differentiates capital as such from property generally or from an inert hoard of money. Impersonal logics of competition do drive capitalist development, but individual capitalists don't and can't know in advance whether particular investments or accumulation strategies will be successful. As David Harvey puts it:

> The coercive laws of competition force individual or collective agents (capitalist firms, financial institutions, states, cities) into certain configurations of activities which are themselves constitutive of the capitalist dynamic. But the 'forcing' occurs after the action rather than before. Capitalist development is always speculative – indeed, the whole history of capitalism can best be read as a whole series of minuscule and sometimes grandiose speculative thrusts piled historically and geographically one upon another.[41]

All capital, then, is fundamentally speculative. Financial relations are in this sense necessary and integral to the basic logics of capitalism, not deviations from them.[42] Financial practices are in the first instance means by which capitalists – and others governed by the mute compulsions of capital accumulation including working classes and states – seek to manage or displace the tensions between the impersonal compulsions generated by capitalist social relations and the uneven geographies of actually existing exploitation. Our critiques of contemporary capitalism, then, need to be able to keep in view the whole circuit of social relations through which value is unevenly realized.

In order to develop this argument, the book draws and elaborates on Harvey's useful suggestion that finance capital must be understood as a contradictory *process*.[43] Rather than treating finance capital as a discrete 'power bloc' within the wider bourgeoisie, Harvey argues, we must understand finance capital as a particular form of circulation process centred on the credit system, but always integrally (if unevenly) wrapped up with the wider circuits of production, reproduction, and exchange. Financial profits are in need of continual realization through the concrete exploitation of labour and nature, and through the sale and circulation of commodities, which are uncertain at all points. These processes generate contradictions which must be continually navigated, displaced, and governed. Notions of 'financialization', which tend to assume the ever-wider power of finance capital as a 'power bloc' over all aspects of social life, leave us ill-equipped to unpick and understand, and ultimately to resist, the process of financial accumulation and its implicit tensions and contradictions.

This approach clears the way for more historically rich analyses, and ultimately for more politically productive understandings of the place of finance in present-day capitalism. The financialization narrative implies a kind of epochal logic which often closes off meaningful considerations of key developments prior to the 1970s. Yet contemporary financial accumulation is clearly enmeshed with deeper-rooted patterns of imperialism and uneven development on a global scale. Seeking to locate finance capital in the diverse and uneven processes of exploitation and dispossession making up actually existing capitalism allows us a vital lens on the relationships between financial accumulation and the complex histories of racial and gendered hierarchies, enduring colonial legacies, and entangled histories of capitalist natures. While this book is largely programmatic, and as such doesn't contain much extensive historical analysis, it does nonetheless suggest some useful ways we might approach these questions.

More importantly, this perspective offers a more productive diagnosis of the crises marking twenty-first-century capitalism and the prospects for building a more just world. Accounts of financialization overestimate or mischaracterize the power of finance. It matters a good deal in articulating responses to the depredations of neoliberal capitalism whether we attribute these to the more pervasive spread of financial logics backed by a cohesive power bloc, or to the continued unfolding of capitalist dynamics of exploitation. The book's approach ultimately helps us to capture the continued centrality of uneven and contradictory forms of exploitation of labour and nature to contemporary capitalism. In other words, the approach here helps us to see that 'confronting finance', in itself, offers no shortcuts out of the crises of contemporary capitalism.

The rest of the book is organized as follows.

Chapter 1 provides an overview and initial critique of the concept of 'financialization'. I outline a working definition of 'financialization'. Despite a good deal of stretching and twisting as the concept has come to be more widely used, I argue that we can point to a common core to 'financialization' stories, which revolves around three premises: (1) 'Financialization' is a discrete periodization of capitalist history, dating roughly to the 1970s; (2) Financialization represents a shift in the orientation of capital away from productive activities and towards finance; and (3) Financialization is expansionary; finance seeks out ever-wider terrains to subject to speculative accumulation. I trace the origins and evolution of this narrative, running from Phillips and Arrighi through to a set of influential publications in the 2000s which helped consolidate 'financialization' as a discrete literature, and a post-2008 boom in 'financialization' studies. The chapter closes with a preliminary critique of financialization.

I move in Chapter 2 to laying out the groundwork for an alternative understanding of finance in capitalism. Here I trace recent debates about finance and 'value' in contemporary capitalism, drawing on Harvey's notion of finance capital as a 'process' rather than a 'power bloc' to try to steer between the poles of a dogmatic insistence on 'labour' as the font of all 'real' value, on one hand, and the dismissal of the continued relevance of labour and production, on the other.

The three chapters that follow develop both the critique of financialization as well as the 'process-based' alternative by reconsidering three particularly important dimensions of relationships between finance and capitalism in the twenty-first century. Chapter 3 revisits the relationship between finance and production, developing a critique of ideas about the contemporary 'stagnation' of productive capitalism, and an alternative view which aims to place an analysis of contemporary financial accumulation within the uneven restructuring of global production and within a longer historical trajectory of global capitalism. This sets the stage for closer analyses of two particular problems in the following two chapters. Chapter 4 considers the relationships between finance and nature. I show how, contra narratives of the 'financialization of nature' emphasizing the expansionary character of finance and the intensification of efforts to subordinate nature to financial speculation, finance is an ever-present feature in the capitalist production of nature. Chapter 5, finally, looks at the relationship between finance and the state, by way of a reinterpretation of the political logics of increasingly prevalent financial solutionism. Rather than a reflection of the political power of finance capital, the recurrent turn to mobilizing private finance to solve multiplying social and ecological problems in twenty-first-century capitalism can be understood as the path of political least resistance for capitalist states in the context of intensifying contradictions.

I move in the final chapter, by way of concluding, to a more direct consideration of the political stakes of the arguments that developed in the preceding chapters. I do this through sympathetic critique of recent perspectives on 'de-financialization', the 'democratization of finance', and the politics of mass indebtedness. Rather than seeing regulating or transforming finance as core strategies for bringing about a more just, more democratic society and economy, there is a need for strategy and analysis which confronts the core operations of capitalist value relations.

1

What is Financialization?

This book makes the case that, while understanding the place of finance in contemporary capitalism is vital, the predominant way of doing so in contemporary critical scholarship, journalism, and activist conversations – namely, through stories of 'financialization' – is limited in important ways. This chapter starts to flesh out this claim. If I'm to pursue the argument in later chapters that we need different conceptual tools to make sense of finance in contemporary capitalism, it's a necessary first step here to explain which ones we've been using and what's wrong with them. So, this chapter is a brief history of 'financialization' debates, and an outline and critique of some of the core premises of financialization narratives.

The chapter starts with the admittedly difficult task of defining 'financialization'. The diffuse origins and proliferating uses of 'financialization' make for a challenge here. Developing a critique of a malleable and multiple conceptual apparatus, especially one that's often used quite loosely, can be tricky. Nonetheless, I'll make the case shortly that talking in terms of 'financialization' – maybe especially where it's not used with much care – generally *does* invoke a core narrative about the ways that global capitalism has changed and is changing. In brief, the 'financialization' narrative asserts that, somewhere around the 1970s, the dominant tendency in core capitalist economies shifted from accumulation based on 'real' productive activities towards accumulation through finance. In the ensuing decades, this shift has occasioned the ever-wider search for new bits of the web of life which can be made into sites of speculative profit.

That definition established, the bulk of the chapter moves on to a consideration of where this narrative came from and how it was consolidated and diffused. I show how the concept picked up the concerns reflected in the 'casino economy' debates in the

1980s with which I started this book. In order to do this, I focus on two key texts, one whose role in financialization debates is widely recognized and one which has been relatively forgotten. The former is Giovanni Arrighi's landmark *The Long Twentieth Century*, the latter is former US Republican Party strategist Kevin Phillips' *Boiling Point*. *Boiling Point*, which was published about a year before Arrighi's opus. Arrighi actually credits the term 'financialization' to Phillips. Though they build in very different political directions, both are heavily indebted to Fernand Braudel and influenced by the 'casino economy' debate going on around them. Taken together, Arrighi and Phillips help to demonstrate how the 'financialization' narrative builds out of earlier debates in the 1980s, whose blind spots it often inherited as well. After discussing Arrighi and Phillips, I briefly trace out two other tributary streams of debate – the 'financialization of daily life' thesis, first articulated by Randy Martin, and debates about changing organizational dynamics in leading US firms, which by 2000 increasingly centred on a critique of the ideology of 'shareholder value'. I then show how a handful of key texts published in the 2000s helped to consolidate these emerging strands of debate into a more-or-less unified core narrative of 'financialization', whose use then exploded after the 2008 Global Financial Crisis. The chapter concludes with a preliminary critique of the financialization narrative.

DEFINING FINANCIALIZATION

One initial challenge of the task undertaken in this chapter is that 'financialization' means many different things to many different authors. Indeed, overviews of 'financialization' often settle on emphasizing the inherent plurality of the concept. Natascha van der Zwan, in an influential review published a decade ago,[1] groups financialization debates into three clusters – dealing with 'financialization as a regime of accumulation', 'financialization of the firm', and 'financialization of daily life'. The first cluster refers to studies tracing the growing share of the financial sector in the overall economy. The second group of studies looks at a set of changes to corporate governance wherein firms' operations are increasingly oriented around delivering 'shareholder value' – delivering returns for holders of shares in the form of higher stock prices – rather than profit, per se. The final group refers to the intrusion of financial logics into ever-wider realms of day-to-day life.

The picture is arguably even more complex than this. In the first instance, there are substantial debates and divergences in approach even within these clusters of work – debates on financialization as a 'regime of accumulation', for instance, include a range of Marxist, post-Keynesian, and institutionalist perspectives. For that matter, there are quite bitter disputes even within these perspectives, maybe especially amongst the Marxist camp.[2] And 'financialization' debates do not necessarily neatly fall into these three boxes in practice. One review written shortly after the 2008 Global Financial Crisis located 17 different definitions of financialization.[3] Equally importantly, debates on financialization have only continued to mushroom. To give one notable example: van der Zwan's review was written largely before a more recent raft of studies on the financialization of commodities, the financialization of nature, and the financialization of development.[4] All of these, in different ways, centre on the problem of how and why things – land, raw materials, food, development projects – are rendered into assets and subjected to financial speculation, and with what consequences (I take up some of these ideas further in Chapters 4 and 5). This problem is taking on growing importance in both academic debates and beyond, but is not really directly captured by any of van der Zwan's three categories.

Some critics have argued that the fundamentally contested character of 'financialization' as a concept itself risks rendering it inchoate and unhelpful. Brett Christophers, for one, suggests that, insofar as the concept 'increasingly stand[s] only for a vague notion of "the (increased) contemporary importance of finance"', it tends to leave begging as many questions as it actually helps us answer.[5] A similar criticism is often levelled at 'neoliberalism',[6] but Christophers suggests that the contrast between 'financialization' and 'neoliberalism' in this respect is informative insofar as, despite proliferating uses, 'neoliberalism' retains a kind of conceptual core that 'financialization' doesn't. Christophers doesn't specify exactly what this 'core conceptual thread' to neoliberalism is, though we can probably assume he means something like 'a programme of governance based on privatization of state functions and the expanded role of markets in organizing social life'. He argues that, by contrast, it is hard to pinpoint the theoretical 'value-added' of 'financialization' itself in most cases absent this kind of a conceptual core. He asks, rhetorically, to what extent the (sometimes considerable) insights generated by studies invoking 'financialization' actually depend on the concept of 'financialization'.[7]

With due caveats, though, I think we *can* pull out something like a conceptual core to 'financialization' that goes beyond the 'increased contemporary importance of finance'. It's probably true that the (sometimes considerable) insights produced by analyses of financialization arrive despite rather than because of the concept itself. Equally, financialization debates are definitely methodologically and theoretically fragmented, and many people use the concept loosely and unreflexively. But invoking financialization does nonetheless do something significant to analyses – maybe especially where it's done without much direct reflection. 'Financialization' is perhaps best thought of as a kind of orienting meta-narrative as much as it is a 'concept' or a 'research programme', certainly in the way it is most often used. It invokes a particular story about the crucial transformations of the global political economy over the last half-century. By using this story to frame their analyses, authors are implicitly or explicitly folding the specific objects of their analysis into a wider narrative and critique of capitalist restructuring. Of course, this isn't a defence of the concept. It does, though, point our critiques in a different direction. The main problem is not that 'financialization' as a concept is incoherent or empty, but rather that it invokes a story about how the global political economy has changed and is changing which is ultimately analytically and politically unhelpful.

So, what is this narrative? Costas Lapavitsas encapsulates most elements of the core 'financialization narrative' in the following, admirably succinct, passage:

Since the late 1970s, real accumulation has witnessed mediocre and precarious growth, but finance has grown extraordinarily in terms of employment, profits, size of institutions and markets.

There has been deregulation, technological and institutional change, innovation, and global expansion. Finance now penetrates every aspect of society in developed countries while its presence has grown strongly in the developing world. While real accumulation has been performing indifferently, the capitalist class has found new sources of profits through the revamped mechanisms of finance.[8]

If we break down what Lapavitsas says here, financialization is:

(1) *A discrete periodization of global capitalism.* That is, 'financialization' describes a series of transformations 'since the late 1970s'. The precise date here is debated and debatable. Many accounts highlight the breakdown of the post-war Bretton Woods monetary system – the so-called 'Nixon shock' – when the US unilaterally abandoned the gold exchange standard and floated the dollar in 1973 as a key moment. But the main point is that 'financialization' describes the present era of capitalist development. It is often seen as a counterpart to the neoliberal era, with many authors seeing neoliberalism as being driven by the financialization of the economy.[9]

(2) *A shift in orientation by capital from 'real' activities to 'financial' ones.* Faced with falling rates of profit in production, capital has increasingly moved into financial speculation, and 'finance capital' has become increasingly dominant over productive capital, and over the orientation of the economy and politics more generally. This shift, importantly, implies the possibility of a meaningful separation of 'real' from 'financial' or speculative capital. Here financialization debates tread terrain fairly similar to Hilferding or Keynes. Keynes' references to turning over the investment allocation function to 'the casino', quoted in the Introduction, are a case in point.

(3) *Expansionary.* Finance 'permeates every aspect of society'. The above shift in orientation has conditioned a search, by finance capital, for ever-wider spheres of social life to be subjected to financial profit seeking. This is, I would argue, an assumption that marks out financialization debates from earlier perspectives. That

finance is expansionary was a core component of many arguments about finance capital at the turn of the twentieth century. Classic analyses around the turn of the twentieth century from Hobson, Hilferding, Bukharin, and Lenin, among others, linked the rise of finance capital to the intensification of European imperialism.[10] But the 'financialization' narrative carries with it connotations of depth even more so than geographical breadth. As Mezzadra and Neilson put it, finance is taken to have an 'ongoing and violent tendency ... to penetrate and subsume economic activity and social life as a whole'.[11] Financialization points to the appropriation of ever-wider swathes of social life as financial assets – the 'capitalization of almost everything' in Leyshon and Thrift's evocative phrase.[12] It also, increasingly, points to efforts to convert the non-human world – from shifting weather patterns to biodiversity – into sites of financial speculation.

Taken together, these three ideas cut across most uses of the concept. Something like the story Lapavitsas succinctly outlines in the quoted passage is common to most readings of financialization: falling rates of profit in 'real' economies since roughly the 1970s have led to a boom in financial speculation, which in turn has led to finance capital seeking to colonize ever-wider areas of society. To be clear, this is not to suggest that everyone writing about financialization would necessarily accept all (or even any) of Lapavitsas' specific arguments about why this is happening or its implications. There is much at stake in debates over how to explain or interpret these different aspects of financialization, and in choices to focus on one or the other dimension of the story. I'll get into some of the nuances of these debates in the remainder of this chapter and elsewhere in this book. For the moment though, I've quoted Lapavitsas in particular here because this passage gives us an admirably concise summary neatly tying together the different aspects of the overarching financialization narrative.

The term 'financialization' is not strictly necessary to tell this story. Magdoff and Sweezy (as summarized in the Introduction above), for instance, manage to articulate a quite similar narrative to the one Lapavitsas lays out without it. So, more recently, does Robert Brenner's influential analysis of the 'long downturn' of leading capitalist economies.[13] In short, some of the problems with financialization arguments are not reducible to the term 'financialization' itself. The points about the theoretical separation of 'financial' and 'real' economies are true of Keynes' or Hilferding's arguments as much as they are about more recent debates actually using the concept 'financialization'. Though, of course, the fact that 'financialization' narratives reflect deeper-lying parts of our critical common sense about finance rather than introducing new ideas wholesale implies, if anything, a greater need for the kind of project undertaken here.

I think it's nonetheless fair to say that 'financialization' has become the dominant conceptual framework for summing up this narrative, and that most uses of the term point to something like these three premises. In short, most invocations of the financialization story – whatever their differences – share politically and theoretically significant underpinning assumptions. As is probably clear, I think this story and the assumptions it rests on are ultimately deeply limiting. The rest of this chapter fills out this sketch of the conceptual core of financialization, showing the intellectual genealogy of the narrative, and highlights some core problems with it. The next two sections map out a brief genealogy of the concept of 'financialization', showing how the elements highlighted here have emerged and taken shape. The concluding section outlines a preliminary critique.

A BRIEF GENEALOGY OF 'FINANCIALIZATION'

The term 'financialization' is sometimes credited to Giovanni Arrighi's *The Long Twentieth Century* – although Arrighi only actually uses the term a handful of times and without precise definition. The term 'financialization' itself is almost an afterthought that Arrighi cribs from a largely forgotten book published the year previous by US political commentator Kevin Phillips, titled *Boiling Point: Democrats, Republicans and the Decline of Middle-Class Prosperity*. Phillips' influence on Arrighi doesn't really extend much beyond the term, and Arrighi's is without doubt a much more rigorous and substantive book. But taken together the two texts are a useful starting point insofar as they do meaningfully point to the context out of which financialization debates emerged and some of the blind spots they inherited from the beginning.

Arrighi and Phillips both very much responded to the same sense shared in the 1980s and early 1990s by many commentators on the left and right of a financial system growing out of control at the expense of the 'real' economy. In important respects, both represent continuations of the debates about the 'casino' economy, with which I opened the book. Explicit articulations of 'financialization' from Phillips, Arrighi, and others to follow put into words a sensibility and encapsulated a set of debates that had been developing for at least a decade prior. Phillips and Arrighi also both respond, albeit with very different normative valences, to related geopolitical debates about the ostensible decline of US hegemony in global politics. There is scant space here to dig into the debates about US decline in the 1980s and 1990s in any detail. But it's notable that the narrative of US decline was contested at the time Phillips and Arrighi wrote, too. Susan Strange's analysis of 'structural power' in the world economy, for instance, offered up a particularly astute critique of US 'declinism' contemporary to Arrighi's work.[14] Strange is arguably very much guilty of the same brand of methodological nationalism as many others in this debate, but nonetheless noted perceptively that the sources of power for US firms and the US state were more 'structural' than direct. US actors, Strange argued, retained dominant positions in global structures of finance, production, knowledge, and military power despite the erosion of formal mechanisms of US dominance and the growth of competing economies in Japan and Germany – perhaps none more important than the enduring global role of the dollar. As Strange insisted, the end of the Bretton Woods system had in fact bolstered the centrality of the US dollar to global financial markets even as its formal role was abandoned – the very depth of global transactions denominated in dollars has rendered the dollar's international role very difficult to displace.[15] And from the vantage point of the 2020s, US power was and is much less weakened than the 1980s common sense had it. The US dollar, for instance, despite periodic predictions of its imminent demise and replacement, retains a central place in the global economy, which continues to be periodically weaponized by US policymakers.[16]

Their veracity aside though, presumptions about US decline had a status adjacent to common sense at the time Arrighi or Phillips wrote, much the same as the vague sense that finance was growing out of control. Both Arrighi and Phillips explicitly, and perhaps less directly Buffett, Bianco, and many of the other 'casino economy' commentators, were concerned with the perceived stagnation and crisis of US-centred capitalism. US decline was a formative concern for Arrighi, who had written extensively on the erosion of US hegemony for at least a decade prior to the publication of the *Long Twentieth Century*.[17] The origins of the concept of financialization lie in efforts to connect the dots between these two sets of anxieties.

Boiling Point is a remarkable artefact in this respect. Phillips was a political adviser to Richard Nixon, and is often credited with Nixon's profoundly racist 'Southern Strategy'. Phillips had risen to prominence in the US on the back of a 1969 book, *The Emerging Republican Majority*, which suggested that the route to a semi-permanent electoral majority for the Republican Party lay in stoking and mobilizing racial resentments against Black and Latinx voters increasingly identified with the Democratic Party.[18] For Phillips, doing so would swing national elections by enabling Republican dominance in the then-still-Democrat-voting former Confederate states. Whether the strategy should really be credited primarily to Phillips or not, Nixon's trademark dogwhistle appeals to 'law and order' very much reflected this approach, which was taken up by subsequent Republican candidates for office. Phillips was in any case quite happy at the time to make himself the face of Nixon's approach – notably in a fawning profile in the *New York Times* in 1970.[19] He eventually left the Nixon administration to write a syndicated newspaper column. By the 1980s, 'Southern Strategy' racial politics had laid much of the political groundwork that made possible large-scale financial deregulation, privatization, and welfare retrenchment.[20] Amidst the wreckage, Phillips styled himself as an ersatz spokesperson for the 'American Middle Class'. He would eventually leave the post-Reagan Republican Party altogether. *Boiling Point* was an encapsulation of this self-recasting. One of the cover blurbs (alongside an endorsement from Nixon himself!) even called Phillips 'the Karl Marx of the Great American Middle Class'.

Boiling Point spoke in important ways to the same concerns and debates about US capitalism with which I opened this book and discussed above. Phillips opened by noting how financial deregulation, tax cuts, and cutbacks to social safety nets adopted across the G7 in the late 1970s and early 1980s had 'proved to be an elixir for global stock markets, property values, and business opportunities',[21] while increasingly leaving out 'the middle class' as real wages and (in a statement that was true at the time, at least) home values stagnated or fell. The end result, Phillips argues, was that

> Middle-class householders found themselves sitting down more and more often with a figurative pencil and piece of paper. *Somebody* had profited enormously in the 1980s, with all that whipped cream and meringue in the financial markets, boardrooms and lawyers' offices, and now *somebody* else – a lot of somebodies – would lose their jobs, pay higher taxes on incomes with lower real purchasing power and otherwise foot the bill for the decline that followed (as declines usually do) the debt-and-speculative boom.[22]

It's notable in this respect that we never really get a concrete definition of the 'middle class' from Phillips. The closest he comes is 'middle income ranks, *not precisely definable* by dollars or purchasing power'.[23] The 'middle class', for Phillips, were more than anything the bearers of what is elsewhere often called the 'standard employment relationship' of mid-twentieth-century Fordist capitalism,[24] that is, people employed in stable, permanent jobs, earning comfortable but not extravagant incomes. This loose definition was implicitly coupled by Phillips with some dubious assumptions about what people in those economic situations were like – especially that they lived in single-family nuclear households and were politically 'moderate'. We can see the implicit assumption about 'middle-class' families in the 'householders' reference in the passage quoted above.[25]

'Financialization' in Phillips' framing is thus incomprehensible without the backdrop of the fraying Fordist compact. Phillips' anxiety about financialization was clearly rooted in the concern that the grand class compromise in the mid-twentieth-century core – which Charles Maier famously characterized in terms of a 'politics of productivity', wherein overt class conflict was moderated through a trade-off of improving pay, job security, and benefits for selected workers paid for out of constantly rising productivity[26] – had come undone. Of course, you'll find no mention in *Boiling Point* of the role that 'Southern Strategy' racial politics had played in enabling this renewed assault on labour. Indeed, in Phillips' telling the same earnest, hardworking, implicitly white, middle-class family supposedly under fire on all sides from criminality and taxes was now also repositioned as the bearer of the assault by finance capital.

The equation of middle-class prosperity with political stability is central to the argument in Phillips' book. Episodes of 'middle-class' decline, for Phillips, 'have always been the stuff of political upheaval'. He proceeds in the following half page to give a bizarre litany of examples to support this point.[27] These range from the Batavian revolution in the late eighteenth-century Netherlands, to rising 'class politics' exemplified in the birth of the Labour Party in the early twentieth-century UK, to the rise of 'social welfare schemes' in agricultural semi-peripheries in the early decades of the twentieth century (he specifically cites New Zealand, Australia, Argentina, and Uruguay), to the rise of the Nazi party in Germany, to the victories of the nominally 'socialist' New Democratic Party in provincial elections in British Columbia, Saskatchewan, and Ontario in Canada at the start of the 1990s. The historical analogies here verge on nonsense. But such assumptions nonetheless presage analyses linking 'white working-class' support for the far right to the erosion of secure employment in the face of globalization, particularly after the election of Donald Trump as president in the US and the 'Brexit' vote in the UK in 2016.[28] Similar assumptions are prevalent in analyses of precarious work more broadly. Guy Standing's writing on the 'precariat', for instance, explicitly worries about the vulnerability of newly precarious workers to mobilization by demagogues in terms not overly distant from Phillips'.[29] Notably, Standing likewise attributes the rise of the 'precariat' to the growing dominance of finance capital, the 1980s onwards representing a 'period when the economy was "disembedded" from society as financiers and neo-liberal economists sought to create a global market economy based on competitiveness and individualism'.[30] What's critical for the moment here, though, is that Phillips' arguments about financialization are reflective of a wider malaise with the decline of the twentieth-century Fordist compromise and the supposed decline of the US as a world power.

Phillips explicitly connected these concerns about the rise of finance, 'middle-class' precarity and political instability to wider geopolitical anxieties about the decline of US hegemony. Drawing on a loose reading of Fernand Braudel and Eric Hobsbawm,[31] among others, he argued that 'financialization' – in the sense of a boom in speculative activity at the expense of 'middle-class' incomes – was a common symptom of hegemonic decline. In Phillips' words,

> While many ordinary Americans found their eroding circum-stances economically painful and politically frustrating, they were hardly unique. Nor was the larger decline overtaking the United States unique. Holland and Britain had also fallen from their middle-class zeniths when manufacturing, trade, nation-alism and bourgeois spirit gave way to 'financialization' – the cumulating influence of finance, government debt, unearned income, *rentiers*, overseas investment, domestic economic polar-ization and social stratification.[32]

Phillips' articulation of 'financialization' here is, above all, rooted in a racialized, moralizing nostalgia. Financialization represented a shift from good, equitable manufacturing and trading economies towards irresponsible speculation, predation, and decadence.

Phillips' direct influence on the debates that followed around financialization was relatively minimal, mostly amounting to the term itself, usually laundered through Arrighi's adoption of it. And Arrighi's engagement with Phillips *is* passing at most. Arrighi credits the term 'financialization' to Phillips, approvingly notes his engagement with Braudel and Hobsbawm, and cites some of Phillips' arguments about the distributional implications of the rise of finance.[33] But Phillips' arguments are nonetheless important here insofar as they speak very clearly to the context and concerns in which arguments about 'financialization' were first articulated. Phillips also makes clear, in a particularly strong form, some of the political stakes of analyses of 'financialization'. Some version of Phillips' nostalgic binary – an imagined past economy rooted in 'good' 'productive' activity, increasingly replaced by the froth and distortion of speculative finance – is also latent in much of the financialization debate (though not normally aligned to quite so regressive a vision of 'class' politics). And more importantly, Phillips undoubtedly spoke to the much more pervasive sense – shared, by the mid-1980s, by the strange collection of billionaires, financial regulators, Marxist critics, and the business press discussed in the Introduction – that finance had slipped the bonds of a productive economy whose activities it increasingly threatened to undermine, and that US power in the world was on the wane.

It's in this context that Arrighi's *Long Twentieth Century*, ultimately of considerable importance in bringing 'financialization' into critical political economy, needs to be read. At its core, the *Long Twentieth Century* is an effort to grapple with the crisis and restructuring of the global economy from the 1970s onwards from a world historical perspective. Arrighi traces the rise and fall of different 'world hegemonies' from the late-medieval period, passing from Genoa, to the Netherlands, to Britain, to the US. Arrighi's concept of 'hegemony' here emphasizes the degree to which a state retains 'the power to exercise functions of leadership and governance over a system of sovereign states'.[34] In this respect, the analysis in the *Long Twentieth Century* is part of a much longer-term effort on Arrighi's part to grapple with the implications of the crisis of Fordist capitalism and supposed decline of US hegemony. In important respects, the later analysis clearly builds on a long 1982 essay in which Arrighi emphasizes the ways in which US hegemony, and particularly the transformation of leading segments of US-based capital in the post-war period, had laid the groundwork for US hegemony, but increasingly came to undermine it. 'The transnational expansion of US capital', Arrighi argues in the earlier essay, 'tended to undermine the imperial framework that had provided the scaffolding for its growth.'[35] In particular, he notes that the tensions inherent in the mid-century Bretton Woods system had given direct rise to a tendency for US capital to 'hoard profits in a supranational money market and to invest them in speculative activities against the dollar'.

This analysis is both made more systematic and extended backwards in *The Long Twentieth Century*. Arrighi emerges in the book with a thesis highlighting a longer-term alternation between two distinct phases of capitalist development, in which a phase of 'material expansion' through commodity production and trade coincides with the emergence of a new hegemonic power and rests on organizational innovations providing the basis for expanded productive activity. Arrighi's main emphasis is on the close links between the emergence of vertically integrated multinational corporations and the rise of American hegemony in the twentieth century. As the 'material expansion' phase proceeds, however, the initial gains from productive innovation are eroded by competition, and along with them the hegemony of the leading power. Capital is thus shifted towards a phase of 'financial expansion' in which profits are derived primarily through speculative activity.

In making the leap from an analysis of the breakdown of Bretton Woods to cycles of hegemony over five centuries, Arrighi takes considerable inspiration from Fernand Braudel's monumental *Civilization and Capitalism* trilogy, both empirically and conceptually. Arrighi declares in introducing his own book that he has 'discovered', in the latter two volumes of *Civilization and Capitalism*, a straightforward 'interpretive scheme' which offers up an explanation of the malaise of late twentieth-century capitalism. 'Finance capital', Arrighi's argument runs, 'is not a particular stage of world capitalism, let alone its latest or highest stage. Rather, it is a recurrent phenomenon which has marked the capitalist era from its earliest beginnings in late medieval and early modern Europe.'[36] Arrighi finds in Braudel a theory of hegemonic change through 'financial expansion'. Throughout the history of capitalism, moments of 'financial expansion' have 'signalled the transition from one regime of accumulation on a world scale to another'.[37]

There are two particularly important facets to this argument which Arrighi draws from Braudel. The first is the idea of 'financial expansion' as a necessary cyclical aspect of hegemonic transitions.

Braudel's discussion in *Civilization and Capitalism* of the turn of Dutch capitalists in the late eighteenth century to lending, particularly to European sovereigns, is particularly formative for Arrighi's argument. Braudel notes that, by the last quarter of the eighteenth century,

> Holland's prosperity led to surpluses which were, paradoxically, an embarrassment, surpluses so great that the credit she supplied to the traders of Europe was not enough to absorb them; the Dutch therefore offered loans to modern states who were particularly adept at consuming capital, if not at repaying it on the promised date.[38]

Braudel is explicit here in, first, drawing the comparison to Genoa two hundred years earlier, and second, in using this comparison to suggest that this shift has a systemic or cyclical basis. In a passage, which Arrighi quotes in setting up his own argument,[39] Braudel asks

> Was this burst of financial activity an aberration as some historians, taking a moral tone, have suggested? Was it not rather a normal development? Already in the latter part of the sixteenth century, another period where capital was superabundant, the Genoese had followed the same itinerary, as the *nobili vecchi*, the official lenders to the King of Spain, gradually withdrew from commercial activity. It looks very much as if Amsterdam, repeating this process, dropped the bird in hand to go chasing shadows, abandoning the money-spinning entrepôt trade for a life of speculation and rentierdom, and leaving all the best cards to London ... But then, did Amsterdam really have any choice? Indeed, had the rich Italians of the sixteenth century had any choice? ... At all events, every capitalist development of this order seems, by reaching this stage of financial expansion, to have in some sense announced its maturity: it was a sign of autumn.[40]

Braudel prevaricates about how systematically this tendency is replicated. But for Arrighi, the phase of 'financial expansion' is part and parcel of the cyclical development of capitalism.

The second major thing Arrighi credits to Braudel is a way of thinking about capital itself which explains this tendency. Braudel suggests (again, in a passage quoted directly by Arrighi),[41] that an 'essential feature' of historical capitalism is its 'unlimited flexibility, its capacity for change and *adaptation*'.[42] Capital is characterized, for Braudel, above all by its fungibility, its ability to 'slip at a moment's notice from one form or sector to another, in times of crisis or of pronounced decline in profit rates'. Indeed, contra perspectives (Marxist and otherwise) which saw in the industrial capitalism of the nineteenth century onwards the realization of the internal logic of capitalist development, Braudel makes these observations towards the end of a 200-page discussion of the activities of capitalists from the fifteenth to the eighteenth centuries, in which capital 'often made incursions' onto the 'foreign territories' of agriculture, industry, and transport, but 'often withdrew quickly as well'.[43] For Arrighi, this amounts to a 'restatement' of Marx's general formula for capital, M-C-M',[44] in which 'Money capital (M) means liquidity, flexibility, freedom of choice', while 'commodity capital (C) means capital invested in a particular input-output combination in view of a profit', and 'hence means concreteness, rigidity, and a narrowing down or closing of options'.[45] It is in the form of money that capital most easily retains its liquidity and flexibility, and hence, for Arrighi, particularly when capitalists do not expect investments in productive capital to yield increased rates of profit, capital will tend to prefer to 'revert to more flexible forms of investment – above all, to its money form'.[46]

Arrighi's core premise here is that direct investment in production comes at considerable risk for capital, particularly in terms of the loss of liquidity and flexibility. It follows here that capital will invest in production only under certain conditions and will tend back towards financial circuits when these conditions are not met. This much is generally true. From this somewhat promising starting point, though, Arrighi quickly takes us in a less helpful direction. Marx's 'general formula' for capital (M-C-M') can thus be, in Arrighi's words 'interpreted as depicting not just the logic of individual capitalist investments, but also a recurrent pattern of historical capitalism as a world system'. The crux of this pattern is an alterna-

tion between phases of 'material expansion', which Arrighi equates
to 'M-C' phases of capital accumulation and phases of financial
expansion, corresponding to the phase C-M'. In the former, money
capital "'sets in motion" an increasing mass of commodities' and, in
the latter 'an increasing mass of money capital "sets itself free" from
its commodity form, and accumulation proceeds through financial deals (as in Marx's abridged formula M-M')'. Taken together,
the phases of material expansion and financial expansion 'constitute a full cycle of accumulation (MCM')'.[47] There's an important
elision here of capital – in the generic and transhistorical sense of
owners of money and productive property in which Braudel uses
the term – with capitalism as a mode of production. And compounding things, in reifying 'capital' in this way, Arrighi makes it
very difficult for us to peer into the actual workings of capital accumulation. Most importantly, capital cannot in fact 'set itself free' of
production under any circumstances.

If their form is somewhat different than Lapavitsas' neat articulation, we can see most of the elements of the financialization
narrative outlined above. The idea of a 'financial expansion', in
which capital increasingly 'frees' itself from the bonds of 'particular input-output combinations' through speculative accumulation,
spells out particularly sharply the assumption that 'financial' forms
of capital are able to more or less 'detach' themselves from the
sphere of production, and that in so doing finance capital takes on
an expansionary imperative. This is perhaps most evident in Arrighi's elevation of 'capital circulating M-M''' from a shorthand to a
label for a discrete species of capital,[48] or even a whole 'phase of
accumulation' unto itself.

In less obvious ways, Arrighi's argument also reflects the particular periodization implicit in the first premise of the financialization
narrative introduced above. Arrighi's diagnosis of the post-1970s
was, in essence, that it was a repetition of secular cycles of capitalist
development. This is a framing, of course, potentially at odds with
the periodization implicit in most later uses of 'financialization'.
These often take the 1970s as a watershed moment, ushering in
an unprecedented period in capitalist history. Yet, Arrighi's main
object was nonetheless, explicitly, the same post-1970s crisis. This
is evident in the first place in the way that the 1994 book builds

on his previous analyses more squarely centred on the US and the preceding quarter-century.[49] But in any case, *The Long Twentieth Century* makes no secret of its presentism. Arrighi's aim is explicitly to engage with longer historical trajectories in order to explain the crisis of advanced capitalism after 1970. 'Over the last quarter of a century', Arrighi opens, 'something fundamental seems to have changed in the way in which capitalism works.'[50] He is quick to add that 'the situation is not as unprecedented as it may appear at first sight', and indeed that the object of the book's historical investigation is to uncover the conditions under which periods of 'crisis, restructuring, and reorganization of global capitalism take place'. But the direct aim is nonetheless to uncover the roots of the period of ostensibly 'financialized' capitalism post-1970 – the historical excursus of the *Long Twentieth Century* is avowedly a 'strictly instrumental' exercise, aimed at more clearly illuminating the key drivers of the contemporary restructuring of global capitalism.[51]

Indeed, it's perhaps notable that Braudel's opus was also written against the backdrop of the early inklings of the same crisis, and in part shaped by it. The question of how the 1970s crisis might reflect longer-run processes frames much of the final volume of *Civilization and Capitalism*:

> Whether a double or single turning point, the change that began in 1973–74 has certainly opened up a long recession. Those who can remember the crisis of 1929–30 have a memory of an unexpected hurricane blowing up out of a clear sky – but which did not last very long. The present crisis which refuses to go away is more sinister, as if it cannot manage to show its true face, or find a label or model which would explain it or reassure us. It is not so much a hurricane as a flood, with the water rising slowly but alarmingly, under a sky obstinately grey and waterlogged. All the foundations of economic life and all the lessons of experience past and present seem to be being challenged.[52]

The precise nature of the crisis is quite obscure here – reflecting a sensibility that would also run through the casino capitalism debates of the 1980s. Something important had changed, something was wrong, though it's not really clear what. Braudel doesn't, in fact, offer much more than the 'dark hints and ominous warnings' that Magdoff and Sweezy would locate in the 'casino economy' debates later on.

Arrighi closes the *Long Twentieth Century* in slightly less ambivalent terms. He notes that each 'cycle of accumulation' had created larger and more complex organizations aimed at resolving the previous crisis of overaccumulation. In his words, 'the crises of overaccumulation that marked the transition from one organizational structure to another also created the conditions for the emergence of ever more powerful governmental and business agencies capable of solving the crises through a reconstitution of the capitalist world-economy on larger and more comprehensive foundations'. But this process, sooner or later, 'must reach a stage at which the crisis of overaccumulation cannot bring into existence an agency powerful enough to reconstitute the system on larger and more comprehensive foundations'.[53] But on the question of whether this might be the case now, or what might bring it about, Arrighi avers. He wonders whether the rapid growth of East Asian economies constituted the 'material expansion' phase of an emergent cycle, or, indeed, in the last words of the book, whether the denouement of US hegemony might lead us all to 'burn up in the horrors (or glories) of the escalating violence that has accompanied the liquidation of the Cold War world order'.[54] Capitalism might end, Arrighi notes, in a reversion to 'the systematic chaos from which it began six hundred years ago', concluding that 'Whether this would mean the end just of capitalist history or of all human history, it is impossible to tell'.[55] It's notable that in the end Arrighi shares a certain apocalypticism with Phillips (though, I hasten to add, apocalypticism of a radically different kind – you'll find none of Phillips' reactionary nostalgia in Arrighi). For both, the analysis of financialization is dominated above all else by a sense that something significant in the way the world was organized was changing and the end result would likely be chaotic. They lapse in other words, into 'dark hints and ominous warnings'.

Arrighi had used the specific word 'financialization' sparingly in all this, though the analysis of 'financial expansion' was a core feature of his book. But the concept was clearly one of the main things that readers took away from the book. In 1996, for instance, in an extended article seeking to place emerging debates about 'globalization' in their world historical context, Samir Amin would present the 'financialization' of the world economy – a process in which 'financial preoccupations have gradually assumed more importance than those concerning economic growth or the expansion of systems of production' – as a crucial element of the contemporary restructuring of world capitalism.[56] Amin's analysis here drew heavily on Arrighi's – though he criticized Arrighi for having followed Braudel in abandoning the 'law of value'[57] and argued that, if the latter were kept in view, the contemporary financialization of global capitalism actually dated to the 1880s, marked by a 'permanent trend towards the concentration of capital', which had 'toppled the competitive form of the productive system ... and ushered in a new oligopolistic form' in ways that had permanently altered the ways in which financialization as such took place and its import.[58] Greta Krippner's work a decade or so later on likewise drew considerable inspiration from Arrighi, even as she sought to put some of Arrighi's claims about contemporary 'financial expansion' on firmer empirical grounds.[59]

For the moment, the point is that it's out of these debates and this unease with the restructuring of late twentieth-century capitalism that the core of 'financialization' as a concept and a narrative emerges. Present-day financialization debates are shaped less directly by the arguments these authors develop and much more by the way that loose ideas about 'financialization' were consolidated in the 2000s, and then propagated in the aftermath of the 2007–08 Global Financial Crisis. In the process, the debates about American hegemony, and the more generally Braudelian historical thrust of Arrighi's and Phillips' arguments, were sloughed off – and with them, to a considerable extent, the question of the end of capitalism (and/or the end of the world).

EXPANDING AND CONSOLIDATING 'FINANCIALIZATION'

Post-2000 debates about financialization saw the development of different strands of financialization arguments, and particularly after 2008 the consolidation of financialization into a more singular narrative. Natascha van der Zwan, in an influential 2014 article, mapped out three different strands of financialization research, which she labelled, respectively, 'financialization as a regime of accumulation', 'financialization as shareholder value', and the 'financialization of the everyday'.[60]

The first strand of work here – financialization 'as a regime of accumulation' – took up the broad problematic established in Magdoff and Sweezy and Arrighi's work fairly directly, while narrowing the latter's historical scope considerably. Perspectives on financialization emphasized that 'something fundamental seems to have changed', increasingly without Arrighi's insistence that 'the situation is not as unprecedented as it may appear'.[61] These studies were concerned generally with the growing importance of finance in the economies of leading capitalist countries. The most notable contribution here is probably an influential article from Greta Krippner on the 'financialization of the American economy'.[62] Krippner notes (rightly, I ought to add) of Arrighi and Phillips that neither actually establishes much of a systematic empirical basis for the claim that the US economy has been substantially 'financialized'. She describes her article as, in essence, an attempt to do so. This is in effect the reason for dropping Arrighi's longer historical lens. Krippner is explicit in a later book building on her 2005 article that financialization does not necessarily represent an 'entirely novel phase of capitalist development', but that her analytic focus was confined to the post-war US.[63] The loss of Arrighi's historical sweep was the cost of a shift towards more rigorously conceptualizing and quantifying 'financialization'.

A collection of essays edited by Gerald Epstein, published around the same time as Krippner's article, introduced similar concerns into heterodox economics.[64] The essays in the Epstein collection, in a vein not totally dissimilar to Krippner's article, are predominantly focused on empirically substantiating the scope and extent of the growth of the financial sector as a proportion of the world economy since the 1970s.

A related question thrown up by post-2000 financialization work, and particularly highlighted in the Epstein book, concerns the relationship between neoliberalism and financialization. Of course this relationship between the financial deregulation of the

1970s and 1980s and the rise of finance is a pressing concern for much of the 'casino capitalism' debate – Madgoff and Sweezy note its importance, as described above, Phillips identifies the importance of regulatory reforms even as he obscures his own role in laying the groundwork for them. There is a very clear sense in much of this debate that the phenomena of financialization and neoliberalism are related, but it's less clear exactly how. In one chapter, co-authored with Arjun Jayadev, Epstein traces the rising 'rentier share' of income in OECD countries. The rising incomes of the 'rentier class', which Epstein and Jayadev more or less equate with finance, were facilitated by financial deregulation and other shifts in monetary and financial policy, which in turn enabled the further entrenchment of economic and monetary policies privileging rentier interests. Rentiers, in their argument 'have been able to push for greater political power: In promoting independent central banks and inflation targeting to keep real interest rates high, in exhorting low budget deficits to reduce inflationary pressure, and in repressing labor which threatens to reduce their share of rents'.[65] 'Rentier' incomes, in short, have 'benefited handsomely from neoliberal policies'.[66] This general narrative was widely shared in both heterodox economics and wider Marxist debates by the early 2000s. David Harvey succinctly encapsulates this narrative when he suggests that when US-led Fordist capitalism had begun to break down in the 1970s, it drove a shift towards a more finance-led model of accumulation, which

> entailed shifting the balance of power and interests within the bourgeoisie from productive activities towards institutions of finance capital. This could be used to attack the power of working class movements either directly, by exercising disciplinary oversight on production, or indirectly by facilitating greater geographical mobility for all forms of capital.[67]

Gérard Duménil and Dominique Lévy make a similar claim that 'neoliberalism is the expression of a desire of a class of capitalist owners and the institutions in which their power is concentrated, which we collectively call "finance", to restore ... the class' revenues and power, which had diminished since the Great Depression and

WWII'.[68] This is a particularly clear illustration of the framing of finance as a 'power bloc' introduced in the previous chapter.

Yet this is a troublesome reading in many ways – the fact that neoliberal reforms have fostered the interests of finance capital does not, in and of itself, mean that the interests of finance as a bloc are a sufficient explanation for neoliberal reforms. There have been relatively few efforts to actually unpick the regulatory decisions of neoliberal policymakers. In her later book, Krippner notes that from Arrighi's 'lofty' long-run vantage point it is often quite difficult to grasp the actual actions of state managers or of capital, or indeed to differentiate one from the other.[69] Krippner lumps 'Marxist' and 'World-Systems' accounts of financialization together here, taking Arrighi as the main exemplar of both. This is, at best, a debatable choice.[70] But Krippner's core methodological argument – that the world historical lens adopted in Arrighi's argument comes at the loss of much serious consideration of how and why state managers foster financial accumulation under particular circumstances – is probably nonetheless correct. And she is absolutely right that the result is to overstate the coherence of the leading 'bloc' of finance capital, as well as the efficacy of the financial 'fix' to flagging profitability. I return to the role of the state and its relationship to finance capital in Chapter 5, but for now the point is that the relationship between neoliberal reforms and processes of financialization was a particularly important question thrown up by 2000s debates, but also particularly difficult to resolve satisfyingly within its own confines.

But the wider narrative of 'financialization' also came about not just by extensions of Arrighi's general problematic, but through their fusion and interpenetration with other largely parallel strands of debate. I turn to these in the next two subsections.

Shareholder Value

A few years after Arrighi, there was a reconsideration of shifting patterns of corporate governance and the rising importance of 'shareholder value'. Here we can point to a heterogeneous community of scholars, centred on a handful of interdisciplinary journals (notably *Economy and Society* and *Competition and Change*) and positioned at the intersection of critical management studies, heterodox economics, political economy, and sociology in developing and popularizing analyses of 'shareholder value' orientation among leading firms, as well as developing the concept of 'financialization' itself.

William Lazonick and Mary O'Sullivan, in a particularly influential contribution to a 2000 *Economy and Society* special issue, traced a shift in the funding and governance models of major corporations, particularly in the US, from 'retain and reinvest' to 'shareholder value'.[71] Prior to the 1980s, a 'relatively small number of giant corporations' dominated the US economy, organized around principles of 'retain and reinvest' – 'these corporations tended to retain both the money they earned and the people whom they employed, and they reinvested in physical capital and complementary human resources'.[72] This organizational principle ran into difficulty in the 1960s and 1970s, as major firms were over-extended into 'too many divisions in too many different types of business', and (in something of a parallel to Arrighi's arguments) increasingly intense competition from Japanese firms in leading industries. Financial economists increasingly offered an alternative in the form of 'agency theory' – emphasizing the superiority of 'market' forms to managerial control in the efficient allocation of resources, and the need for a 'takeover mechanism' to discipline management on behalf of shareholders. These ideational shifts, for Lazonick and O'Sullivan, were given impetus by the rise of institutional investors – the widening participation of pension funds, insurers, and mutual funds in stock and bond markets, encouraged by the gradual loosening of regulatory restrictions. Corporate managers in this context were increasingly oriented towards the promotion of shareholder returns, driving a shift from 'retain and reinvest' models to 'downsize and distribute': 'Under the new regime, top managers downsize the corporations they control, with a particular emphasis on cutting the labour forces they employ, in an attempt to increase the return on equity'.[73] The crucial consequences of these shifts were, on one hand, a growing tide of layoffs and labour force downsizing, and on the other, a growing emphasis on redistributing profits to shareholders in the form of dividends and stock buybacks.

It's notable in the first instance here that this approach seems to imply a more constrained definition of 'financialization'. Lazonick and O'Sullivan trace a specific shift in the way that managers and investors understand and operationalize profit itself and the implications this has for the operations of firms. Studies of the influence of 'shareholder value' doctrines on corporate activity in particular sectors have generated fine-grained insights about the impacts of these changes on the process of production itself, documenting (inter alia) the growing significance of financial market imperatives in shaping firm-level decisions – ranging from choices about the sourcing of clothing in global value chains to brewery closures and the growing reliance of car manufacturers on profits from sales financing in the face of low profit margins on manufacturing activity.[74] Studies across a number of sectors point generally to the growing trend for firms beholden to equity markets to prioritize share buybacks and dividends to the detriment of investing in productive capacity, and very often to the detriment of workers.[75]

As with the growth of the financial sector relative to the overall economy, all of these are real enough trends. In some instances, they have been misinterpreted, exaggerated, or overgeneralized. Joel Rabinovich, for instance, argues persuasively that the narrative where a growing share of the income of non-financial corporations comes from financial activities is probably overstated – both in the sense that it has declined in aggregate since the early 2000s and that some nominally 'financial' profits are in fact side-effects of other activities or other forms of restructuring (notably, tax avoidance and the internationalization of production).[76] More importantly, a perspective emphasizing the power of finance as the motive force behind the patterns of restructuring traced here threatens to obscure as much as it reveals. George Liagouras notes that such perspectives underplay the importance of wider structural shifts in corporate form – notably the articulation of global networks of production and the growing importance of intangible assets poorly captured by categories derived from industrial capitalism.[77] Perhaps even more importantly, the assumption that these shifts are driven on or on behalf of finance capital obscures other contested and contradictory drivers of these shifts (a point I'll return to further in the concluding section).

The Financialization of Daily Life

The expansionary character of finance has been given much of the emphasis in the growing debate on the 'financialization of daily life', following Randy Martin's book of the same title.[78] For Martin, the point was to explore a growing sense that financial relations constituted an increasingly important part not just of 'the economy' as such, but of the ways that people made and understood themselves. Martin underlines in this sense the ever-wider 'invitation to live by finance'. Paul Langley, a few years after, would publish a landmark study of the production of financial subjectivities along lines similar to those laid out by Martin. Langley emphasized a growing shift from discourses of savings and thrift towards an emphasis on 'investment' accompanying the neoliberal privatization and retrenchment of pensions and social security. As Langley rightly notes, there are important differences between deep-rooted logics of 'thrift' and the invocations of 'investment' favoured in neoliberal interventions – particularly in relation to their respective articulations of risk and calculation: 'While thrift and insurance calculate and manage risk as a possible hindrance, danger, or loss to be minimized, risk is represented through the calculations of everyday investment as an incentive or opportunity to be grasped.'[79] The rise of finance, in short, asked people to understand their transformed relationship to risk as a crucial site through which they would produce their own livelihoods and life-courses.

The broad agenda that's followed Martin's and Langley's work is probably the most coherent and self-contained of the wider financialization debates. Much of the emphasis in the literature on the financialization of daily life has been on mapping the particular modes of calculation and subjectivity through which financial subjects are expected to manage their own existence – or, in Sarah Hall's evocative terms, everyday uses of financial techniques and subjectivities have become increasingly 'inescapable'.[80] Recent studies have closely examined lived subjectivities of engagements with financial products and markets in a variety of contexts.[81] An important strand of literature here emphasizes the kinds of agency, and even possible resistance, exercised in and through consumer engagements with various financial instruments. A particular point of emphasis for Langley is that everyday users of financial services are frequently framed as 'passive dupes of the power and agency of globalising finance capital.'[82]

The financialization of daily life is certainly – as Christophers concedes in his critique of financialization – one of the most distinctive strands of research to emerge under the banner of financialization. 'Perhaps only', Christophers argues, in the strand of work following Martin, 'does financialization provide original and forceful theoretical insight.'[83] Christophers insists though, rightly in my view, that the 'financialization' narrative here nonetheless offers up an unduly restricted historical optic on the production and reproduction of financial subjectivities. The responsibilizing thrust of contemporary neoliberal policymaking, for instance, finds parallels in a much longer history of promotion of investment activities in the metropolitan core,[84] and indeed in responses to colonial crises.[85] Likewise, the focus on financial subjectivities can risk pulling attention away from the ways that the restructuring of mass investment is in many ways profoundly linked to the restructuring of work and livelihoods more broadly. Susanne Soederberg argues in this sense that 'much of the literature on financialisation and consumer society stops at the realm of exchange without venturing into the wider capitalist relations of production and by extension, accumulation.'[86]

A Post-2008 Explosion

Although the groundwork had been laid for close to two decades, it wasn't really until after the 2008 financial crisis that the 'financialization' story really took off as a kind of common sense about how the global economy works. In 2009, introducing what would turn out to be an influential collection of articles in *Competition and Change* on the relevance of 'financialization' studies for making sense of the then-unfolding Global Financial Crisis, Johnna Montgomerie and Karel Williams could still talk of 'financialization' studies as being carried out by a 'diverse minority within the political and cultural economy'.[87] Ewald Engelen, in the same issue, could describe a growing interest in financialization which was nonetheless being carried out by a small community which had work to do in order to 'convince the wider social science community of its descriptive and explanatory value-added'.[88]

Suffice to say that the wider social science community appears to have bought into the concept. Figure 1.1 gives an admittedly crude measure of this growing consensus, based on a keyword search for 'financialization' in Scopus.[89] Some caveats are in order, as this is far from a comprehensive sample. Scopus results are limited to academic publications, and they are not comprehensive even of all academic publications (Scopus' coverage of books is particularly poor). The results shown include only articles with 'financialization' as a keyword – a small subset of those that talk about 'financialization' in some capacity or take on board parts of the narrative as background. The results also don't include studies that have used the somewhat less common British spelling ('financialisation'). So the numbers here are far from a comprehensive sample. The number of academic journals and articles published during this period has also itself grown, which doubtless accounts for some of the growth in 'financialization' articles. But with all due caveats, the pattern here is nonetheless extremely clear and highly unlikely to be solely an artefact of the database or search parameters: there are eleven articles in the Scopus database published in 2008 with 'financialization' as a keyword; for 2022, there are 287.

It's difficult or impossible to encapsulate all of these overlapping debates at this point – though I deal further with some more recent examples in Chapters 4 and 5 in particular. But ironically, the rapid pluralization of 'financialization' studies has probably made it easier rather than harder to boil 'financialization' down to a relatively cohesive core narrative. The 2008 Global Financial Crisis has clearly served as a significant spur for this rapid expansion of financialization debates. It's notable that Lapavitsas' definition cited at the beginning of this chapter was published in 2009, one of many reflections on the politics and political economy of global finance occasioned by the crisis. Van der Zwan's 2014 article itself played a notable role in this, linking together three relatively insulated

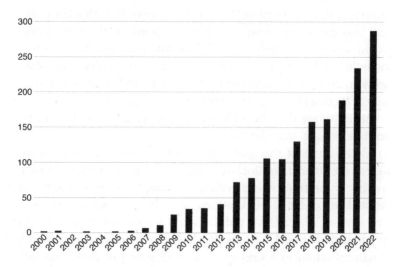

Figure 1.1   Scopus keyword search results for 'Financialization' by year
of publication, 2000–22
Source: Author.

strands of research into something like a single research programme. We'll deal with some of the more specific iterations of this
programme in the later chapters of this book, especially Chapters 4
and 5. For now it's probably worth noting that it's especially in the
proliferation of work on financialization post-crisis that Ouma's
shift from 'explanandum to explanans' truly takes place. Where for
Arrighi, and Krippner, 'financialization' was something that needed
to be explained, and for shareholder value debates it gestured at a
specific tendency in the restructuring of leading firms and value
chains, in a growing proportion of work on financialization the
increasing generalized power of finance capital itself increasingly
stands in as explanation for diverse social phenomena.

CONCLUSION: A PRELIMINARY CRITIQUE
OF FINANCIALIZATION

In the foregoing, I've traced the broad outlines of a consensus
around the meaning of 'financialization', and placed this within
an intellectual genealogy of debates about the place of finance

in capitalism. By the mid-1980s, both the business press and the academic left had come to the similar conclusion that the financial system had run amok, to the detriment of the economy as a whole. This 'casino capitalism' narrative was the backdrop against which Phillips uses the term 'financialization' to describe a threat to 'middle-class' wellbeing. Arrighi cribbed the term 'financialization', in passing, from Phillips, in the midst of an expressly Braudelian analysis linking financial expansion and the decline of American hegemony. It's nonetheless from Arrighi in particular that the term was quickly taken up in critical analyses of capitalism. Other strands of 'financialization' debate started emerging in the late 1990s and 2000s, through analyses of shareholder value ideologies and the 'financialization of daily life'. These debates were increasingly consolidated through a few influential analyses in the 2000s and took off dramatically in the aftermath of the 2008 Global Financial Crisis.

What's wrong, then, with the financialization story? I flesh out some of these problems, alongside tracing the further development of financialization debates, in subsequent chapters. For the moment, I want to sketch the outlines of a critique. Taking the key precepts of the financialization story in turn (a post-1970s periodization, the presumption of the expansionary character of finance, and the separation of financial and real economies), I'll discuss briefly in this section how each poses important limits on our discussions of finance and capitalism.

A Constricted Historical Lens

I've noted above that much of Arrighi's – or for that matter, even Phillips' – historical sweep has been excised from recent discussions of financialization. This isn't, in and of itself, a problem. Krippner, for one, is quite explicit in trading historical breadth for empirical precision. But epochal readings of 'financialization' nonetheless pose some significant constraints on analyses of the shifting role of finance. Some of these are neatly captured by Christophers' critique of 'optic' limits of financialization.[90] Christophers argues that studies of financialization have tended to focus almost exclusively on the post-1970 period and to blur what is in some cases a justifiable methodological choice to restrict the scope of analysis with an overarching global periodization. The result is that 'studies of financialization are in important respects predisposed' to overstating the novelty of contemporary patterns.[91] For Christophers, this matters insofar as 'Looking at financialization in the present through a strictly presentist lens ... can only ever furnish a partial perspective on its constitution.'[92]

I return to some more detailed engagements with this problem of the historical lineages of contemporary finance in some of the discussions of the shifting terrain of global production in Chapter 3, of land and nature in Chapter 4, and of 'Development' practice in Chapter 5. For the moment, one brief example might suffice. A range of recent pieces have shown that, from the perspective of much of the global south, many of the contradictions commonly associated with contemporary processes of financialization – especially the seeming divorce of 'financial' from 'real' activities, persistent underinvestment, and persistent financial instability – are the historic norm going back much farther than the 1970s, particularly in colonized countries. As Kai Koddenbrock and colleagues insist in a long-run historical analysis of Senegal and Ghana, the 'divorce' of productive economies from financial profits ought to be read as a symptom of colonial economies rather than a recent product of financialization.[93] And attention to this longer history opens up a much wider range of analytical resources, and offers means of considering the lineages of the present in much more complex terms. Samir Amin, for instance, was writing insightfully about the 'inertia' implicit in colonial financial and monetary systems as an obstacle to development in the 1960s and 1970s.[94] The historical richness of our analyses aside, moreover, absent this kind of consideration, a lot of the debate about financialization risks mistaking the exceptional experience of post-war Fordism in a handful of core economies for the historic norm.

Financial Expansion and Its Limits

Another key problem concerns the presumption of the 'expansionary' character of finance. The presumption of expansionary finance tends to lead towards a kind of 'positive case bias' in studies of financialization. That is to say, we tend to look at cases where this or that phenomenon has been subjected to speculative trading, overlooking the places where efforts to build financial markets have encountered resistance, or simply failed.[95] But the more important problem here is not just that studies of financialization are marked by a failure to recognize the empirical limits of processes of 'financialization', but that the assumption of finance capital's expansionary tendencies can lead us to misdiagnose the drivers of 'financial expansion' itself where it does take place. To put it simply, if we presume that finance capital is (a) dominant, and (b) inherently expansionary, it is seductively easy to attribute disparate social and economic phenomena to the unfolding interests of finance capital.

I return to several more concrete examples related to this point in Chapters 4 and 5. For now, a brief example will hopefully suffice of the ways this set of assumptions can mislead us. At the level of the firm, Sam Knafo and Sahil Dutta have recently compellingly shown that the so-called 'shareholder revolution' of the 1980s was 'the unintended outcome of political contests *among* different groups of corporations, rather than the product of the external imposition of *shareholder preferences* on corporate America as a whole'.[96] They point to the significance of corporate conglomerates in the 1960s, a group of smaller challenger firms predominantly in the US, using high levels of debt and access to credit in order to finance aggressive strategies of acquisitions. For Knafo and Dutta, the conglomerate strategies represented not just a mechanism for diversification – creating the type of sprawling corporations to which Lazonick and O'Sullivan, among others, viewed the shareholder revolution as a response – but a radically different, and profoundly contested, shift in the orientation of corporate strategy which was later picked up by the 'corporate raiders' 1980s.[97] Rather than the embodiment of structural forces, raiders represented a different strand of managerial practice:

> Corporate raiders ... were managers in their own right. Just like the conglomerates before them, they leveraged on financial markets as a means to capture other firms. While it is true that they legitimated their actions in the name of shareholders,

their concerns were primarily managerial. At stake was a matter of gaining control over firms and capturing assets, not simply exerting voice or threatening exit to influence managers.[98]

The primacy of shareholders, they argue, was a largely unintended consequence of these managerial strategies. Raiding managers often couched their actions in appeals to the interests of shareholders, a process which did open up more space for shareholders to advance claims of their own, but shareholders nonetheless played a predominantly reactive role in the financialization of the firm. As Knafo and Dutta summarize:

> That shareholders have gained handsomely in the era of shareholder value and joined in on the spoils of financialized management is without question. Yet the evidence is much weaker, if not contrary, when it comes to the impact of shareholder agency and their ability to drive change.[99]

For present purposes, the point is that assimilating the rise of shareholder value orientation into a wider story of the growing power of finance leads us to a superficially compelling diagnosis of changes in corporate governance as the product of the growing power of finance. In practice, though, this intuitive story leads us potentially to miss the much messier, more contested story underlying the rise of the shareholder as a key figure in corporate governance. Equally, it leads us to overstate the direct power exercised by shareholders, and more importantly, to misinterpret its origins and drivers.

Bifurcating Finance from Capitalism

Finally, the financialization narrative invites the idea that capital accumulation increasingly takes on forms 'divorced' from the 'real' economy. I've already, to an extent, highlighted some of the problems this creates in the discussion of the historical optic of financialization above. Many of the problems we tend to attribute to 'financialization' are, in fact, much deeper-rooted. More to the point, a focus on the growing reach and power of finance per se offers up a truncated and partial lens on the restructuring of contemporary capitalism. I'll elaborate on some of the problems this creates in the chapters that follow, but for now it's worth noting that a focus on the power of finance creates both analytical and strategic problems. I highlighted the kind of circularity that invocations of financialization can introduce in the previous subsection. But maybe more importantly, the assumption that contemporary forms of finance are particularly marked by the power of finance capital has implications in terms of both how efforts to build a more just world must be targeted and how and by whom they might be carried out. A focus on financialization as the predominant structural tendency in contemporary capitalism risks gearing these struggles overly onto financial terrain (to put in the simplest terms a point to which I'll return in Chapter 6), and misrecognizing the power of finance itself. As I'll show in the chapters that follow, what we need both analytically and politically is not merely to be able to confront or to democratize the power of finance, but to be able to cut to the root of capitalist relations of value in the first place. In the next chapter, I start to develop some tools for doing this, drawing on Marx's notes on money and the credit system in conjunction with more recent Marxist debates.

2

Finance as Process

If not through narratives of 'financialization', how should we understand the place of finance in contemporary capitalism? In this chapter, I want to sketch the first cut of an alternative approach. Of necessity, this chapter is probably the densest and the most abstract part of this book. I can only promise that the claims here will be fleshed out more concretely in later chapters. Here, I draw on engagements with Marx and subsequent Marxian debates about money, value, and finance capital to argue for a 'process' view of finance, centred around the continual dynamic interplay of abstract and concrete labour. The 'process' view articulated here draws on David Harvey's distinction between conceptions of finance capital as a 'power bloc' – 'a particular configuration of factional alliances within the bourgeoisie' – and of finance capital as a 'process' – 'a particular kind of circulation process of capital which centres on the credit system'.[1] A process view suggests a way of framing the relationships between finance and wider processes of capitalist accumulation that allows us to keep the exploitation of labour and nature in view in our analyses of financial accumulation.

But before we get to that, we need to reckon with the problem of 'value'. I want to avoid two parallel traps into which discussions of finance in recent years have tended to fall. On one hand, we are often confronted with the dogmatic assertion that finance capital is somehow inherently 'fictitious',[2] or a parasitic imposition on the 'real', 'productive' economy, which is the site in which value is produced. Some Marxist perspectives on finance and financialization have a bad habit of doing this.[3] What could be called the 'orthodox' Marxist view asserts that financial operations cannot generate 'value' as the latter can only be produced in the labour process. As such, financial profits are a mix of parasitic rents and speculative froth which will be brought down to earth in the next financial crash. On the other hand, one of the great problems with 'financialization' narratives is precisely that they often wind up by telling us, wrongly, that labour and production as such no longer matter very much, or that finance capital has 'detached' itself from them and now accumulates in a recursive and self-referential process. A number of more recent perspectives within and outside of Marxist traditions assert that the growing dominance of finance capital detached from labour means that labour itself is no longer central to the operation of value. As such, our politics need to start not from labour and the workplace, but from assets and the calculation of risks. These perspectives are effectively two sides of the same coin: they both treat financial profits as somehow capable of being 'detached' from the labour process, but disagree about how to interpret that detachment. They also both lean, as I'll argue further below, on an unduly narrow and inflexible understanding of labour, production, and exploitation under capitalism.

A more productive starting place, I think, is from the premise that all capital, including finance capital, is in Marx's words, 'value in process'. That is, capital is so many organizationally discrete bundles of money and commodities recirculated through processes of production and exchange in hopes of realizing surplus value. This fact of circulating in search for returns is what distinguishes money in its form as capital, as such, from money as revenue to be hoarded or spent on consumption goods. But, critically, putting value into motion as capital also means putting it at risk. In order for anticipated returns to take the concrete form of profit, they must be realized in and through the concrete exploitation of labour and nature, on one hand, and through the sale of finished commodities, on the other. These movements are risky, costly, and always prone to failures, big and small. They also necessarily involve a degree of spatial and temporal displacement – capital in the form of money is spent at one point in time, in hope that it returns with profit at some more or less definite point in time in the future. In the meantime, capital in circulation must manage to mobilize labour and nature at a cost and a level of productivity consistent with the value embodied in the original capital, otherwise, in Harvey's words, 'capital is lost because the individual concrete specific conditions of labour do not correspond to the conditions for embodying concrete labour.'[4] The point here is that it does very important things for how we understand finance if we accept that abstraction, risk, leverage, and speculation are inherent to the accumulation of capital, not just to a specifically 'financial' form thereof.[5] The twin corollaries of this are both that financial profits can only ever be divorced from production in appearance, and on the other hand, that there are no capitalist relations of value without finance. Finance capital is inherent to capital's most basic laws of motion. Harvey's 'process' view is particularly useful here insofar as it enjoins us to analyze the specifically 'financial' activities of capital firmly within the wider circuits of capital accumulation. This helps get us beyond the unhelpful stalemate of some recent debates about finance, labour, and value.

The remainder of this chapter develops this argument further in three sections. The first section below outlines and develops a critique of the post-2008 revival of 'value' debates, specifically as they pertain to finance. The next section makes the case for an understanding of value rooted in risk – or maybe more precisely, in the uncertain valorization of 'abstract', socially necessary labour through 'concrete', embodied labour. The final section turns to Harvey's 'process' approach to finance capital to outline the place of finance in relation to this wider tension.

FINANCIAL CRISIS AND THE CRISIS OF VALUE

By now it's a cliché to open a discussion like this one by noting that the years post-2008 have seen a marked revival in engagements with Marxist theory on X. I cannot, unfortunately, think of a better way to mark out this section. The crisis and its aftermath directly prompted myriad reconsiderations of the concept of 'value' itself and its relationship to labour exploitation and to finance in particular. This revival is clearly not unrelated to the post-crisis boom in studies of financialization noted in the previous chapter, but it has also taken place in no small part in parallel to, or in critical dialogue with, ideas about financialization. The set of traps into which these debates have tended to fall are instructive about the way towards a more helpful understanding of finance, value, and capitalism.

If there's such a thing as a 'conventional' or 'orthodox' reading of exploitation and value in Marx, it centres on the discussion of surplus value in the first volume of *Capital*.[6] Here, Marx seeks to demonstrate that, even where all commodities are exchanged at a 'fair' price reflecting their underlying value in terms of socially necessary labour time, it is the exploitation of labour that generates surplus value for capitalists. The basis for the argument is that, if the value of commodified labour reflects its own cost of reproduction – the hours of daily work it takes to clothe, house, and feed a worker – then capital is able to expand itself by appropriating surplus value through its capacity to extract more hours of work from the worker than is required for their reproduction. Labour power is thus unique among commodities in its capacity to produce surplus value.[7] Marx's key claims here are, first, that capital exploits *even when* workers are paid 'fairly' for their labour power, and, second, that capitalist forms of exploitation are in this sense uniquely veiled by the nominally 'free' market exchange of commodities. Exploitation under capitalism is not direct, but rather takes the appearance of a market exchange between nominal equals. This reading of surplus value is sometimes – both by allegedly 'orthodox' Marxists and by their critics – spun into a rigid reading where value can only be 'created' through wage work in production organized along very narrowly defined capitalist lines (note in the first instance the slippage between 'surplus value' and 'value' here).

This kind of reading creates some notable difficulties in articulating a Marxist perspective on finance. If value can only be 'created' in the sphere of production, then by definition financial activities cannot 'create' value. Lapavitsas' reliance on the term 'expropriation', rather than 'exploitation' to describe the turn by financial institutions in the US in particular 'to the personal revenue of workers and others as sources of profit', is a case in point.[8] Financial expropriation, for Lapavitsas, 'is an additional source of profit that originates in the sphere of circulation', as distinguished from 'exploitation', which 'occurs in production and remains the cornerstone of contemporary capitalist economies'.[9] If we frame 'value' in this way, then the question quickly becomes one of how finance can (as in the title of a subsequent article and book from Lapavitsas) 'profit without producing'.[10] Lapavitsas points to stagnating profitability in productive sectors marked by mature 'monopoly capital' and a consequent boom in financial activity: 'an asymmetry has emerged between the sphere of production and the booming sphere of circulation'.[11] Cédric Durand offers a somewhat similar perspective in which financial profits are inherently contradictory. Finance for Durand is 'split between the predatory logic inherent in its incapacity to generate value by itself' and its role in 'organising capital accumulation, which favours innovation'.[12] Financial profits for Durand are necessarily parasitic, but finance cannot be reduced to parasitism because it is necessary for the organization of capital.

Productive stagnation and falling real wages appear in these framings as a kind of ultimate *limit* on financial profits – that is, finance can't ultimately 'expropriate' more than workers earn in wages. Durand's emphasis on the contradictory nature of finance capital and financial profits is one example. Lapavitsas, similarly, is careful to insist that financialization is an *asymmetry* between finance and productive capital rather than 'the escape of capital to the realm of finance'.[13] In this case, the ostensible decline of productive capital, resulting in falling wages and the growing precarity of employment, are in the final analysis a fetter on the continued expansion of financial profits. Lapavitsas and a co-author highlight this dynamic clearly in a more recent article, suggesting that falling wages and employment had created a 'watershed' moment for financialization in the US.[14] In this respect, Lapavitsas is correct and the distinction between exploitation and expropriation is useful up to a point. But this is nonetheless to drive much too clean a dividing line between the exploitation of labour in the workplace and through debt, and between productive and financial activity on the part of capital. And ironically, this is a move that lets Lapavitsas and others largely bracket out much direct consideration of the concrete practices of exploitation at work in the 'real economy', in favour of large-scale aggregates of the labour share, and how these intersect with the shifting terrain of finance. The main stumbling block here, as I'll show further in the next section, is to do with the assumption that value is a tangible quantum with a specific origin – or in other words, the assumption that value is a thing that must be 'created' at a specific point in the circuit of capital.

The other side of the coin here are a series of sympathetic critiques of Marx's value theory. The common basis for these latter arguments is that Marxist approaches ostensibly cannot account for finance as a 'value-generating' sphere of activity so long as they hinge on the idea that labour is the font of all value. This is often seen as rendering Marxian value theory obsolete or needing updating in order to render it compatible with twenty-first-century capitalism. As Dick Bryan and colleagues put it, 'if theories of value cannot incorporate finance in a central role, then they are disengaged from the frontiers of capital accumulation'.[15] The starting point here is undoubtedly a right one – finance has always been an integral part of capitalist relations of production and a theory of value which cannot accommodate finance is of limited use. However, what is actually being rejected in these discussions is typically the 'orthodox Marxist' view introduced above, taken to hinge on a Ricardian 'labour theory of value' (of which Marx's discussion of surplus value is in fact a critique).[16]

One notable direction here has been to draw on a particular reading of 'value form'[17] Marxisms, particularly the work of Moishe Postone.[18] While a full critical account of Postone's argument in his landmark *Time, Labour and Social Domination* is beyond my scope here, it is worth pulling out a couple of key points. Postone's main contribution is an insistence that capitalism is characterized not so much by a particular property regime or the operation of markets, but by the operation of value through abstract and impersonal – in a word, alienated – modes of social domination. Capital 'subjects people to impersonal structural imperatives and constraints that cannot be adequately grasped in terms of concrete domination (e.g., personal or group domination)'.[19] A key plank of Postone's argument is the claim that in Marx's writing, 'labour' refers not to the general, transhistorical, concrete act of performing work, but to the specific, alienated form that labour takes under capitalism. Importantly, commodity-producing labour under capitalism is animated by depersonalized compulsions, but also naturalized such that it appears indistinguishable from 'labour per se'. Thus, for Postone, 'two sorts of necessity are conflated in the form of an apparently valid transhistorical necessity: one must labor to survive'.[20] A reading of value similar to this one is, I think, useful for thinking about finance. However, efforts to apply this perspective to the problem of value and finance have often fallen into some common traps.

Geoff Mann's 'Value after Lehman' – an insightful critique of orthodox Marxist perspectives that asserted the 2008 financial crisis represented the inevitable collapse of a 'fictitious' economy of speculation somehow separate from the 'real' economy of production – is a good example.[21] Mann argues that value must be understood as 'a form of social wealth constituted by a spatially and temporally generalising social relation of equivalence and substitutability under, and specific to, capitalism'.[22] In this sense, Mann argues rightly that neat distinctions between 'real' and 'financial' (or 'fictitious') value are untenable. If value is a relation of equivalence, it is not an absolute object created at a particular place and time. The particular form of value, in this reading, must be understood historically and relationally. So far, so good. But critically, for our purposes at least, to Mann this includes the possibility of value 'decoupled' from labour: 'Abstract labour remains a crucial manifestation of this relation, but our current condition demonstrates that value itself is not beholden to labour.'[23] If Mann's framing of value as a 'spatially and temporally generalizing social relation' is useful, this insight needs to be followed in the direction of exploring its operation across the whole circuit of capital. The claim that value is potentially 'not beholden to labour' ultimately does something methodologically quite similar to Lapavitsas' claim that financial processes of expropriation originate in the sphere of circulation. It lets us treat financial returns as something separable from the profits generated in the 'real' economy of production, and thus implies an analysis of finance qua finance divorced from the whole circuit of accumulation.

Carolyn Hardin's more recent *Capturing Finance* makes a similar argument, drawing on Mann and Postone among others.[24] Hardin starts from the disjuncture between the nearly ubiquitous presence of 'arbitrage' in business school and practitioner discourses about finance, and its near-absence from critical studies of finance. 'Arbitrage' refers, in essence, to trades taking advantage of different prices for the same thing in different markets. For financial market participants themselves, arbitrage is a crucially important means of making profits, and the construction of opportunities for arbitrage has profoundly shaped the development of financial practices and institutions. Hardin asks what a critique of finance might look like that puts arbitrage at the centre. She interrogates the material, technological, and social relations that make arbitrage possible. For Hardin, focusing on arbitrage reveals a financial system organized around the systematic structuring and 'capture' of differential returns.

Hardin uses this analysis to set up a broader engagement with the question of 'value' and critique of finance in capitalism. Drawing, like Mann, on an extension of Postone, Hardin suggests that 'for finance, the principle that enacts abstract domination within society and is the condition of possibility of the capture of value is risk.'[25] The key examples through which this claim is fleshed out are a discussion of mutual fund 'timing' and of the US subprime lending boom in the buildup to the 2008 financial crisis. The finer details of these accounts are beyond the scope of the present discussion. The critical thing for our purposes is that Hardin suggests that large-scale arbitrage profits through these means have been enabled by wider social and political changes which have compelled more and more people to borrow, and invest, in order to secure their own livelihoods. As Hardin puts it, 'One may easily revise Postone's concise statement "One must labor to survive" as "one must invest to survive".'[26] Here, Hardin suggests that finance capital derives surplus value by capturing something like 'surplus risk', generated by the growing subjection of people to the impersonal compulsion to engage with financial instruments. It's notable that Hardin makes Postone's statement somewhat more 'concise' than it is in the original, and that what is excised is precisely that commodity-producing labour under capitalism is a historically distinct social form often naturalized through its conflation with the transhistoric category of 'labour'. Postone's original statement is a comment about how a historically particular form of labour relations is reproduced. Ironically, in revising Postone's statement, this distinction between labour under capitalism and labour in general is mostly lost. One consequence is that Hardin often seems to discuss dynamics of financial risk-taking and labouring as if they were analogues – the mute compulsion to participate in financial risk and the mute compulsion to labour are framed as separate processes which are alike in illuminating ways. This is not unique to Hardin by any means. Other recent efforts working from other broadly Marxist perspectives also aim to rethink the sources of financial value suggest a similar move from labour to 'risk' as the font of specifically financial value.[27] Brett Christophers also makes a cognate argument by way of analogy: 'if the abstraction that occurs in labour markets enables labour-power to bear value ... then the abstraction that occurs in financial markets enables risk – financial risk in the form of financial assets – to bear value.'[28]

In Hardin's case, the political stakes of this move are explicit. Hers is one of a number of recent contributions to argue that the axes of vulnerability, stratification, and power in contemporary capitalism have less to do with 'work' than they may have used to,[29] and, as a result, a progressive politics able to deal with the real operations of finance will need to be articulated on the terrain of 'risk' rather than labour. The basic problem with this view is that in practice the terrains of labour and of risk remain intimately entangled. The very compulsion to 'invest in order to survive' – and to borrow in order to do so – stems from transformations in wider labour regimes, and in turn intensifies the compulsion to work.[30] To put it in the simplest terms, for the vast majority of everyday 'investors', investments remain intimately linked to their employment – whether directly part of their remuneration through pensions, or slightly more indirectly through the investment of savings (i.e., wages not needed for immediate consumption). The largest single investment asset owned by the median household in the metropolitan core, and for that matter in more affluent segments of working classes in many peripheral countries, is a house. Houses are virtually always bought on credit, with the consequence that homeowners must continue to sell labour in order to make mortgage payments. In this respect, mortgage debt is reflective of the experience of indebtedness more generally. One of the chief effects of widespread indebtedness globally is that people owing debts feel the compulsion to work more acutely.[31] Both the compulsion to save for retirement (which often now takes the form of 'investment') and the frequency of indebtedness are given in the commodification of labour power.

Indeed, we can read indebtedness as a common historical form of appearance taken on by the more general operation of the alienated compulsion to sell labour power. Søren Mau usefully suggests that the latter in its most basic form is akin to a relationship of indebtedness: 'The historical creation of the capital relation can ... be seen as the original incurment of a debt which is inherited by every new generation of proletarians ... from this perspective, surplus labour is a kind of interest the worker has to pay in order to live.'[32] For now, the point is that recent debates about finance and value have taken on board the argument about the abstract character of value from Postonian value form theory much more readily than Postone's effort to reframe *labour* itself. This has been to the detriment of considering how the shifting terrains of risk, debt, and capitalist labour regimes are entangled.

Postone's own reading of 'financialization', interestingly, does something different, though ultimately shares some of the same problems.[33] For Postone, financial accumulation represents, in effect, a truncated flight from value relations in crisis. Faced with falling productivity and a growing inability to produce surplus value, Postone suggests that capital has retreated into a 'frenzied attempt to transform everything possible into sources of future wealth'.[34] While the accumulation of 'value' (in the sense of the objectification of socially necessary labour time) is in crisis, for a time

the crisis of value production is masked by the financially mediated attempt to transform more and more dimensions of life into the 'raw materials' of price and profit – into forms of purported wealth that supposedly will guarantee ever more complex so-called financial instruments, as if such 'wealth' were independent of value in capitalism ... However, it does not, I suggest, entail the accumulation of value, but modes of the extraction of purported wealth to compensate for the absence of such accumulation.[35]

Thus, financialization, for Postone

can be understood as an unintentional effort to abolish value within a framework that remains structured by value. As the accumulation of value slows down, the search for wealth becomes perversely reflexive, like an autoimmune disease – it begins to feed on the substance of society and nature.[36]

Postone's terms here are not functionally all that different from Durand's or Lapavitsas' – emphasizing capital's turn to 'the extraction of wealth' rather than the 'production of value'. Finance features here as an imposition ('like an autoimmune disease') on value accumulation rather than an integral part of the total circuit of capital. If Postone has not conflated concrete labour with abstract labour in the manner of other recent efforts at reinterpretations of value, this argument appears to make the opposite mistake, falling into precisely the trap that Mann highlights of mistaking finance for something 'outside' of capitalist value relations. We've found our way back to the original impasse about the detachment of financial from productive economies.

The cross-cutting problem with both 'orthodox' Marxist and many other approaches, I think, is that they risk treating 'financial' value either as a contradiction in terms or as a separate species of value somehow different in form and operation from 'productive' value. This is true whether finance is framed as a parasitic imposition on value created in production or as a separate process of accumulation altogether such that value can be 'created' outside the labour process. Even where authors seek not to dismiss the continued importance of labour, they often nonetheless fall into a curious kind of analogism in which financial values are *like* productive values, generated by different but parallel processes: 'Risk is to financial value as labour is to productive value.' As I'll show further in the next section, part of the problem here is that these approaches, both those trying to work through an 'orthodox' reading of Marx or to critique the ostensible Marxist orthodoxy, lean on a problematic reading of both labour and risk as they figure in capitalist value relations. As I'll argue in the next section, we don't need to 'risk' value theory so much as recognize the ways that risk is already embedded, if implicitly, in Marx's understanding of value.[37]

LABOUR, ABSTRACT AND CONCRETE

It's helpful, in getting beyond this debate, to begin by acknowledging that there is a grain of truth (though, to be clear, no more than a grain) to capitalist ideologues' dictums about 'risk' and 'reward'. Risk and uncertainty are inherent facets of valorization processes under capitalism in general, not only in finance. That is, profits that accrue to capitalists *are*, in an important sense, reliant on risk-taking. Of course, this doesn't support the conclusion that capitalist profits are a justly earned reward for bearing risk. Even more sophisticated liberal commentators are sceptical on this point. Frank Knight is often cited as the progenitor of dictums about risk and reward. Yet, while he does make the claim that a speculative willingness to bear uncertainty is the source of capitalist profits, Knight also makes clear that profit nonetheless cannot meaningfully be a 'just reward' for doing so. For Knight, judgements about uncertain future conditions are inherently based on incomplete information, and hence subject to a good deal of luck. In this sense, capitalists 'deserve' their profits in much the same way lottery winners 'deserve' their prizes.[38] Equally, this is not to deny that, contra liberal mythologies, actually existing capitalists often do everything in their power to minimize those risks or pass them on to others. And, most importantly, even Knight's framing in its emphasis on luck occludes the often-brutal processes of exploitation that must go on in the background in order for capitalist profits to be realized. Nonetheless, the core grain of truth here is that it is not possible to make profits without taking on exposure to risks. All capital is speculative.

This basic insight does operate in the background of Marx's framing of money and capital. In Marx's 'general formula for capital',[39] M-C-M', money is exchanged for specific commodities (M-C), which are combined with commodified labour, power and reconverted into money through exchange (C-M'). Critically, in this understanding capital is a social relation and hence more a recurrent process than a thing. Through circulation 'value ... becomes value in process, money in process, and, as such, capital'.[40] Money, as a universal equivalent, is necessarily fungible. Marx differentiates the 'money form of revenue' from the 'money form of capital'.

The distinction is precisely to do with how money is deployed. The former refers to money used for consumption goods (including by workers, as well as that appropriated by capitalists for their own consumption), the latter to money put into circulation as capital.

Yet, the actual realization of value through concrete processes of exploitation is always uncertain. In the phase M-C, Marx later argues in a discussion of circulation in the second volume of *Capital*, the capitalist 'advances himself money against the surplus value he still has to hunt out'.[41] Before capital can return as profit, concrete labour must be mobilized at a cost and a level of productivity consistent with the 'abstract' labour embodied in the initial 'M'. There is never any guarantee that this can or will be achieved in practice – indeed, as I'll show further below, there are some engrained and structural reasons why localized valorization processes will tend to fail over time. The initial movement M-C is always speculative, and always carries the risk that capital is lost somewhere in circulation.[42] As Marx puts it, in situations where surplus value is not realized – for instance, because the productivity of labour employed by the particular capitalist falls below the socially necessary average, because finished commodities do not sell in the quantities anticipated, because prices fall – 'the anticipatory character of the money spent against future surplus-value clearly emerges'.[43] Equally, in framing capital in this way, we can see how finance is always already imbricated across the whole circuit of capital at multiple points – a point to which I will return shortly.[44] Money is needed in order to set this whole circuit in motion, to keep it moving, and to close it, and so mechanisms are necessary to move money from where it is to where it's needed.

To get at why this matters, it is worth returning to the 'labour' in the 'labour theory of value'. As Simon Clarke notes, the 'orthodox' reading of Marx is 'economistic' insofar as it

> assimilat[es] Marx to the conceptual framework of classical political economy, seeing the foundation of his 'economics' in the classical labour theory of value, reinterpreted as a theory of exploitation according to which the appropriation of surplus labour in the form of profit was based on the ownership of the means of production by the capitalist class.[45]

For the classical political economists, the 'labour theory of value' is in essence a theory of price formation, in which the price of any given commodity will tend more or less to reflect the labour that went into producing it. Marx's discussion of surplus value in the first volume of *Capital*, as noted above, takes as given some of the core assumptions of liberal political economists in order to illuminate the ways that exploitation operates under capitalism, veiled by its appearance as 'free' contract between nominal equals. It is generally on the basis of an overextension of this argument to an absolute claim that value must be 'created' by labour that Marxist readings of 'exploitation' and value are dismissed as ill-suited to contemporary financial capitalism.

But this isn't the only, or indeed the most useful, way to read Marx on this point. Dianne Elson rightly highlights a kind of 'misplaced concreteness' in the orthodox labour theory of value.[46] Marx draws a crucial distinction between 'embodied'/'concrete' and 'socially necessary'/'abstract' labour. It is the latter which is both distinct to capitalism and at the core of value relations. When we take these distinctions seriously, in Clarke's words, value under capitalism must be understood as 'labour whose social character has been abstracted from the activity of the labourer to confront the labourer as the property of a thing; labour whose human qualities have been reduced to the single quality of duration; dehumanised, homogenous, in a word, *alienated*'.[47] From this perspective, as Elson aptly notes, Marx's theory of value is not an attempt to explain prices or profits with reference to the labour embodied in commodities, but rather an attempt to explain why labour takes the peculiar alienated form that it does under capitalism.[48] Value, in this sense, is not a quantity of surplus labour time so much as it is 'an objectification ... of a certain aspect of that labour-time, its aspect of being simply an expenditure of human labour power in general, i.e. abstract labour'.[49] The task for analysis, then, is to unpick historically the social relations through which, in Marx's words, 'concrete labour becomes the form of the manifestation of its opposite, abstract human labour'.[50]

The stress on 'abstraction' and alienation here is critical. It indeed militates against the 'misplaced concreteness' of value as a direct embodiment of labour power (in the manner stressed by Hardin,

Mann, and others discussed above). But importantly – and this latter point is less well taken up in recent finance debates – it also suggests that financial manifestations of value, the labour process, and the sale of labour power are always intrinsically linked. 'Value' as such is not directly extracted from or 'created by' concrete labour and embedded in commodities. Rather, value is expressed as an anarchic and competitive compulsion to valorize, to realize in the concrete 'socially necessary' costs and rates of productivity per unit of labour across the whole circuit of capital. Value is not 'created' at any particular point, but rather produced in the continual operation of the whole circuit. As Marx notes in his *Contribution to the Critique of Political Economy*, 'Commodities are the direct products of isolated independent labour, which have to be realized as universal social labour through their alienation in the process of private exchange, that is to say, labour based on the production of commodities becomes social labour only through the universal alienation of individual labours.'[51]

Moreover, the compulsion to valorize requires the completion of the whole circuit M-C-M', and hence is always already speculative at all points. Once commodities have been produced, they are of little use to the capitalist unless they can be sold – value must always be realized in the form of prices. But price is always an imperfect and speculative approximation. Marx notes that 'although price, being the exponent of the magnitude of a commodity's value, is the exponent of its exchange-ratio with money, it does not follow that the exponent of this exchange-ratio is necessarily the exponent of the magnitude of the commodity's value.'[52] Marx gives the example here that, given the opportunity, the capitalist will almost certainly overcharge for the commodities they seek to sell, and may under some circumstances be compelled to accept less than the nominal value of their commodities:

> Suppose two equal quantities of socially necessary labour are respectively represented by 1 quarter of wheat and £2 ... £2 is the expression in money of the magnitude of the value of the quarter of wheat, or its price. If circumstances now allow this price to be raised to £3, or compel it to be reduced to £1, then although £1 and £3 may be too small or too large to give proper

expression to the magnitude of wheat's value, they are neverthe-
less prices for the wheat, for they are, in the first place, the form
of its value, i.e. money, and, in the second place, the exponents
of its exchange ratio with money.[53]

Critically, for Marx, this possible divergence between price and
underlying value 'is not a defect, but, on the contrary, it makes this
form the adequate one for a mode of production whose laws can
assert themselves as blindly operating averages between constant
irregularities'.[54] Marx is clear that this system of 'blindly operating
averages' is intimately connected to the alienation of labour:

> In this difference between price and exchange value lies the
> demonstration of the fact that the particular individual labour
> contained in a commodity has first to be expressed through the
> process of alienation in terms of its counterpart, i.e. as imper-
> sonal, abstract, universal, and, only in that form, social labour
> viz. money.[55]

Value, then, is indeed usefully read as an abstract form of domination. But critically, in this sense it is a compulsion towards
'socially necessary' forms of labour that can only ever be unevenly,
partially, and temporarily fulfilled. Socially necessary abstract
labour must be realized as concrete, embodied labour, and then
the commodities generated in the process must in turn realize
their value in the concrete form of prices. Neither is guaranteed. As
Harvey notes, the compulsions of capitalist competition inevitably
apply in the realization of value after the fact.[56] Concrete labour
is indeterminate, and the very reorganization of space, technology, labour and nature needed to carry out concrete labour in its
various forms tends ultimately to undermine the social and ecological conditions for the maintenance of socially necessary levels
of productivity. Valorization can be interrupted in the shorter term
by disruptions of different aspects of the production or circulation process – for instance, bad weather, power cuts, or failures
of transport and communications infrastructures. Indeed, insofar
as the maintenance of these conditions of production is systematically externalized by capital, capitalist relations of production

will tend over time to degrade them such that 'accidents' become more likely.[57] There is also a considerable risk to capital stemming from the simple fact that workers are active and concrete agents in the production process. Labour in its concrete form is perpetually 'indeterminate'. As Elson argues, labour 'is a fluidity, a potential, which ... has to be socially "fixed" or objectified in the production of particular goods, by particular people in particular ways'.[58] More generally, concrete labour can only ever approximate socially necessary labour time and productivity, as the latter is an average whose realization in particular instances is reliant on an array of factors, one of which is the irreducibility of individual workers and concrete labour processes themselves. Marx gives the following illustration in his discussion of cooperation in the labour process in *Capital*:

> For example, let the working day of each individual be 12 hours. Then the collective working day of twelve men simultaneously employed consists of 144 hours; and although the labour of each of the dozen men may diverge more or less from average social labour, each of them requiring a different amount of time for the same operation, the working day of every one possesses the qualities of an average working day, because it forms one-twelfth of the collective working day of 144 hours ... But if the twelve men are employed in six pairs, by six different 'small masters', it will be entirely a matter of chance whether each of these masters produces the same value, and consequently whether he secures the general rate of surplus value.[59]

Here Marx suggests that the compulsion to realize socially necessary average levels of production in and through the activity of variable individual workers is the origin of both a tendency to centralize capital and of coercive workplace discipline. But this can and does backfire. The impulsion to speed circulation times and raise productivity in capitalist enterprises often translates into a tendency to kill and maim workers, and more generally to simply deplete workers' productive capacities over time.[60] The worst consequences of these tendencies are borne by workers who are killed, maimed, and depleted, but these processes do both disrupt the realization of value in the short term and potentially degrade productivity over the longer run without the capacity to continually replace workers. The exploitation of concrete labour is also necessarily mediated through historical patterns of social difference and through variegated free and unfree labour regimes. In Stuart Hall's phrase, 'the law of value ... operates through and because of the culturally specific form of labour power, rather than in spite of it'.[61] If value is in need of continual realization, it is given concrete form only through 'blindly operating averages between constant irregularities', and hence is always at risk.

It is worth noting at this point that Marx's discussion of these questions in the initial chapters of the first volume of *Capital* takes place under a highly formalized set of assumptions and simplifications. He looks first at capital in its 'simple reproduction', a single circuit M-C-M'. This discussion of capitalism under 'simple reproduction' is a thought experiment aimed at teasing out some key dynamics, not a condition that has ever existed in history. Historical capital exists only under conditions of 'expanded reproduction' – in which many overlapping iterations of the circuit M-C-M' take place simultaneously between competing capitals arrayed unevenly through different geographic and institutional settings. We can only ever meet capitalism, and the impulse for valorization, *in media res*. Evidently capitalism did come from somewhere. There is an extensive debate – the so-called 'transition debate' – about how capitalist social relations came about historically.[62] But for present purposes what matters is that, as an emergent property of several interconnected historical currents, actual historical capitalism has never existed in a state other than one of expanded reproduction. The move from simple to expanded reproduction is Marx's intellectual move to admit more complicating dynamics within a simplified formal model rather than a historic development of capitalism itself.

If risk is always already fully present in capitalist value, particularly under conditions of expanded reproduction, if the 'speculative' operations of financial capital are reflective of the inherently speculative nature of capital in general, then finance capital itself can't be understood as a bloc of capital somehow separate, detached or 'divorced' from 'productive' capital or any 'real' economy. Instead it has to be seen in the context of the whole circuit of capital. Leda Paulani usefully highlights a contradictory tendency towards the 'autonomization' of value, inherent in the social form of the commodity itself, and expressed most fully in the operations of credit. In her words,

> With the development of money, fully constituted, in its figure of credit … the accumulation process becomes autonomous from the production and realisation of the surplus value, but internalises in credit the contradiction that constitutes this process between the dialectical impulse of indefinitely valorising value in general and the dependence that such valorisation has on the production of material and concrete wealth.[63]

Credit relations, in other words, represent the fullest logical development of an immanent tendency in the commodity form towards the operation of value as an abstract impersonal compulsion. But credit cannot escape from the concrete realities of production.

The point is that this reading of labour and value puts us on a better footing to make sense of finance in capitalism, insofar as it implies that value isn't a thing 'created' at any particular point in the circuit of capital, but rather valorization is a dynamic property of the circuit as a whole. Thus, in Clarke's words, 'production and circulation are not *independent* spheres between which relations of dependence or independence can subsequently be established, they are differentiated *moments* of the circuit of capital which is itself a totality'.[64] Value must be continually approximated in the concrete at every point across the whole circuit M-C-M' through a system of 'blindly operating averages'. In this sense, two points are critical for an analysis of the place and power of finance: (1) risk and speculation are already inherent, if often implicitly, in the operations of value under capitalism, and (2) finance and production both need to be understood in the context of the circuit of capital as a whole. This includes not just through the process of production itself, but also through multiple acts of exchange and circulation, payment and repayment, which of necessity take place over time and across space. There is an important distributional struggle that goes on across the circuit of capital between particular capitalists over their respective shares of surplus capital (this is discussed further in concrete terms in the next chapter), which is bound up with patterns of restructuring over time, with concrete state actions favouring certain kinds of accumulation over others, and so on. These historical determinations are, of course, hugely important in practice. But as a first analytic principle, the aim has to be to understand the circuit of capital as a whole.

This raises the question, though, of how to talk meaningfully of 'finance capital' as a discrete sphere of activity. In the next section, I'll show that David Harvey's 'process view' offers us probably the most useful starting point.

FOR A 'PROCESS' VIEW OF FINANCE CAPITAL

Harvey pulls out an important thread from Marx's notes, emphasizing the integral embeddedness of finance capital in the circuits of capital accumulation more generally, and the way that financial operations inherit and amplify the crucial risks and tensions introduced in the preceding discussion of value. Marx, as noted above, doesn't use the term 'finance capital'. His explicit discussions of credit and the banking system in Vol. 3 of *Capital* introduce a dizzying array of terminology – among others, 'interest bearing capital', 'fictitious capital', 'userer's capital' – to refer to a range of different configurations of money and finance.[65] His analysis of the role of finance isn't entirely consistent over time either. A significant portion of Marx's analysis of July Monarchy-era France and the 1848 revolution in *The Class Struggles in France* rests on what could be read as a 'power bloc' reading of finance. He stresses the dominance of what he calls 'the finance aristocracy' – a collection of 'bankers, stock-exchange kings, railway kings, owners of coal and iron and forests, a part of the landed proprietors associated with them' – rather than the French bourgeoisie as a whole. It's perhaps notable that in this discussion Marx describes the financial segments of the bourgeoisie acting as an 'aristocracy' rather than finance *capital* as such. The finance aristocracy, Marx suggests, 'sat on the throne, it dictated laws in the Chambers, it distributed public offices, from cabinet portfolios to tobacco bureau posts.'[66] This is clearly an approach to finance which is useful up to a point in the context of the analysis of unfolding historic class struggles, but much less so for understanding the dynamics and unfolding of capital accumulation.[67]

Harvey argues that Marx's later notes on money and finance in *Capital* imply a definition of finance capital as 'a particular kind of circulation process of capital which centres on the credit system'.[68] This contrasts with more explicit uses of the term in later Marxist writing, starting with Hilferding and Lenin in particular, which have tended to talk about finance capital in terms of 'a power bloc which wields immense influence over the process of accumulation in general'.[69] Harvey's discussion here predates the term 'financialization', but the latter conception of finance capital as a power bloc could nonetheless quite comfortably encapsulate much of the debate traced in the preceding chapter – centring, as Harvey notes, 'on the manner in which a power bloc called "finance capital" is constituted and the relative importance of this power bloc vis-à-vis other power blocs'.[70] As I'll show here, we usefully follow Harvey's insistence on a process view of finance capital, 'with particular emphasis upon ... [the] internal contradictions' of this process. This remains, with a few exceptions,[71] a somewhat underexploited conceptual framework. Harvey's contribution is heavily indebted to Suzanne de Brunhoff (especially her *Marx on Money*).[72] But Harvey's terminology ('process' versus 'power bloc' readings) itself is highly useful, and folded into a discussion of some of the dynamics of spatiality and risk in a way that helpfully builds on de Brunhoff's exegesis, and complements the view on value laid out above. A process view of finance calls our attention to the ways in which financial practices in particular – various mechanisms for borrowing, investing, hedging or speculating on changes in prices – are entangled with the whole circuit of capital.

Harvey's critique of 'power bloc' readings of finance capital primarily takes the form of a critique of Lenin and (especially) Hilferding's analyses of finance capital. Hilferding's arguments in particular are worth recapping briefly. Hilferding's *Finance Capital*, originally published in German in 1910 and one of the first actual uses of the term 'finance capital', traces what he calls the 'latest phase of capitalist development', marked by the ostensible rise of 'finance capital'.[73] The rise of 'finance capital' to Hilferding marks the culmination of a cycle initiated by the growing concentration of large-scale industrial capital. This in turn drove, on one hand, the 'elimination' of competition through the formation of industrial cartels, and on the other, 'br[ought] bank and industrial capital into an ever more intimate relationship'. For Hilferding, it is through this tight relationship between banks and monopolistic industry that 'capital assumes the form of finance capital, its supreme and most abstract expression'.

The mechanism Hilferding stresses here is considerably different from what is highlighted in contemporary studies of financialization. (Of course, this makes sense given Hilferding is talking about a very different time period, namely, late nineteenth and early twentieth-century Germany and Austria.[74]) For Hilferding, rising industrial concentration requires ever-greater pools of readily available finance, and as a result, industrial capital becomes increasingly reliant on 'bank capital' – in this way, 'an ever-increasing proportion of the capital used in industry is finance capital, capital at the disposal of the banks which is used by industrialists'. This development, he argues, completes a 'cycle in the development of capitalism'.[75] Money capital, as 'userer's capital', plays a major role in the emergence of capitalist production, but is gradually subject to increasing resistance from, and eventually subjugated to, 'productive capital'. The subsequent expansion of industrial production drives a growing need for credit, and concomitantly the 'power of the banks increases and they become founders and eventually rulers of industry, whose profits they seize for themselves as finance capital'. In this way:

> bank capital was the negation of userer's capital and is itself negated by finance capital. The latter is the synthesis of userer's and bank capital, and it appropriates for itself the fruits of social production at an infinitely higher stage of social production.[76]

Hilferding moves on to connect this rise of finance capital to a range of consequences, including the growing centrality of speculation 'disconnected' from production to the operation of financial markets and their consequent vulnerability to crisis, the intensification of imperialism as monopolistic finance capital sought new markets and cheap inputs, and the increasing intensity of struggles between labour and capital in the core.

Finance capital, in this discussion, takes on the character of a powerful fraction of capital whose interests increasingly drive the actions of the state and the restructuring of the economy as a whole. Or, in short, it operates as a 'power bloc'. If the specific mechanics of Hilferding's analysis don't hold very well for twenty-first-century capitalism, this aspect of his argument anticipates the implicit or explicit claims of much of the financialization debate. There's a notable slippage in Hilferding's argument here – he moves from a reconstruction of Marx's theory of money to an analysis of the formation of 'finance capital' as a phase in the evolution of capitalism to a discussion of some aspects of early twentieth-century capitalism from the vantage point of the driving role of 'finance capital'. Having developed through the 'negation of bank capital', finance capital increasingly takes on a life of its own. Thus, having reconstructed the rise of finance capital, Hilferding offers the unfolding interests of a unitary 'finance capital' up as explanation for a variety of developments. In this sense, de Brunhoff attributes to Hilferding a tendency to divorce the examination of credit and banking systems from the underlying theory of money and value (and, hence, from production) – noting that 'this dissociation has probably been one of the reasons for the overestimation of "finance capital"'.[77] What's critical here is that Hilferding's 'dissociation' of finance from money in general (and, implicitly, from the tension between abstract and concrete labour through which money relations operate) is integral to his ability to reconstruct finance capital as a 'power bloc', and hence to explain subsequent developments as functionalist outcomes of the interests of that bloc.

Harvey's 'process view', by contrast, which he develops by way of an exegesis of Marx's notes on the credit system (heavily influenced by de Brunhoff's account), positions finance in the wider circuit of capital as 'value in process' introduced above. Finance is implicit in the wider circuit of capital in a range of different ways – the credit system offers a variety of means of smoothing out the spatial and temporal dislocations implicit in the circulation of capital, but creates new contradictions in the process. If we see finance capital in this way, we can develop some schematic notes about how credit is integrally entangled with the wider circuits of capital.

First and most obviously, as noted above, capital must be made available in the form of money prior to the process of production. Under actually existing conditions of expanded reproduction, this inevitably requires credit, as de Brunhoff in particular emphasizes. Marx underlines this point in his notes on the banking system in Vol. 3 of *Capital*: 'the industrial capitalist does not "save" his capital but rather disposes of the savings of others in proportion to the size of his capital, and the credit that the reproductive capitalists give one another, and that the public give them, he makes into his own source of private enrichment'.[78] The same is true of the point of sale needed to close the circuit M-C-M' by reconverting commodities into money.[79] Marx makes a distinction between money serving as 'means of purchase' and 'means of payment' with respect to the latter, particularly in the *Critique of Political Economy*. Purchases must often take place on credit, through various contractual means, such that the creation and circulation of credit instruments is functionally often the dominant form of monetary circulation. Marx elsewhere notes that the varied circulation time of capital – in effect, the time it takes for commodities to get from the point of production to the point of sale, during which time they are bound up in the form of money or commodities and cannot be valorized – constitutes one of the 'material bases for differing periods of credit' and highlights on this basis the importance of overseas trade for the historical development of the credit system.[80] For the moment, the critical point is that while credit relations are necessary to the circulation of capital, credit contracts give concrete form to the compulsions of value, and in the process tighten them. As Marx notes in the *Critique of Political Economy*, when commodities are purchased on credit, 'In order to pay at the expiration of the contract, [the buyer] must have sold commodities before that. Thus, entirely apart from his individual wants, the movement of the circulation process makes selling a social necessity of every owner of commodities.'[81]

Rendering labour as a commodity also requires the subjection of workers' revenues to the same temporal disjunctures. The subjection of labour to the 'mute compulsion' of the market depends on the subjection of processes of physical and social reproduction to the social power of money – capital must be able to stand between workers and their basic survival needs.[82] Yet the inevitable spatial and temporal distance between the sale of labour power and its concrete manifestation means that the performance and reproduction of labour also do not coincide with the payment of wages. Or, for the worker as the seller of commodified labour power, the labour contract (whether formally written or otherwise) usually operates as means of purchase, but not means of payment. As a consequence, Marx notes, 'Everywhere the worker allows credit to the capitalist. That this credit is no mere fiction is shown by the occasional loss of the wages the worker has already advanced, when a capitalist goes bankrupt, but also by a series of more long-lasting consequences.'[83] In a footnote, Marx elaborates on these 'more long-lasting consequences' in terms of workers' need to borrow against future wages for subsistence items.[84] As in the discussion of means of purchase and means of payment among capitalists above, credit relations enable workers to survive until payday only by tightening the 'mute compulsion' to labour expressed through money. Indebted workers must continue to sell labour power in order to repay their debts when they fall due.

These pressures are amplified further by the fact that employment is not normally constant – workers may or may not find a willing buyer for their labour power at any given point in time. Cyclical patterns of capitalist restructuring tend to continually produce and reproduce some 'relative surplus population' not directly engaged in wage work – capital 'depends on the constant formation, the greater or less absorption, and the reformation of the industrial reserve army or surplus population.'[85] Crucially, Marx notes of this relative surplus population that 'every worker belongs to it during the time when he is only partially employed or wholly unemployed.'[86] Yet, the mute compulsion of capitalist social relations entails the continued need for money even on the part of workers not presently in the labour force directly. Marx's historical discussion of relative surplus populations, notably, puts considerable emphasis on exploitation through debts and rents as crucial forms of the mute compulsion of capital. He points, for instance, to mutually reinforcing links between debt, the reconfiguration of urban space for housing capital, and the degradation of working conditions and vulnerability of workers to hyper-exploitation, with the result that 'the mines of misery are exploited by house speculators with more profit and at less cost than the mines of Potosi ever were.'[87] He likewise notes that agricultural labourers in nineteenth-century England were subject to severe forms of exploitation by housing speculators 'who buy scraps of land, which they throng as densely as they can with the cheapest of all possible hovels.'[88] The end result of this process is that 'the pauperism of the agricultural labourers is ultimately ... the chief source of their miserable housing, which breaks down their last power of resistance and makes them mere slaves of the landed proprietors and farmers.'[89] These forms of exploitation, given in the subjection of social reproduction to the power of money, alongside being means of accumulation in themselves, can play a critical role in subjecting labour to the domination of capital. Not only do the short-run temporal disjunctures implicit in wage labour, then, rely on patterns of credit and indebtedness, but capitalist relations of production tend structurally to produce workers not directly engaged in wage labour, but who remain subject to the 'mute compulsion' of the market. Credit relations are thus an intrinsic part of the continued operation of discipline of value.

With these considerations in view, we can start to understand why Marx is explicit that the notation M-M' – often used as a stand-in for 'interest bearing' or 'finance' capital in financialization debates – is shorthand.[90] It designates a circuit better represented as something like M_1-M_2-C-M_2'-M_1', or more realistically but even less elegantly, a web of many partially overlapping Ms and Cs. Money capital is advanced as credit, cycled through the operations of productive and commercial capital at several points, and (assuming the latter more or less go to plan) returned with interest. Marx notes that 'it is precisely this process of M as capital which the interest of the lending money-capitalist is based on and from which it derives.'[91] As Bonefeld argues, 'While money asserts itself as the source of its own self-valorisation, M ... M' exists only in and through the ability of capital to harness labour as the variable component of exploitation.'[92] For Marx, using the shorthand M-M' is not just for convenience, but at least partly intended precisely to draw attention to the troublesome processes of abstraction through which 'everything that happens in between' the payment of credit and its repayment with interest is hidden from view.[93] Insofar as financial profits appear to be 'decoupled' from productive activities, or purely speculative, then, they represent 'the capital mystification in its most flagrant form'.[94] There *is* a potential distributional struggle between holders of financial capital and holders of productive capital implicit here over the share of total surplus value that is returned as interest, fees, or other forms of financial revenues. But interest remains premised on the profitable realization of the rest of the circuit of capital.

What's critical is that, seen from a process view, credit relations both stem from and ultimately raise the stakes of the gamble that's already implicit in the circuit M-C-M' – not only might capital be lost if the process of valorization is not realized, but borrowed capital needs to be repaid whether or not it is valorized. Harvey cites Marx's claim in the *Grundrisse* that credit 'suspends the barriers to the realization of capital only by raising them to their most general form'.[95] Harvey interprets this primarily in terms of a tendency for the credit system to generate crises insofar as 'it can only deal with problems that arise in exchange and never those in production',[96] and as such is prone to speculative excesses. This is partly true – credit enables the continual circulation of commodities and labour power, but can't in itself directly modify the concrete production process, and can certainly set in motion circulations of capital which cannot be completed. But the exchange vs production framing Harvey lapses into here also perhaps misses the importance of temporality and circulation. Money and credit are, in Mann's terms, the 'stitch of space-time' under capitalist relations of production – they are necessary in order to enable the continued circulation of capital, but exacerbate contradictions and potential points of failure in the process.[97] Marx's actual sentence in the *Grundrisse* notably continues that credit suspends barriers by 'positing one period of overproduction and one of underproduction as two periods'.[98] Value in motion is necessarily value at risk; credit relations smooth the motion of value only by amplifying risk. Credit locks in the productive valorization of concrete labour by particular capitals in advance, anticipating its future realization and hence intensifying the compulsion to valorize.

At the same time though, this means that finance capital likewise depends on the future mobilization of concrete labour at the price and level of productivity implied in the credit transaction, or for workers the continued payment of wages at levels sufficient to enable both the payment of debts and the purchase of means of survival. Any 'separation' of financial and productive activities is thus only ever partially achieved.[99] As Bonefeld rightly observes, 'the disproportion between production and circulation cannot be explained by reference to the autonomization of one form from the other'.[100] The implication here is that financial markets do not impose on productive economies from the outside so much as emerge from, intersect with, and amplify the contradictory patterns of uneven development implicit in capitalist relations of production.

CONCLUSION

I've tried in this chapter to pull together the basis for an alternative view of finance in capitalism, drawing on Marx and Marxian discussions of value theory and Harvey's 'process' view of finance capital. The crux of the preceding sections is: Capital is, in Marx's terms 'value in process'. If we take this notion seriously, then value isn't 'created' anywhere in particular, but is rather a speculative approximation that must be, but often isn't, continually *realized* through the whole circuit of capital. There is no doubt a concrete distributional question about the accrual of surplus value between particular capitals – higher profits in the financial circuit, all else being equal, do come at the expense of wages and of the profits accruing to owners of productive and commercial capitals (to the extent, anyway, that these are actually different people than the owners of finance capital).[101] In this sense, there is value in Durand's claim that financial profits are inherently 'predatory' in some sense. These distributional struggles are consequential for particular capitals, states, and workers. But it nonetheless raises methodological and political problems for us to try to analyze the operations of finance capital in isolation from the operation of other circuits of capital. The increased share of total social profit captured by the financial sector is ultimately, as Beverly Best argues, a concrete historical 'form of appearance' of underlying dynamics of capital accumulation and value. A stress on linking finance capital with concrete processes of exploitation within wider circuits of capital asks us to examine the concrete social relations – the embodied social practices through which profit is created, and the wider networks of social relations making these practices possible – through which abstract value is realized in concrete form. Finance capital understood as a 'process' must, then, be situated in relation to the whole circuit of capital and its inherent tensions.

What would it mean to study finance and the relationships between financial and productive activities from this angle? In the following chapters, I take up the question of how these processes unfold in more concrete terms, and how they reframe our understandings of finance capital. For now, a few general guiding questions are in order. A process approach requires in the first instance that we foreground the relationships between particular configurations of finance capital and everything that must 'go on in between' to enable continual repayment. So we have to ask: What configurations of space, labour, and productive capital are needed to enable particular forms of financial accumulation, and vice-versa? How durable are they and how far *can* they be brought into existence? How do existing patterns of restructuring shape and constrain processes of financial accumulation? And, crucially, do these dynamics help to explain the uneven character of the development of new financial markets?

3

Finance and Production

One of the key tenets of financialization debates (outlined in Chapter 1) is the rapid expansion of finance capital and the stagnation of production. This premise certainly chimes with some observable facts about the contemporary global political economy. Real wages have stagnated or fallen globally for decades, as has the labour share of global income.[1] Processes of deindustrialization are starkly visible in much of the global north (and increasingly in much of the global south as well).[2] The share of the financial sector in overall profits and GDP as a whole has risen across the core capitalist countries. Not unrelatedly, income and wealth inequalities have spiralled. To put it bluntly, financiers have very visibly got richer while most of the rest of us have got poorer. Indeed, this trend seems only to have been accelerated by the increasing frequency and severity of financial crises, perhaps most clearly encapsulated in what Jeremy Green and Scott Lavery neatly term the 'regressive recovery' from the 2007–08 financial crisis in core economies.[3]

There's a striking degree of consensus on most of these points. Already in the mid-1980s, in the proto-financialization debates about 'casino capitalism' with which I opened this book, liberal commentators were preoccupied by concerns that 'Wall Street' was booming, surfing a wave of speculative excess, while 'Main Street' stagnated. Most major Marxist accounts of financialization in particular – all the way back to Magdoff and Sweezy or Arrighi[4] – not dissimilarly link the rise of finance to the seeming stagnation of wider productive economies. Robert Brenner's parallel arguments about the 'long downturn' of global capitalism avoid the term 'financialization' but likewise posit finance as the exception to a global erosion of capitalist profitability, centred in particular on the manufacturing sector.[5] Brenner's more recent discussions, suggesting that the core activity of US capitalism has shifted towards processes of politically enabled financial 'predation', echo similar themes – 'money making has been de-linked from profitable production, especially in a weak economy'.[6]

These diverse accounts differ on a number of important fronts. Marxists disagree with each other almost as intensely as they do with Buffett and the like (maybe more so). But the stagnation of 'productive' sectors and consequent degradation of pay and job stability nonetheless figures across all as cause and consequence of financialization. The falling profitability of production has ostensibly driven a redeployment of capital towards financial circuits, encouraged by leading states.[7] For (post-)Keynesian takes on financialization in particular, the redirection of investment towards speculative activity in turn has exacerbated the falling profitability and productivity of production through the misallocation of resources – as in Keynes' reference, cited in the Introduction above, to the consequences of leaving the investment function to the financial 'casino'. As one working paper from staffers at the Bank for International Settlements memorably puts it, referring to the tendency for banks and hedge funds to hire physics and maths graduates from highly ranked universities, 'finance literally bids rocket scientists away from the satellite industry'.[8]

These are all real trends in aggregate. Quantitative studies, mainly focused on OECD economies, have highlighted correlations between rising financial profits and falling wage shares, rising precarity and inequality.[9] There can be little doubt that the recorded GDP of core economies is increasingly stagnant. Figure 3.1 shows the annual rates of GDP growth in the five largest OECD member economies (the US, Japan, Germany, the UK, and France), as well as the total across the whole OECD, since 1971. The overall trend, despite volatility from year to year, is unmistakably towards slowing growth. Neither is there much question that the share of finance in reported profits and in the overall GDP of core capitalist economies has increased.[10] However, this has happened to a lesser extent than financialization narratives can imply. The latter trends appear to have levelled off. Figure 3.2 shows the relative share of gross value added by finance (bolded lines) and manufacturing (un-bolded) across the five largest OECD member economies since 2000. Notably, only for one year in one country (the UK in 2009) has the share of value added attributed to finance actually exceeded that attributed to manufacturing, and even then only fractionally. Of course, this doesn't discount the fact that the share of finance *had* expanded significantly in most of these economies in the decades prior to 2000 – as some authors have shown in considerable detail.[11] It does, however, suggest important limits to any process of 'financial expansion' that may have taken place.

This is perhaps the first clue that analyses stressing capitalist 'stagnation' and the accompanying rise of finance miss out on deeper-lying patterns of restructuring that have taken place over recent decades, which ultimately matter a good deal for understanding the nature and extent of transformations to the financial system and capitalism more generally. Specifically, the stagnation and financialization story too easily glides over two issues with crucial political implications. First, a financial system inclined towards underinvestment in productive capital is certainly not unusual, indeed it is arguably the historic norm of capitalist development in most of the world.[12] Capital accumulation has always depended on the extractive appropriation of cheap or unpaid labour, from marginal people and landscapes often rendered disposable through processes of gendering, racialization, and colonization.[13] Capitalist relations of production certainly can generate innovation and productivity growth in places, but those productivity booms inevitably lean on the appropriation of cheap labour, energy, and raw materials – in short, stagnation and depletion – elsewhere.[14]

Second, the stagnation story ironically often brackets out considerations of the actual concrete restructuring of production, finance, and most of all how the two intersect. A closely related problem is that the dominant analyses of stagnation all largely abstract from the materiality of production as a metabolism between labour and capitalized natures. This tendency has created important blindspots in analyses of stagnation and restructuring. Ratios of profitability and/or productivity viewed at a very high level of aggregation ultimately obscure as much as they reveal. To stress a recurrent theme of this book: We must be able to keep the whole circuit of capital in view, and we should be careful of diagnosing any widespread 'crisis of value'. Doing so helps us grasp, on

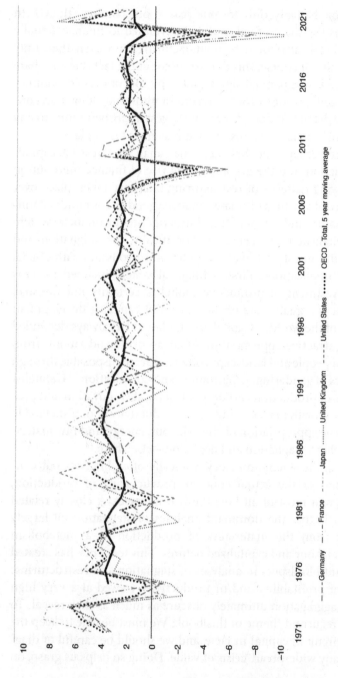

Figure 3.1 Annual GDP growth rates in OECD and selected economies, 1971–2022
Source: Author based on OECD data.

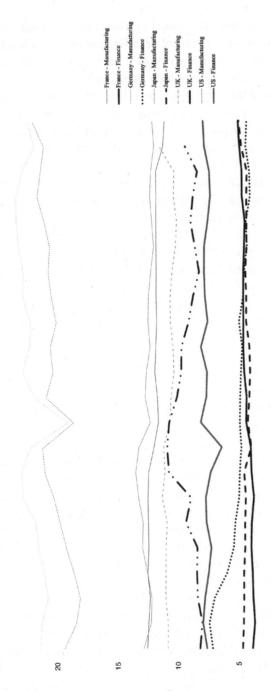

Legend:
- France - Manufacturing
- France - Finance
- Germany - Manufacturing
- Germany - Finance
- Japan - Manufacturing
- Japan - Finance
- UK - Manufacturing
- UK - Finance
- US - Manufacturing
- US - Finance

Figure 3.2   Gross value added in manufacturing and financial sectors, as per cent of total output, in selected economies, 2000–21

Source: Author based on OECD data.

one hand, the connections between the primary transformations of financial accumulation over recent decades, and on the other, the concrete restructuring of production as it has taken place through patterns of uneven development *on a global scale.*

This chapter thus further reconsiders the relationships between finance capital and production, building out the 'process' view of finance outlined in the previous chapter. The aim here is to reposition the relationships between finance and the visible restructuring of production over recent decades in a way that allows us to talk about the shifting place of finance, while keeping in view the whole circuit of capital. The chapter does this in four broad steps. The first section below recapitulates and develops a preliminary critique of debates about productive stagnation and financialization in late twentieth- and early twenty-first-century capitalism, concentrating primarily on Marxist debates. The next develops a conceptual argument, building on the 'process view' of finance capital developed in the previous chapter, coupled with arguments about the continual and contradictory restructuring of capitalist production through spatial, ecological, and organization transformations. It is argued this move, from aggregate 'stagnation' to an emphasis on finance as imbricated in continual, uneven patterns of restructuring, gives us the leverage to better place the uneven development of finance in the transformation of global production in recent decades, and vice versa. The final two sections develop, necessarily in broad strokes, some empirical propositions about how this conceptual move helps us to reframe the turbulent transformations of global production and global finance over the last 70 years. I do this first by reframing the crisis of profitability in the 1970s as a *global* crisis engendered by the conjuncture of a global transition from coal to oil in the mid-twentieth century with the political breakdown of European empires and completion of the global state system on the other. In the final section, I consider the organizational and geographical restructuring of global production in the period since roughly 1980, emphasizing, on one hand, the interplay of financial accumulation with the uneven development of production, and, on the other, the way that this restructuring has been profoundly shaped by developments highlighted in the earlier period.

FINANCIALIZATION AND THE CRISIS OF
PRODUCTIVE PROFITABILITY

There are several somewhat different, though clearly partially related, explanations offered for the falling profitability of production in recent decades. I'm going to focus primarily on Marxist analyses here, primarily because they represent the most systematic and sophisticated attempts to articulate the 'stagnation' hypothesis and link it to the rise of finance.

Chapter 1 discussed Arrighi's analysis. For Arrighi, US hegemony (as with Genoese, British, and Dutch hegemony in preceding centuries) was rooted in a phase of 'material expansion' driven by specific innovations in productive organization. In the case of the US in the 'long twentieth century', Arrighi felt these derived from the 'internalization of transaction costs' enabled by the rise of the vertically integrated corporation.[15] The 'economies of speed' created by the internalization of the production of inputs within a single enterprise ostensibly allowed US manufacturing firms to achieve higher rates of profitability domestically and to expand operations internationally over the first half of the twentieth century.[16] But this advantage could only last for a time, until the widespread emulation of those innovations ate away at profit rates, prompting US capital to shift towards financial expansion. In short, productive stagnation, for Arrighi, was driven by competitive emulation which gradually eroded the super-profitability of US firms. At the same time, as he had stressed in earlier essays on the shifting structures of US imperialism, US firms had tended increasingly to hoard overaccumulated profits in emergent global money markets.[17] The organizational form of US dominance, in short, ultimately proved self-undermining.

Probably more common, at least in Anglophone debates, are arguments emphasizing the role of 'monopoly capitalism', on one hand, or 'overcapacity', on the other. The former could be termed the *Monthly Review* school, as many of its most significant contributions have been published in or by authors closely associated with that journal and associated book press. The *Monthly Review* school has generally stressed the tendencies towards stagnation inherent in 'monopoly capitalism' in 'mature' capitalist systems. Magdoff and

Sweezy give us probably the first coherent and systematic Marxist account linking the rise of finance and the stagnation of productive economies. Responding to the 'casino capitalism' debates emerging in the mid-1980s, they argue that what was happening was different from the periodic speculative bubbles that had previously seized hold of financial markets. The 'casino' was not simply a product of finance growing out of control. 'Beginning as long ago as the 1820s', they wrote, 'speculative excesses of this kind became a normal feature of the capitalist business cycle, getting under way in the later stages of the boom and foreshadowing the panic and collapse to come.'[18] The rise of finance in the 1980s, however, was in Magdoff and Sweezy's estimation something different, 'very far from being an end-of-boom phenomenon.'[19] For them, it was nothing less than a secular restructuring of the US economy, with deep roots and profound consequences.

Magdoff and Sweezy suggest that the US, as a 'mature monopoly capitalist society', had inherent tendencies towards stagnation. The argument here was rooted in Sweezy's earlier work on monopoly capitalism with Paul Baran, which emphasized a tendency towards increasing concentration inherent in capitalist relations of production.[20] While growing concentration generates massive surpluses for a handful of monopolists, the very concentration of capital also introduces increasing barriers to the profitable redeployment of these surpluses. For Magdoff and Sweezy, these constraints had been (as it turned out, only briefly) allayed by specific conjunctural circumstances after World War II (WWII) – not least the need for investment to restore wartime damage, the expansion of global trade under US hegemony, and the Cold War arms race. These forces had run out of steam by the 1960s and 1970s – indeed, they were 'self-limiting', insofar as investment 'not only responds to a demand, but satisfies it'. Banks, meanwhile, were faced with the stagnation of demand for credit in industrial investment, and increasingly pushed to look for alternative customers. They found ready borrowers in many newly independent governments through the 1970s, and 'at home' drove the creation of ever-more complex, ever-more self-contained financial products. The 'financial sphere', in Magdoff and Sweezy's argument, always 'has the potential to become an autonomous subsystem of the economy as a whole, with an enormous capacity for self-expansion'.[21] In theory, this could have been reined in by governments. But with the industrial economy faltering, governments increasingly did the opposite in leading economies – facilitating financial expansion 'in the belief that this was one way, perhaps the most effective way, of countering stagnation'.[22] Crucially, for Magdoff and Sweezy, financial expansion was a response to productive stagnation rather than a cause of it – financial activities enabled the profitable redeployment of capital that would otherwise sit idle. Magdoff and Sweezy's emphasis on 'monopoly capital' has been taken up by a range of publications in and around *Monthly Review*.[23]

Another alternative explanation, most clearly represented in Brenner's work, leans less on monopoly and more on 'overcapacity'. Brenner, much like Magdoff and Sweezy, sees the mid-twentieth-century boom as reflective of a unique set of conditions that ultimately proved self-limiting. Brenner puts more emphasis on the Depression in creating conditions for the boom in the US – crediting the 'huge reductions in the cost of production' enabled by the 'enormous shakeout of obsolete capital stock', the creation of a 'backlog of unused innovations', coupled with rapid reductions in real wages and the destruction of labour militancy under the pressure of mass unemployment.[24] Coupled with the demand stimulus generated by WWII, US manufacturing capital achieved unprecedented rates of profit through the 1940s. Nonetheless, the rapid expansion of production also meant the absorption of surplus labour, and technological advance rapidly created masses of sunk fixed capital. From the 1950s onwards, US capital was increasingly incentivized to invest abroad. US rates of profit accordingly began to fall. The 'later developers' – Germany and Japan in particular – by contrast, could continue to draw on a much larger pool of surplus labour for much longer, and (by virtue of being 'technological followers') were relatively unburdened by 'sunk fixed capital embodying obsolescent technology'.[25] US firms, in this context, 'turned out to have over-invested, and were prevented [by lower-cost competition from Germany and Japan] from raising prices in line with labour and capital costs'.[26] The end result was that, system-wide, global aggregate rates of profit began to fall, resulting ultimately in a 'global crisis of over-capacity and overproduction'. For Brenner, much of the economic history of the following decades could be told through the lens of desperate state efforts to stave off stagnation through monetary interventions without allowing the violent shakeout of excess productive capacity that was needed, with different states at different points in time trying to capture greater shares of saturated export markets through currency devaluations or stoking asset bubbles in hopes of generating new financial sources of investment in manufacturing.

The Endnotes collective outlines a similar story to Brenner's, again emphasizing the role of overcapacity, and the growing importance of finance in efforts to maintain profitability.[27] Global economic history from the 1980s onwards can be 'envisage[d] ... as a game of musical chairs in which the spread of productive capacity across the world, compounded by rising productivity, continually aggravates global overcapacity. Excess capacity is then kept in motion by a continual process that shifts the burden of this excess on to one inflated economy after another.' The latter flows of surplus capital can only be managed through escalating indebtedness, facilitated by low interest rates, leading to an endless series of speculative bubbles. This narrative is couched, to be fair, with an explicit critique of 'financialization' as a concept – not inaccurately characterized as 'an ambiguous term suggesting the increasing dominance of financial capital over industrial or commercial capital' – which ultimately masks the sources of surplus capital sloshing around the system, and the reasons why it must be continually reinvested in financial markets even as these themselves struggle to retain high rates of return. Like Brenner, in rooting an analysis of the rise of finance in the wider restructuring of productive relations, the Endnotes narrative avoids some of the pitfalls of what elsewhere in this book I've called 'power bloc' analyses of finance capital. But finance nonetheless appears here as crisis deferred, rather than a constitutive moment in the valorization process; and debt as a consequence of the collapse of production rather than a key force in organizing its restructuring. And some wider problems with the entire narrative of productive stagnation nonetheless remain.

There are real debates here about the source of the falling profitability of manufacturing. But in the broadest terms the story is similar across the board: The profitability of manufacturing in particular in leading capitalist economies began to fall in the 1960s and 1970s, prompting a rash of responses including a shift towards finance as a key locus of profitability. It is common enough in analyses of financialization to simply take for granted this stagnation of manufacturing and continue the analysis from there. Lapavitsas, for instance, gives an overview of Marxist and mainstream debates about post-1970s stagnation early on in *Profiting without Producing*, but is largely concerned with the fact of stagnation itself as a context for the growing 'asymmetry' of finance and production. Cédric Durand, like Arrighi, echoes Braudel in pointing to the rise of finance as a 'sign of autumn' for contemporary capitalism, but focuses more on the role of various forms of 'fictitious capital' in delaying the oncoming crisis: 'for a time, the increasing sophistication of finance allowed a certain concealment of the growing disconnect between, on one hand, the exhaustion of the productive dynamic, and, on the other, the needs of capital and popular aspirations.'[28] Stagnation is more often treated as a starting point for the analysis of financialization rather than something that needs to be established or explained.

Some initial points about this overarching narrative are in order. Whatever their other differences, Brenner, Magdoff and Sweezy, and even Arrighi (who, despite his world-historical focus ironically perhaps does the most to obfuscate the difference between leading capitalist firms and their home states) offer up what are fundamentally methodologically nationalist analyses.[29] That is, analyses that take the nation-state as a self-contained unit within which economic activity takes place. Analyses of stagnation generally focus on the slowing of growth in what are frequently described as the 'mature capitalist' economies – mainly the UK, US, Germany, and Japan – tracing from there an ostensibly 'global' crisis of profitability.

As noted in the previous chapter, one of the core contradictions of capitalism is that the valorization of capital in general can only be achieved through the competitive interactions of concrete particular capitals. Critically, 'capital-in-general' is by definition an abstraction: it can exist, in Simon Clarke's words, 'only in the form of particular capitals, and the relationship between these capitals is essentially contradictory'.[30] In linking a similar line of thought to stagnation debates, David McNally notes, rightly, that 'Capital does not invest in order to boost Gross Domestic Product ... it invests in order to expand itself via the capture of shares of global surplus value'.[31] To the tension between particular capitals and capital in general also has to be added a scalar mismatch between the operations of capital (which are global) and the concerns of the state (which are on the national scale). This matters here insofar as 'economic growth' is de facto a methodologically nationalist concept, concerned not with capital accumulation in general per se, but primarily with concrete manifestations of value within the territory of the state(s) doing the counting. This broader conceptual problem is also mirrored in a more practical way in an inherent scalar disjuncture between the scope of operations of capitalism and of economic measurement, which has been intensified by the particular concrete form of global restructuring in recent decades.[32] If we could articulate a non-methodologically nationalist reading of growth in concept, our actually existing measures of growth nonetheless necessarily reproduce methodologically nationalist frames.

Measures of productivity, profitability, and economic growth are not passive recordings of economic activity, but measures of those aspects that are materially most relevant for the states collecting them. Measurements of 'the economy' are first and foremost instruments of statecraft.[33] As Brett Christophers rightly notes:

> It is no coincidence that national accounts materialized as a technology of political calculation and intervention in the period in modern human history that witnessed ... the strictest protectionism of national economies ... National accounts were the accounts of *nations*, delimited precisely as such ...[34]

Christophers goes on argue, I think persuasively, that the expressly national scale of national accounts data has exaggerated measures of 'financialization' of leading economies.[35] A considerable portion of the growing share of profits of banks and other financial institutions in the US and UK is accounted for less by the growth of the financial sector per se, and more by the growing internationalization of these firms' operations, coupled with the way that profits from operations abroad are reported. More generally, a number of authors have noted that the globalization of economic activity, in the context of a national frame of measurement and accounting, generates important difficulties and renders economic statistics increasingly unreliable.[36] For present purposes, the important thing to note is that there's a mismatch between the country level at which measures of economic activity are pitched and the global scope of capital in general.

'Advanced' capitalism has always existed in an uneven and combined relation to the areas underdeveloped through the reproduction and expansion of capitalist relations of production. Capitalism must, then, be grasped as an unevenly developed totality operating on a global scale, which always generates a kaleidoscopic picture of growth in some places and stagnation and decline in others. The very concept of self-contained, 'mature capitalisms' – stagnating or otherwise – is antagonistic to understanding capitalism as a whole in this sense. The need for a global scope is moreover especially salient in the context of the concrete forms of productive reorganization we have witnessed in the last few decades. For all that 'globalization' debates in the 1990s and 2000s led down multiple political and intellectual culs-de-sac and have (rightly) gone out of fashion, the organizational form of capitalist production has indeed become more directly and consciously global in important ways. Productive processes are increasingly coordinated through hierarchical global production networks[37] and accompanying 'global wealth chains' (to borrow Leonard Seabrooke and Duncan Wigan's useful phrase).[38]

Nominal stagnation within national territories *does* offer important bases for understanding the role that capitalist *states* have played in liberalizing and deliberately promoting the expansion of financial activity. Brenner's analysis of the ways that US, Japanese, and German policymakers struggled to retain manufacturing productivity and profitability within their own jurisdictions, increasingly through various interventions in monetary and financial policy both nationally and internationally, remains compelling even if we don't fully buy his analysis of the roots and extent of the profitability crisis.[39] Jack Copley has done something similar in the case of the Thatcherite financial deregulation in the UK, albeit with a much more fleshed out theory of the state and the failure-prone dynamics of capitalist statecraft.[40] We should nonetheless be wary of what a story of productive stagnation actually tells us about the global organization of capitalist production or its relation to finance capital.

Accounts linking the rise of finance in recent decades to the stagnation, overcapacity, or falling profitability of production are also, relatedly, all missing an account of capital's production and reconstruction of nature in and through the process of accumulation. Extrapolating from aggregate statistics in a few core economies has ultimately led to major omissions from the story of stagnation, not least around the interconnected bundle of issues surrounding energy and ecology, the end of formal empire in the mid-twentieth century, and the contradictions of postcolonial capitalisms. The notion of a widening imbalance between financial and productive accumulation likewise misses the complex interplay of financial and productive circuits over the longer run.

FROM STAGNATION TO RESTRUCTURING

I outlined a process view of finance capital in the previous chapter, arguing that financial accumulation must be understood as integral to the circulation of capital and the operation of value more generally. Here I want to extend this perspective somewhat to think about the shifting configurations of productive relations over time. My basic claim is that a more productive starting place for an analysis of how finance as a process relates to the organization of production is to centre the always uneven processes of spatial, ecological, and organizational restructuring endemic to capitalist social relations in our account.

A worthwhile starting place here is with a recognition that, as noted above, 'capital' taken in general is always an anarchic aggregation of competing particular capitals. If there is some truth to the monopoly capitalism thesis, it lies precisely in the fact that larger capitals are often much more readily able to escape the limits of the market and impose prices and levels of turnover on others (on which, more in the next section). Any fall in aggregate profitability will inevitably be unevenly felt between different particular capitals. Particular capitals are indeed subject to a variety of tendencies towards falling profitability, which can manifest as more generalized crises of accumulation at different scales. However, it's important to note that these tendencies are better understood as geographically bound and realized unevenly rather than secular tendencies of capital as a whole.[41]

Neil Smith's 'production of nature' thesis is relevant here.[42] Capital operates by restructuring the metabolism between nature and labour, both in the sense that the 'alienation' of the worker from their own basic subsistence is the basis of capitalist exploitation, and in that the labour process itself entails the qualitative transformation of this metabolism. As Marx emphasizes, 'labour is, first of all, a process between man [sic] and nature, a process by which man ... regulates and controls the metabolism between himself and nature. He confronts the materials of nature as a force of nature.'[43] For Smith, the corollary here is that the constitution of capitalist accumulation entails not just the domination or depletion of an 'external' nature but the production of alienated capitalist natures themselves – Smith uses the phrase 'second nature' to describe the historical natures produced through capitalist relations of production. By this, he means that capitalist production requires ways of assembling a metabolic relation between labour and other commodities (an important one of which, as emphasized in the next section below, is nearly always a source of external energy) with the means of production in a particular time and place. In Smith's words, 'Unless space is conceptualized as a quite separate reality from nature, the production of space is a logical corollary of the production of nature.'[44] The crucial point here is that capital in this way 'produces distinct spatial scales – absolute spaces – within which the drive towards equalisation is concentrated'.[45] Smith's perspective is useful in the first instance insofar as it highlights the necessarily geographically uneven nature of both accumulation and crisis – overproduction and overaccumulation happen within historically produced 'absolute spaces' of variable scale. In this sense, insofar as we do see meaningful tendencies to overproduction and overcapacity, they are primarily concentrated within particular sectors or particular spaces. At the time of writing, for instance, problems of overcapacity in the manufacturing of solar photovoltaic panels, centred in particular on Chinese firms, represent a growing policy and geopolitical concern insofar as they represent a significant drag on profitability and further investment in SPV panel manufacturing, and threaten to undercut US and European manufacturers of solar panels.[46] However, precisely because these tendencies are geographically bound, spatial and organizational restructuring can and does offer capital a route out of crises of overaccumulation – in Harvey's words, if 'the frontiers of the region can be rolled back', the devaluation of capital can be avoided.[47]

However, while the production of nature and space is necessary for the valorization of the circuit of capital, capitalist natures also pose important fetters on processes of capital accumulation. In particular, there is a fundamental contradiction between an alienated compulsion to maintain 'socially necessary' levels of productivity and capital's tendency to deplete and toxify the wider web of socio-ecological relations with which it is enmeshed. James O'Connor notes that there is a contradiction between capitalist relations of production and the 'conditions of production'. This is an instance of the fundamental contradiction between particular capitals and capital in general insofar as the conditions of production must be maintained in order for accumulation to proceed, but as a rule all or most particular capitals will seek to pass the costs of maintaining them on to other actors (whether other capitals, working classes, or the state). Capital must produce its own natures, but cannot reproduce them indefinitely, and must continually restructure both its own social, spatial, technological and organizational form, and capitalist natures in order to navigate its own tendency to destroy them.

The logic here is not miles off Marx's argument about the 'general law of accumulation', outlined in Chapter 25 of *Capital*, which stresses the need for the continual technological and organizational restructuring of capitalist production.[48] For Marx, the expansion of production drives an increased need for labour, while depleting and impairing the extant workforce. This threatens to drive up the price of labour, but this tendency is checked, Marx argues, by the continual formation and reformation of 'relative surplus populations' through the spatial, organizational, and

technological restructuring of relations of production and reproduction.[49] O'Connor's argument takes a relatively similar form,
but emphasizes the 'external' (or, better, externalized) social and
physical conditions necessary for production to take place including the availability of productive land, labour, water, and energy.[50]
These conditions are 'naturalized', insofar as, in Rudy's words, 'in
the normal operation of capital, production conditions are treated
as freely available, naturally reproduced and effectively inexhaust-
ible factors of production'.[51] Capitalist relations of production
thus, in O'Connor's words, tend to 'self-destruct by impairing or
destroying rather than reproducing their own conditions'.[52] Capitalist production as a metabolic relation also simultaneously
generates and externalizes wastes, which can produce dynamics
of accelerating toxification on different scales – the most notable
example (though far from the only one) is planetary climate
breakdown caused by carbon emissions.[53] O'Connor gives a list of
examples of mechanisms by which capital destroys its conditions
of production, including the warming climate, acid rain, saliniza-
tion of water tables, toxic wastes, soil erosion, and the 'pesticide
treadmill' which all result from the progression of capitalist production, as well as the breakdown of communal solidarity and
family structures, depletion of workers' bodies, and costs linked
to processes of urbanization. All of these raise costs of production and/or undermine productivity and profitability, and thus
'destroy profits as well as nature'.[54] Jason Moore notes that underproduction in this sense is a conjunctural phenomenon, where the
depletion of inputs that could previously be appropriated cheaply
(e.g., labour, food, energy, atmospheric carbon sinks) become
increasingly degraded.[55] Here again, the tendency to erode ecological surplus produces tendencies towards the opening of new
commodity and waste frontiers, and to more intensive modes of
development through growing 'capitalization and socio-technical
innovation', but often at the cost of accelerating processes of depletion and toxification.[56]

   Alongside conventional Marxist theories emphasizing the
development of capitalist crisis as a result of overcapacity and overproduction (as in, inter alia, most of the arguments discussed in the
preceding section), there is thus also a distinct possibility of crises

of 'underproduction' – in essence, that a growing share of social product must go towards a litany of 'unproductive' uses in order to maintain the externalized conditions of production, rather than the self-expansion of capital.[57] For present purposes, what's important here is that this tendency towards underproduction generates continual parallel pressures for restructuring and re-regulating the relationships between capital and historically produced natures.

But capitalist restructuring is not without limit. It is deeply constrained both by the pre-existing natural processes it encounters, and by the configurations of space and nature produced through previous processes of capitalist accumulation. In Smith's words, 'there is no omnipotence to capital, and what it can do in reality – albeit a reality of its own making – is much more limited'.[58] The redeployment of capital, equally, can only displace contradictions rather than resolving them. In the process, capital produces new contradictions which will inevitably need to be resolved by further restructuring.[59] But the most salient implication of all this is that capital possesses a continual tendency towards crises and restructuring. Faced with the periodic exhaustion of its capacity to capture surplus value in particular 'absolute spaces', capital is compelled to continually build new ones while constrained by existing configurations of labour, nature, and capital. The capacity of different particular capitals to actually do this in practice is uneven, and changes over time. These processes unevenly remake space and nature to the extent that the analysis of particular national configurations will always obscure important parts of the movement of capitalist relations of production as a totality.

Finance is without doubt part and parcel of these processes of restructuring. This is true in the first instance in that financial markets frequently serve as mechanisms for pooling and redeploying overaccumulated capital. Where considerations of finance have entered into analyses of capitalist restructuring and uneven development, it has often been in this sense, stressing how financial capital has acted as an agent accelerating uneven development.[60] Moore, for instance, after suggesting that the tendency to underproduction is often resolved by capital through efforts to dissolve the boundaries between different 'cheap' conditions for production (of which food, energy, raw materials, and labour are particularly important), argues that the twenty-first-century financialization of commodities introduces an unstable extension of this process such that the valorization and circulation of raw materials is increasingly interdependent with that of other commodities (e.g., copper on oil and vice versa) rather than on their own production.[61]

Followed through to conclusion, though, a process view of finance capital suggests that the role of finance is more complicated than this. Relations of credit and debt are necessary to the management of crisis of underproduction and the production of new capitalized natures. O'Connor makes the suggestive point that the expansion of financial activity is itself not only a symptom of overproduction, but of crises of underproduction and the escalating 'unproductive' expenditures they necessitate.[62] Debts, as noted in the previous chapter, also remain a crucial means by which the mute compulsion of the market is retained over relative surplus populations expelled from direct employment as wage labour in and through processes of restructuring.[63]

More importantly, finance is not only a vector of uneven development, but is *itself* unevenly developed as a process of circulation.[64] I mean this in two ways. First, finance capital is not an ethereal, esoteric, dematerialized circuit, but a concrete assemblage of material systems, standards, and routinized human practices. This latter point in particular is one that so-called 'Social Studies of Finance' (SSF) literature often taking inspiration from Science and Technology Studies has been quicker to recognize than Marxist political economy.[65] Though SSF work has generally done so in a way that avoids meaningful engagement with questions of accumulation, power, and exploitation.[66] Finance is undergirded by a material and social infrastructure – by fixed capital in the form of brick and mortar buildings, communications equipment, and by various forms of labour.[67] Some of the latter are infamously well remunerated and involve sufficient command over capital that the people who perform them must be considered to occupy contradictory managerial or even outright capitalist class positions.[68] This is far from universally the case, though. Many of the myriad customer-service, data-entry and like roles necessary to the operations of finance capital have long been carried out on proletarianized terms. Thus, finance capital understood as a circulation process is not just free-floating money, but a capitalized nature of its own through which money and commodities including labour power can be combined and recombined in different forms. The material geographies of financial systems are, in fact, prone to centralization and tend to be quite consistent over time, even as new products targeting different populations are rolled out.[69] The redeployment of finance capital like productive capital is shaped and limited by its existing production of nature.

Second, financial and monetary relations are hierarchical, and again these hierarchies tend to persist over time. Financial systems and financial relations have long played a major role in facilitating, consolidating, and organizing extractive relations. One of the long-run consequences of this dynamic is aptly characterized in terms of 'international financial subordination'.[70] Metropolitan cores of the global political economy are characterized by deep pools of financial capital, and as a result by relative monetary and financial stability. Peripheral people, states, and places are, by contrast, subject to persistent constraints on available resources, and to volatility beyond their control.[71] The uneven development of finance in this sense often poses significant barriers to the restructuring of production. Credit often does not flow easily to the places most in need of investment, nor necessarily even to those most capable of valorizing it – a point to which I'll return in Chapter 5.

The upshot of all this is that the historical trajectories of capitalist production are usefully understood in terms of a continual, uneven restructuring of space, nature, technology, and organization aimed at fighting off these tendencies to over- and underproduction. Finance capital is itself unevenly developed and in a similar process of continual restructuring, closely interpenetrated with the uneven restructuring of 'productive' circuits. Any process of financial expansion is ultimately contingent on the reconfiguration of the whole circuit of capital in a manner that makes possible the accumulation of a larger share of surplus value within financial circuits. From a process view, the task is to understand the place of finance in the perpetual restructuring of capital accumulation. Seen from this angle, narratives of capitalist stagnation are potentially useful, certainly true within some of the 'absolute spaces' of existing capital accumulation, but necessarily incomplete. In what follows, I want to build on this discussion by sketching a (necessarily quite broad) alternative interpretation of the crisis and restructuring of global capital accumulation over the last 70 years.

THE GLOBAL CRISIS OF ACCUMULATION REVISITED

I outlined some key points of debate about the global profitability crisis in the 1970s in the first section above. In themselves, these narratives are not wrong – there was absolutely a crisis of profitability, as well as of social legitimacy, in the capitalist core in the 1960s and 1970s. This crisis remains unresolved, and the conflictual, truncated, and error-prone responses to it have undoubtedly profoundly shaped the contemporary landscape of global capitalism. But the stagnation story is incomplete. What is often framed as productive 'stagnation' in much of the financialization debate is better understood in terms of an uneven geographical and organizational restructuring in response to a global crisis of accumulation, which has exacerbated hierarchical transfers of surplus value in spatial terms from periphery to core and in organizational terms from 'smaller' to 'larger' capitals, while accelerating dynamics of underproduction which were at least partially responsible for falling rates of profitability to begin with.[72] To understand how this has taken place, and why it matters for finance, it's worth revisiting the 1970s crisis itself in terms of the production of nature on a global scale. In order to do this, alongside questions of monopoly or overcapacity we must reckon with two empirical developments in the mid-twentieth century which ultimately had far-reaching consequences: The rise of oil and the end of formal empires.

It is hard to overstate the scope and speed with which, in the middle decades of the twentieth century, oil was adopted as an energy source and petrochemical products became key materials and inputs across a huge swathe of different sectors of the global political economy.[73] We often talk about the rise of fossil capital and the massive expansion in the consumption of fossil fuels through the twentieth century. But the change in form of fossil capital implicit in the mid-twentieth-century transition from coal to oil was significant and hugely consequential for subsequent accumulation in its own right.[74] Figure 3.3 shows, in very broad strokes, the shift in the global composition of energy use from 1900 to 2010. At the turn of the twentieth century, oil accounted for 1 per cent of global energy use, and coal for 47 per cent. By 1940, oil's share had grown to 12 per cent, while coal accounted for 51 per cent. By 1970, the share of coal had fallen to 28 per cent and that of oil had risen to 38.[75] This dramatic shift from coal to oil notably coincides almost exactly with the post-war 'golden age' of global capitalism in the core. It is hard to exaggerate the extent to which oil seeped into all aspects of capitalist productive and reproductive relations during this period. As Adam Hanieh has recently argued effectively, oil matters not only as a source of energy, but also through the incorporation of synthetic materials derived from petroleum (plastics, synthetic fibres, synthetic fertilizers) into a vast array of production processes in place of various natural materials.[76] The shift from coal to oil itself was, equally, a massive impetus to the development of trans-oceanic logistical infrastructures. Relative to coal, oil deposits are (1) geographically concentrated, (2) capital-intensive to extract, but (3) possible to transport over long distances. The shift to oil thus necessitated a massive increase in the logistical capacity for the global circulation of commodities. In 1970, oil shipments represented roughly 56 per cent of world shipping cargo by volume.[77] The rise of oil also facilitated global logistical networks, insofar as oil-based fuels are also used overwhelmingly in oceanic shipping. In accordance with the growing centrality of oil to global capital accumulation, oil markets also took on an increasingly important role in shaping global financial markets – especially in its close connection to the status of sterling, and later the dollar, in global currency hierarchies.

The consequences of the rise of oil for the distribution of global profitability, for capitalist productivity, and in sharpening the contradictions of fossil capitalism in general, are curiously absent from debates about the mid-twentieth-century manufacturing boom or productive 'stagnation' in recent decades. The dramatic shift from coal to oil as a source of energy, and the adoption of petrochemical substitutes for a wide range of natural products, both in the space of a few decades in the mid-twentieth century, are underrated contributors to the post-war productivity boom. Brenner

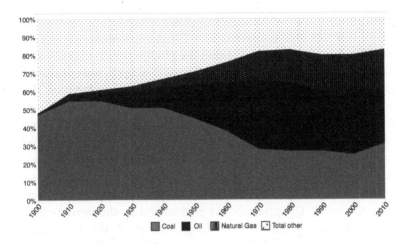

Figure 3.3   Global energy mix, 1990–2010, in per cent of total global energy use

Note: 'Total other' category includes biomass (e.g. wood, charcoal) as well as hydro-electric, nuclear, as well as most forms of present-day 'green' power generation. The composition of this category has changed significantly over time, but the main purpose of the image is to show the changing composition of fossil fuels over time.

Source: Author based on data from V. Smil, *Energy transitions: Global and national perspectives*, 2nd edn (Santa Barbara: Praeger, 2017), Appendix A.

and Magdoff and Sweezy, among others, are absolutely correct in highlighting the importance of the devaluation and destruction of capital associated with war and depression in clearing the way for this technological shift, but miss the qualitative character of the productivity boom itself. Fordist capitalism in the core – both the dramatic expansions of productivity and the class compromise centred on stable employment and homeownership – were profoundly dependent on new applications of oil, as energy and as material, both in industrial applications and in consumer use, mediated through particular histories of class struggle.[78] The long oil boom also laid the conditions for both the most intense contradictions in contemporary capitalism (i.e., the breakdown of the planet's climate), and an underappreciated source of lagging or unstable profitability in other sectors from the 1970s onwards.

The 1970s crisis of capitalist profitability was also an oil crisis in a more immediate sense. The crisis inaugurated a period where a much higher share of total surplus value has fallen to the owners of oil reserves and associated infrastructures. Figure 3.4 gives a crude indication of this – it shows the proportion of 'oil rents' as a share of global GDP from 1970 to 2021. 'Oil rents' are calculated by the World Bank as a measure of the difference between the total monetary value of oil consumed and the cost of producing it. Setting aside the definitional questions that might be raised around the word 'rent' here, it's a reasonable proxy for the share of global surplus value captured by owners of oil extraction rights. Figure 3.4 shows a dramatic spike in the 1970s, in which oil rents shot up from equivalent to 0.4 per cent of the world economy to a peak of 4.7 in 1980. The price shocks engendered by the introduction of production quotas by the Organization of the Petroleum Exporting Countries (OPEC) in 1973 and the Iranian revolution in 1979 drove a dramatic redistribution of total surplus value. This shift exacerbated the falling profitability of manufacturing sectors as the cost of oil drove input and material costs ever-higher. It also exacerbated global relations of financial subordination insofar as it both drove the expansion of core financial centres, particularly New York and London, as these became the main focal points for the recirculation of overaccumulated oil profits, which exacerbated dynamics of unequal exchange in most of the global periphery. After 1980 the share of oil rents fell, reflecting partly the levelling off and growing instability of prices, but also in part the fact that higher prices for oil gradually made profitable the opening up of new offshore (e.g., in the North Sea and Gulf of Mexico) or otherwise difficult to access (the Alberta Tar Sands) oil deposits which were more expensive to exploit. The latter, notably, also played a significant role in allaying the loss of manufacturing industries in several core economies.[79] For oil and gas firms, large swings in profitability from year to year are a function of a wider structural dynamic created by frequent movements in prices.[80] As Gavin Bridge puts it, 'Swings in price cause value to "slosh" back and forth from one end of the chain to the other: a rise in oil prices will distribute value away from consumers and towards producers, while a fall in prices drives value away from producers and towards consumers.'[81] Nonetheless, it's notable that despite considerable price volatility and the further development of more expensive-to-extract deposits (e.g., through fracking), and hence rising average costs of production, oil rents have only very rarely fallen back to their early 1970s levels in aggregate (only in 1998 does the share fall to 0.5 per cent).

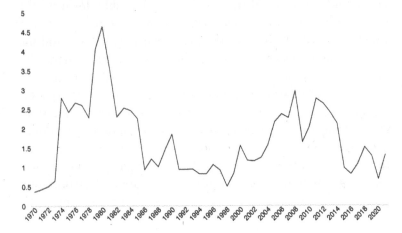

Figure 3.4   Oil rents as percentage of global GDP, 1970–2021.
Source: World Bank Data.

If we want to understand how we got from oil boom to long downturn, though, we need to understand how oil was bound up with the complex political and financial dynamics engendered by the end of formal empires. The interplay of oil and formal decolonization ultimately laid both the financial and material conditions for the restructuring of global production in the latter decades of the twentieth century. If it's true that the tension between the global orientation of capital and the territorial fragmentation of political authority is a core contradiction of historical capitalism,[82] the fragmentation of the world into discrete states was only fully achieved with the disintegration of formal European empires in Africa, Asia, and the Caribbean in the mid-twentieth century. The insertion of dozens of new financially and economically subordinated but politically independent states into the global political economy was one of the most radical structural shifts in the history of global capitalism. Much more so in the context of the global energy shift in the mid-twentieth century because many of the largest oil deposits were found in newly independent states facing a highly hierarchical and uneven global financial system.

Postcolonial states faced an immediate and difficult bind on gaining their formal independence. Critically, the peripheral position of postcolonial states led most to double down on the valorization of natural resource exports initially developed under colonial rule, or to develop new primary exports. Rarely did the aims of anti-colonial projects limit themselves to the formal transfer of state power. Many mid-century anti-colonial thinkers and movements also correctly connected colonial rule to an exploitative global capitalism, and accordingly understood liberation from colonialism as encompassing far-reaching social transformation.[83] The achievement of political sovereignty in nation-state form, in and of itself, was not necessarily the end goal of these movements. The nation-state form assumed by formal decolonization also introduced important contradictions. As Fred Cooper aptly summarizes:

> When, in 1955, people living in the territory of Senegal sought better health facilities and schools and labor conditions equivalent to those in France, they were posing a demand as French citizens. They had representatives – albeit few – in the French legislature. In 1965, they were posing such demands as citizens of Senegal, a poor country whose major source of foreign exchange and government revenue was, literally, peanuts. They could ask for foreign aid but had no say in its distribution.[84]

Of course, the structure and organization of colonial states – not least their status as *capitalist* states[85] – militated against the realization of such claims on the metropolitan core of global empires. But the point is that the nation-state form in and of itself did little to make their achievement easier. The uneven development of colonial monetary and financial systems often exacerbated these problems, imposing significant limits on investment within colonial territories while deepening compulsions to produce crops or minerals for export. In Samir Amin's assessment, the 'inertia' of colonial financial systems constituted 'powerful means of guiding the development of peripheral capitalism in a way that conforms to the needs of the center'.[86]

Postcolonial regimes were also in many instances faced with the flight of colonial capital. This mattered both in terms of exacerbating the pressures of financial subordination, but also for how it helped lay the groundwork for infrastructures of offshore finance which have in turn played a critical role in the later restructuring of global production. The scale of capital flight from formally decolonizing territories is hard to overstate. Vanessa Ogle has shown in detail how the liquidation of colonial assets – as colonial capitalists 'Distrustful of newly independent governments and non-white rule, fearing resentment, increased taxation or possibly even nationalization ... divested from empire.' – gave impetus to the formation of a global infrastructure of tax havens and offshore finance.[87] Tax havens had emerged first in Europe (in, e.g., Liechtenstein and Switzerland) in response to the introduction of income taxes during and after WWI, and had expanded further, predominantly in British dependencies (e.g., Hong Kong, Malta, the Cayman Islands), after WWII. But the large-scale movements of money and capital out of colonized territories gave a significant boost to the development of tax havens globally. Flight capital from British settler territories in Eastern and Southern Africa, especially Kenya in the last years before the territory's relatively late independence in 1963, was predominantly responsible for the establishment of the Bahamas as a tax haven.[88] Not only was the scale of flight capital important, but the perceived need to hide it in order to protect it from taxes, repatriation, or capital controls encouraged the development of increasingly elaborate mechanisms of financial secrecy. Postcolonial states facing this global context thus had few good options, and found themselves compelled to double down on capitalist development.[89] In Kenya, to continue the example above, the flight of settler capital, particularly in the absence of high-value oil or mineral rents, created a growing dependence on attracting foreign investment. Although the post-independence government, spurred by former trade unionist and head of the Economic Planning and Development Ministry, Tom Mboya (eventually assassinated in 1969), initially outlined a nominally 'socialist' approach to development, this 'socialist' strategy was quite explicit that a shortage of domestic capital meant that Kenya needed to 'stimulate the inflow of private capital from abroad.'[90] This approach made sense in a structural situation where 'Neither the government nor the Kenyan bourgeoisie could afford to ... alienat[e] foreign capital.'[91]

In many cases the responses to these constraints involved doubling down on state control over the production of agricultural export crops. Key crops and mineral exports were increasingly brought under various forms of state control. In Ghana, for instance, the late colonial and postcolonial state had sought to loosen the fiscal and monetary constraints posed by the currency board system by capturing cocoa exports directly. State-owned marketing boards gained a monopoly over sales of cocoa in 1947 and were retained by the postcolonial regime. While, on one hand, this provided a source of resources to finance development projects, it also intensified the state's reliance on continued exports of cocoa, even as social and ecological contradictions – in the Ghanaian case, particularly the loss of productivity to soil depletion, deforestation and pests – tightened through the 1970s.[92] These same dynamics elsewhere also spurred renewed oil exploration and the nationalization of oil reserves, expressly understood as a means of reversing unequal terms of trade and loosening the structural constraints of financial subordination.[93] The centrality of oil to mid-twentieth-century monetary hierarchies meant that, in Matthew Schutzer's words, 'The fact that for most of its modern history oil has been sold in strong global currencies has meant that, for oil-importing nations ... the monetary history of oil has not been one of generating national wealth, but of the recurrent production of debt.'[94]

The logic of oil production as a route out of the constraints of financial subordination culminated in the OPEC price spikes, which added to the constraints posed by overcapacity on manufacturing profitability. OPEC must nonetheless be seen in the context of wider efforts at collective structural reform, most notably the movement for the New International Economic Order (NIEO) in the 1960s and 1970s. The NIEO sought to loosen the constraints the international financial system posed on local development, not least by raising prices for the export of primary commodities, but operated within the framework of capitalist development within nation-states. As Samir Amin would observe in a postmortem for the NIEO in 1982, this project ultimately represented the deepening of capitalist social relations, and engendered important contradictions in the process:

> The internal logic of the programme – raising the prices of raw resources exported by the Third World; a new push in export oriented industrialisation geared to developed country markets and based on cheap manpower and the abundance of natural resources; and the acceleration, at reduced cost to developing countries, of technological transfer – reflects the contradictory nature of the accumulation of capital on a world-scale. On the one hand, this programme can only be predicated on a deepening of the international division of labour: by increasing the rate of extractable surplus-value (through the superexploitation of labour in the periphery), the programme permits an increase in the rate of profit on a world scale and can only be read therefore, as a contribution to global capitalist development. On the other hand contradictions emerge within the accepted framework of capitalist development between the strategies of the monopolies and the imperialist states on the one hand and those of the peripheral capitalist states and their bourgeoisies on the other.[95]

Given the centrality of oil to the organization of global capitalism by the 1970s, it should perhaps not be a surprise that it was OPEC in particular which was able to raise export prices successfully. Because of the tight links between oil and global monetary relations, noted above, the spike in oil prices had the effect of further tightening the financial and monetary constraints on national development faced by most postcolonial regimes. The oil crisis, then, exacerbated a crisis of postcolonial capitalist development. If the OPEC shocks represented, on one hand, the one real success of NIEO-style global price controls, they also pushed non-oil-exporting states into fiscal and monetary crisis, compounding what was in many instances the social and ecological exhaustion of postcolonial agricultural development, at the same time as they created vast pools of money needing reinvestment.

The oil price spike in the 1970s not only undercut the profitability of capitalist enterprises reliant on oil as energy or as material
(which is to say, most capitalist enterprises, certainly the vast
majority of manufacturers), but also contributed to a global crisis
of simultaneous over- and underproduction that contributed significantly to the first shoots of financial expansion and the Third
World debt crisis of the 1970s and 1980s. Oil producers in the
1970s suddenly found themselves with vast monetary surpluses,
largely sitting with banks in New York and, especially, in London
in newly liberalized Eurodollar markets – the latter were financial institutions permitted to trade in dollars outside the US.[96]
These funds were increasingly redeployed as loans to states in the
global south through the emerging infrastructure of 'syndicated
loans'. These are loans where a number of banks form a group to
make a loan to a single borrower. As Malcolm Campbell-Verduyn
and colleagues put it, 'an enormous inter-bank market funded
longer-term loans to developing country borrowers from short
term borrowing in international wholesale inter-bank markets,
facilitated by telephone and telex'.[97] Durable relations of financial
subordination form an important part of the context here – even
though oil surpluses were being generated in no small part in postcolonial economies, it was nonetheless financial centres in the core
which retained the infrastructures and deep markets to recycle
them. In a context where surpluses held by oil-producing firms
and states needed to be recirculated, where manufacturing sectors
in the core economies were sclerotic and stagnant, and where the
non-oil-exporting parts of the Third World were in increasingly
desperate need of credit to finance widening balance of payments
deficits, syndicated loans to developing countries took off rapidly.
In 1972, before the OPEC price spikes, US\$7 billion of new syn-
dicated loan facilities were announced. By their peak in 1981 this
figure was US\$133 billion.[98] What happened next is well known
– as interest rates in the US were tightened in the early 1980s,
developing countries already in financial distress were pushed into
default, which kicked off the brutal neoliberal 'ground clearing'
exercise of structural adjustment.[99]

The 1970s crisis was a crisis of overaccumulation, on one hand,
but had its counterpart in the beginnings of an accelerating crisis

of underproduction on a global scale. The impacts of carbon emissions and associated global heating have increasingly undercut the conditions of production unevenly, but globally. To give a sense of the scope of this crisis, a recent study estimates that lost productivity due to the increased frequency of extreme heat events alone account for the loss of trillions of dollars of global GDP between 1993 and 2013 (for all that measures of GDP must be taken with some caution for reasons outlined above). These impacts are universal but unevenly distributed, with costs ranging from 6.7 per cent of GDP per year on average in regions in the lowest income decile globally, to 1.5 per cent of GDP per year in the wealthiest decile.[100]

Notably, we see the first indications of this multifaceted crisis in parts of the postcolonial global south in the 1970s. In Senegal – the first country to adopt a structural adjustment loan in 1978 – the decade previous had been marked by an agricultural crisis engendered by a series of catastrophic droughts, exacerbated by the depletion of soil quality and a growing concern with the prevalence of carcinogenic aflatoxin in the groundnut-exporting regions which had been intensively cultivated.[101] Drought in the Sahelian regions of Africa in the 1970s represented some of the earliest instances of the global crisis of underproduction brought about by carbon emissions. Indeed, droughts across Africa played a significant role in the consolidation of scientific consensus about the impacts of carbon emissions from fossil fuels on the climate.[102] Already from the early 1970s, Senegalese authorities had taken steps to foster the development of foreign investment for horticultural exports, particularly in former groundnut growing areas, as a means of generating an alternative source of export earnings.[103] In this context, the debt crisis was the symptom of a crisis of underproduction as much as it was the product of overaccumulation by oil producers. The brutal 'ground clearing' of structural adjustment represented in this sense an effort to rescue a wider postcolonial project of agricultural capitalization.[104]

In short, the 1970s crisis was a global crisis, in which finance and relations of financial subordination were already closely imbricated at a number of points. The crisis of profitability was, alongside the exhaustion of the post-war boom, effectively a working out of contradictions engendered by the simultaneous rise of oil and decline of formal empires in the mid-twentieth century. The national capitalist development projects engendered by the end of formal colonial rule ironically both drove the spike in oil prices and created severe balance of payments crises for non-oil exporters which facilitated the recycling of surpluses. While manufacturing economies in the core were beset by problems of overcapacity, the debt crisis and subsequent violent ground clearing of neoliberal-ization laid the groundwork for a radical restructuring of global production in the ensuing decades. The networks of tax havens and associated financial infrastructures produced in the flight of capital from politically independent territories, meanwhile, laid the groundwork for the accompanying organizational restructur-ing. I turn to the ways in which these dynamics played out in the following section.

CHANGING GEOGRAPHIES OF MANUFACTURING

With this reconsideration of the wider global, ecological, and financial history of the 1970s crisis, it's now possible to return to the restructuring of global production in recent decades. What we have witnessed in the last five decades is probably best understood not as a global crisis of growth or of productive profitability per se, but rather a radical restructuring of capital which has greatly increased the power of a handful of institutional manifestations of capital, predominantly transnational corporations and their managers, over the organization of production and distribution of revenues globally. This is a restructuring in which the circulation of finance capital has played a key role at many different points, enabling the expansion of financial sectors, but from which the rise of finance as such is impossible to separate.

The Globalization of Production

Perhaps the most immediately notable thing about the global restructuring of capitalism in recent decades is the dramatic shift in the location of manufacturing activity, increasingly centred on China. David McNally, among others, has made the case that, if we take global capitalism as a totality, the decades from the 1970s onwards need to be seen less as one long crisis of overcapacity, and more as a period of 'dramatic social, technical and spatial restructuring of capitalist production ... all of which significantly raised rates of surplus value and profitability, and led to a volatile ... but nonetheless real process of sustained capitalist expansion, centered on East Asia'.[105] Martin Arboleda likewise traces a shift in the centre of gravity of global production towards China in particular and East and South-East Asia in general.[106] This has led, Arboleda argues, to the radical global reorganization of extractive sectors as these increasingly centre on producing materials for Chinese manufacturers. In any case, the point is that we can trace a shifting global division of labour in which manufacturing activities are increasingly concentrated in East Asia generally, and China in particular. This tendency has accelerated since the turn of the millennium. As Figure 3.5 shows, in the last two decades the share of global value added in manufacturing attributed to China in particular has continued to grow rapidly – and, indeed, Chinese growth accounts for much of the global expansion of manufacturing output since 2000. Where China represented about 9 per cent of global manufacturing output in 2004, by 2020 that figure had grown to 29 per cent.

The various stagnation stories outlined above have grappled with the rise of China in different ways. Brenner in particular acknowledges the relocation of Japanese investment and production to lower-wage areas in East Asia in the 1980s and 1990s.[107] He assimilates this development into an account of 'overcapacity' globally – Brenner notes of the rise of manufacturing in East Asia that 'The struggle for markets in a global manufacturing sector that remained haunted by over-supply continued to take the form of a zero-sum struggle, with winners and losers determined heavily by the movement of exchange rates.'[108] The continued growth of Chinese manufacturing does not, in itself, invalidate Brenner's claim about falling profit rates globally – he does, after all, incorporate rising East Asian production into a wider story of global overcapacity. Endnotes, among others, likewise note that the rapid growth of Chinese manufacturing for export has been achieved largely alongside the destruction of socialist-era industrialization and on the basis of the incorporation of low-wage labour into existing labour-saving technology. As such, it hasn't delivered large-scale incorporation of the wider population into industrial manufacturing.[109] By contrast, Arrighi's ersatz sequel to *The Long Twentieth Century*, titled *Adam Smith in Beijing*, argues that the potential scenario of an East Asian 'material expansion' envisaged as a possible future in the final pages of the former book had largely come to pass.[110] Or, in other words, the rise of China is not in itself incompatible with the wider narrative of stagnation. Not least as the manufacturing boom in China has seemed increasingly to be losing steam.

But it is nonetheless notable that China in particular, and East Asia in general, have been the locus of a radical geographical and organizational restructuring of global manufacturing. It's perhaps worth noting to begin here that China is in some senses an outlier to the narrative of oil-induced debt crisis introduced above, but not entirely. As Isabella Weber has recently demonstrated, China's post-Mao transition back to capitalism was gradual (in stark contrast to the brutal 'shock therapy' of privatization and austerity practised across the former Soviet Union and in much of the global

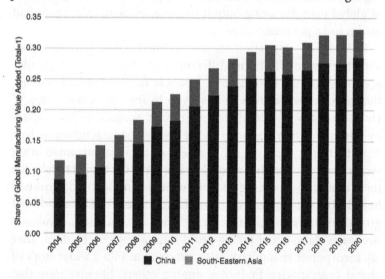

Figure 3.5 Share of global manufacturing value added, 2004–20
Source: Author calculations based on UNSD data.

south), but also very much negotiated both within the Communist Party and in and through relationships with the World Bank among others.[111] China's partial liberalization was in this sense very much entangled organizationally with uneven processes of neoliberalization elsewhere. China's rise as the epicentre of global manufacturing was made possible through the large-scale mobilization and disciplining of rural-urban migrant labour.[112] Equally important was the mobilization of cheap energy, primarily in the form of coal. Visible in Figure 3.3 is a marked revival of coal as a share of the global energy mix between 2000 and 2010. Both in terms of extraction and in terms of use, this global revival of coal has been driven almost entirely by Chinese development. In 1990, China produced 1.08 gigatonnes of coal, which represented 23 per cent of the global total; by 2013, these figures were, respectively, 3.97gT and 48 per cent.[113] The spatial shift of global production towards China, in short, very much rested on the production of a new configuration of nature and space which permitted the restoration of cheap labour and cheap energy.

But this spatial restructuring as such is only part of the story, and the much more complex picture of finance and production in the twenty-first century becomes clear when we move away from the methodologically nationalist frame of so much of the stagnation debate in order to ask about the organizational *form* through which production is carried out. The relocation of much manufacturing to China is a particular manifestation of wider shifts in the organizational form of global production, increasingly organized through uneven and hierarchical production networks, in which core firms are systematically able to offload costs of production to smaller peripheral productive firms, and ultimately to hyper-exploited labourers, while forcing down the prices they pay. Guido Starosta suggests, usefully, that global production networks through which a growing share of production is organized represent in effect 'the social form through which certain normal capitals appropriate the surplus value released by small capitals'.[114] This has been the product of a deliberate shift in managerial practice – described in part in the discussion of 'shareholder value' orientation in Chapter 1 – in which lead firms have sought to unbundle the process of production, retaining ownership of only the most lucrative aspects of the circuit of capital and retaining control of the riskier and less profitable activities by other means. The so-called 'smile curve' has become a widespread organizing logic. The 'smile curve' describes the relative profitability of the activities along the value chain traced by a commodity, suggesting that this tends to follow a 'U-shaped' curve – the first (design, research and development) and last (marketing, branding, and distribution) links in the chain tend to be more profitable than the middle ones (actual manufacturing). Leading transnational firms have increasingly sought to maximize their profitability by retaining ownership over the ends of the chain and divesting from the manufacturing activities in the middle. This unquestionably represents an organizational transformation facilitated by the longer-run tendencies established in the preceding half-century. The extraction of surplus from smaller capitals by transnational firms rests very firmly on reconfigured relations of hyper-exploitation of labour, themselves made possible in no small part by the sweep of structural adjustment and large-scale displacement from agriculture since the 1980s.[115] As Clair Quentin and Liam Campling put it, neatly:

> The less well remunerated productive workers are, the greater the surplus available for appropriation in the entire system. However, given that surplus value can be appropriated without ownership of productive assets, the downward pressure on the incomes of productive workers can be exerted indirectly by the downward pressure on the incomes of firms owning productive assets.[116]

The scale of surplus value appropriated in this sense is significant. An oft-cited example is Apple's iPhone and iPad: Kraemer et al., a decade ago estimated that 30 per cent of the value of a low-end iPad, and 58 per cent of the value realized from the sale of an iPhone 4 (the newest model at the time) accrued to Apple. The profits of various component suppliers and assemblers, in Taiwan (primarily to Foxconn, which actually mainly operated in mainland China), Korea, and Japan, amounted to 5.7 per cent of the total, and 5.4 per cent in total to labourers in China and elsewhere.[117] Apple is perhaps the epitome of a wider process in which value chains have been restructured, with major global firms able to retain the most lucrative activities and divest themselves from costly or less profitable ones. Apple's monopsonistic control over the supply chain for the iPhone allows it to actively and deliberately suppress the profits that obtain in manufacturing activities proper along its value chain. The capacity to indirectly appropriate cheap labour and cheap energy in China and elsewhere in East Asia is a crucial part of Apple's global profitability. This is no doubt, in part, a problem of excess manufacturing capacity, insofar as many suppliers compete to provide inputs. And it is equally no doubt the case that problems of overproduction and overcapacity *do* develop within particular 'absolute spaces' in ways that do weigh on the profitability of leading firms. As I write this, for instance, Samsung has been forced to slash its production of memory chips. Chip production had been ramped up from 2020 – during the Covid-19 pandemic, supply chain disruptions and higher purchases of electronics led to a shortage of chips, and a spike in prices, to which Samsung and other producers responded by ramping up production. This very quickly produced a glut of chips, particularly as demand levelled off, and profits collapsed in 2022 and 2023. Samsung estimated that its operating profits dropped from over 14 trillion won in the first quarter of 2022 to 600 billion in the equivalent period in 2023, a fall of roughly 96 per cent.[118] The competitive dynamics within particular industries, in short, can undoubtedly produce substantial problems of overproduction and overcapacity within particular absolute spaces.

However, to make overcapacity into the lodestone of a generalized theory of diminished profitability is also to miss that the relations between capitals drive both the weak profitability of smaller capitals and the overall high profitability of many dominant firms. Monopoly capitalism perhaps offers more purchase on this set of relationships insofar as relations of concentration and the dominance of some segments of capital over others are hugely important.[119] But at the same time, the global organization of production clearly represents a form of monopoly capitalism restructured in a very different direction than the monopoly capital version of the stagnation/financialization narrative suggests. In any case, it does not make sense to examine 'manufacturing' and other profits here separately. Apple is still wholly reliant on manufacturing activities for its 58 per cent, even if it doesn't own the capital or labour power through which those activities are carried out directly. Branding, R&D, and distribution, to put it bluntly, are lucrative, but worth nothing unless iPhones are made and can be sold, without which there can be nothing to distribute to Apple's shareholders either. Ultimately, we get a distorted picture of what's happening here by looking at sectoral distributions rather than trying to look at the restructuring of the circuits of capital as a whole.

This picture hardly applies to Apple in isolation either. Agricultural production, for instance, has likewise been marked by a dramatic concentration of corporate control over inputs and over marketing by a few large firms, on one hand, in the case of staple crops like corn, wheat, and soy; and simultaneously by the rise of increasingly complex production networks dominated by major supermarkets and global food brands and organized through complex contract and subcontract arrangements for horticultural crops.[120] Philip McMichael has aptly termed the latter 'value-chain agriculture'.[121] As with the organizational restructuring highlighted in the case of Apple, this must be seen as part of a longer-term process of agricultural commercialization driven along by the responses to the crisis of the 1970s. The brutal 'ground clearing' of structural adjustment emerged out of and intensified longer-run processes of capitalization already underway. What's happened in the broadest terms is that the lowest-margin, highest risk, and most competitive aspects of production processes have systematically been outsourced and often relocated. The most important aspect of all of this for present purposes is that the interplay of finance, energy, and capitalist development traced in the previous section have played a critical role in laying the groundwork for this restructuring. I trace out these dynamics across the next two subsections.

Cheap Labour and Debt

The fine margins that obtain in manufacturing and agricultural production under monopolistic global production networks are only possible through an intensified exploitation of labour, both in productive and reproductive settings, and through both formal waged work and increasingly through irregular forms of employment relations in combination with gendered patterns of social reproduction.[122] Ben Selwyn in particular has made cognate arguments about the role of labour and global value chains in development. Against perspectives that frame employment at the fringes of global value chains as a 'first rung on the ladder of development', Selwyn argues that poor pay and working conditions inherent in these settings in fact create new forms of poverty.[123] For the mostly women rural-urban migrants disproportionately employed in light manufacturing activities, increased incomes in monetary terms are accompanied by the intensification of work and rising costs of survival items. For Selwyn, when we centre the relations of exploitation accompanying the diffusion of global value chains, they look less like a 'first rung' and more like 'global poverty chains'. As Elena Baglioni describes in detail in relation to the margins of horticultural supply chains in Senegal, gendered household relations can play a significant role in making women in particular available to be exploited as cheap labour.[124] Importantly, it is precisely the 'ground clearing' carried out under the auspices of structural adjustment, following the debt-fuelled breakdown of postcolonial modes of state capitalism, which has permitted the redeployment of surplus labour into marginal positions in global value chains.

At the level of individual workers, renewed relations of indebtedness also represent in many instances a critical organizing and disciplining mechanism through which this redeployment has been achieved. Livelihoods and work are increasingly precarious. This has happened alongside the privatization and commodification of housing, water, caring labour and other basic infrastructures of social reproduction in the course of social reproduction. In both rural and urban settings, this has been exacerbated by the acceleration of climate breakdown. Taken together, these dynamics have led to crises of indebtedness in both rural and urban settings, in the global north and global south. This is not exclusive or unique to the present by any means. Relations of indebtedness have long served, for instance, as the mechanism structuring the capitalization of agriculture.[125] However, the reconfiguration of relations of indebtedness has nonetheless served as a key mechanism for the organization of labour. The boom in contract agriculture noted above is one example. Debt relations, wherein large firms advance seed, fertilizer, and agri-chemicals on credit, against a claim on the final crop, play a critical role in structuring value-chain agriculture.[126] Relations of indebtedness have also proved crucial in driving the movement of workers towards employment in low-wage manufacturing activities. For instance, the intersections of exploitation through labour and through debts, as Brickell and colleagues demonstrate, coupled with retrenchment of state supports and downloading of responsibility for social reproductive work onto households, have combined in Cambodia's garment sector in a crisis of hunger prompted by the pandemic-era cancellation of orders from major global retailers.[127]

By the same token, the extension of formal indebtedness has been radically uneven and strongly conditioned by the restructuring of production itself. Paying attention to the relations between financial accumulation and 'everything that goes on in between' also suggests that we need to be attentive to the ways in which workers' revenues might shape the uneven development of financial markets. South Africa is a good example. Exclusions from access to credit were, as Deborah James and Dinah Rajak among others have noted, a core feature of apartheid.[128] Post-1994 reforms sought to encourage greater lending to populations often barred from borrowing under apartheid, in large part by encouraging greater competition among lenders.[129] Most major banks subsequently significantly expanded high-interest, unsecured credit operations. This was matched by a dramatic expansion of commercial microcredit operations.[130] However, the overall rapid expansion of consumer indebtedness masked a highly uneven process intimately entangled with wider restructuring of production.

For instance, debts played a crucial role in the remobilization of cheap labour in sufficient quantities to enable expanded platinum production in the early 2000s. Platinum mining in South Africa had historically drawn on colonial- and apartheid-era migrant labour systems that had grown up during the period dominated by gold mining. Employment was thus historically dominated by temporary migrant workers, recruited through the Employment

Bureau of Africa run by the Chamber of Mines, and housed in company compounds. In the 1970s and 1980s, as the National Union of Mineworkers (NUM) was increasingly successful in organization in the compounds and immigration restrictions forced an increased reliance on South African labour, real wages across the mining sector boomed. By one estimate, real wages for mineworkers tripled between 1973 and 1983.[131] Mobilizing labour in increasing numbers without inflating wages took on vital importance as the platinum sector boomed in the 2000s. As Andrew Bowman notes, the pressure to deliver dividends to shareholders meant that longer-term investments that might have raised labour productivity or improved efficiency were generally foregone, and downwards pressures were continually inflicted on wages.[132] Firms systematically dismantled compounds, and the use of contract labour and labour brokers proliferated across the mining industry from the 1990s onwards.[133] By the first decade of the 2000s, roughly a third of platinum mining labour was contracted out.[134] For employers, the growth of labour broking permitted a renewed supply of cheap labour in the context of nominally stringent post-apartheid employment laws – in Kally Forrest's words, it allowed employers to replicate apartheid-era recruitment regimes' 'low wages, low social reproduction costs, and no obligation to provide job or social security'.[135]

The influx of new workers, coupled with the privatization and marketization of housing and local infrastructures, produced a crisis of social reproduction in platinum belt communities, as stagnant or falling wages ran up against spiralling living costs and strains on local infrastructure. Less than 10 per cent of workers at Lonmin's Marikana facility, for instance, were housed in hostels or other company-built housing in 2013,[136] while upwards of 40 per cent of the total population in the Rustenberg Local Municipality lived in informal settlements.[137] A notable consequence here was a boom in predatory lending in the platinum belt, and correspondingly, of indebtedness among mineworkers. Specific numbers are hard to come by, but media reports in 2012 and 2013 (particularly in the aftermath of the killing of 44 striking miners by police in 2012) emphasized the prevalence of unsecured credit providers. Miners interviewed in 2012, for instance, reported that 'most

miners' regularly drew on unsecured credit, on average R1,000–
1,500 with a repayment period of 30 days, often at very high rates
of interest: 'Interest rates of 5% a month are charged, excluding a
service charge of R50 a month and an initiation fee of a maximum
of 15% on the value of the loan. Collection fees for defaulters also
apply.'[138] The redeployment of mining labour into new spaces to
facilitate platinum mining, particularly in the context of the privatization and individualization of workers' housing, both depended
on relations of indebtedness, which deferred but ultimately exacerbated an ongoing crisis of social reproduction, and created an
important site for new forms of financial accumulation.

The point here is that financial relations figure centrally in
the global restructuring of production. On one hand, relations
of indebtedness serve as a particularly important concrete form
of appearance of the wider compulsion to labour. Put in simpler
terms: Debts have driven a growing number of people to seek work
at the margins of restructured global production networks, despite
the reliance of the latter on the continual intensification of extraction of surplus through processes of super-exploitation. On the
other hand, debts have served as mechanisms to postpone (while
in turn exacerbating) the crises of social reproduction engendered
in the process. The 'financialization of daily life', or the rise of
'financial expropriation' such as it has taken place, in short, is profoundly mutually imbricated with the restructuring of labour and
nature implied in the contemporary globalization of production.

The Organizational Transformation of Capital

At a wider level, the patterns of restructuring noted here have been
accompanied by the growing centrality of *managerial* modes of
coordination – the systematically uneven rollout of techniques of
standardization, measurement, and fostering of contained competition organized by leading capitalist firms in conjunction with a
growing army of consultancies, law offices, accountants, and the
like. The contested transformation of firm structures discussed
in Chapter 1, greatly facilitated by particular configurations of
finance, has clearly played a role in fostering contemporary managerialism. Elena Baglioni and colleagues frame managerial forms

of coordination as mechanisms enabling the 'continuous expansion and capture of value'.[139] Starosta rightly notes that the transfer of surplus value through global production networks is strongly conditioned by the capacity of key firms to establish the 'determinate conditions of turnover for each participating capital'.[140] To add complexity to this global reorganization, value chains are increasingly structured in such a way as to minimize the tax and wage obligations of leading transnational firms, with important effects on the global distribution of value[141] – the latter facilitated in no small part by the infrastructure of tax havens laid in the process of formal decolonization.

To give a rough sense of the scope and salience of these shifting organizational forms in the structure of global production, we can point to the growing share of international trade made up of intra-firm and intra-industry transactions. Intra-firm trade refers to imports and exports between affiliates of the same corporate group. Intra-industry trade refers to trade in unfinished goods between firms in the same sector. These measures do need to be taken with some caution. In the first instance, for present purposes, trade is evidently not the same thing as production. Intra-industry trade also does not precisely capture the flow of goods within global production networks. It is, though, a rough indication of the degree to which production is organized through global production networks. Equally, while the volume of international trade has grown rapidly as a share of total production, not all commodities are ever traded across borders. We should also note that statistics on intra-firm trade are unevenly collected and reported – measures are difficult and time consuming to construct, and as such they are typically only collected sporadically. The volume of trade in intermediate goods, in and of itself, still doesn't tell us anything about the qualitative organization of that trade; and global production networks *do* vary widely in their degree of integration and hierarchy. Nonetheless, figures on intra-firm and intra-industry trade do give a good indication that a rising proportion of production and exchange takes place *within* leading transnational corporations and within production networks dominated by them.

And these numbers do paint a very striking picture. By 2009, according to calculations by a pair of OECD officials, 47.8 per cent of US imports and 27.9 per cent of US exports consisted of intra-firm transactions.[142] That is, of goods that US firms bought from abroad, nearly half were from related companies. Brulhart points to a 'secular upward trend' in intra-industry trade, running roughly from the 1960s and levelling off in the 1990s.[143] Unsurprisingly, depending on the precision with which 'industries' are classified, the exact proportion of trade classed as 'intra-industry' varies. But, even using the strictest possible definition Brulhart estimates that intra-industry trade grew from 6.9 per cent of global trade in 1962 to 26.8 per cent in 2006.[144] A growing proportion of intra-firm trade is also for 'intangible' assets and services (e.g., branding, research and development, marketing services, book-keeping). This trade in particular is closely associated with profit shifting and tax avoidance. Bryan et al. note that by 2006, 'intangible' assets had exceeded the value of 'tangible' ones among US-based corporations – for high-tech and pharmaceutical firms, this figure could rise as high as 90 per cent. The shift, they argue, was predominantly down to the coincidence of the globalization of production with the increasing availability of opportunities to shelter profits from taxes in offshore financial centres. Evocatively, they quote an international tax lawyer interviewed by the *New York Times*: 'You can't pick up a factory and move it to the Cayman Islands ... so most of the assets that are going to be relocated as part of a global repositioning are intellectual property. In today's economy that is where most of the profit is.'[145] It is difficult to estimate the exact size and scope of these movements of value, but they are by any measure highly significant. Clausing estimates that globally, more than a trillion dollars was shifted by the world's largest 2,000 firms from high to low tax jurisdictions in 2012.[146] Ludvig Wier and Gabriel Zucman's estimates point to three global trends between 1975 and 2019: First, the corporate share of global income (i.e., the share of total global income classified as corporate profits) has increased by a third from 15 to 20 per cent. This is both because corporations, as opposed to generally smaller non-corporate businesses, control a growing share of global economic activity, and because the share of revenues claimed by capital (at the expense of the labour share) has steadily risen. Second, corporate profits are increasingly multinational. The share of multinational profits

(profits recorded by corporations in jurisdictions outside their home country) has more than quadrupled – from 4 per cent to 18 per cent. Finally, of the latter, the share reported in tax havens has increased from 2 per cent to 37 per cent. Taken all together, the share of total profits shifted to tax havens (and often in the process reallocated from 'primary' or 'manufacturing' activities to 'finance' and 'services') has grown from negligible (0.1 per cent) to 7 per cent in the period examined.[147]

To put it briefly: A non-trivial component of the profitability of manufacturing capital hasn't been eroded so much as offshored. Here again, a restructured financial system has been partially constitutive of the restoration and transformation of profitability through restructured production relations.

One other critical implication of the rapid expansion of global inter-state trade occasioned by the restructuring of production is also that the need for cross-border payments infrastructures and, particularly in the context of globally floating currencies engendered by the breakdown of the Bretton Woods order, the risks of fluctuations in the relative price of different currencies have been amplified. As Edward LiPuma and Benjamin Lee argue persuasively, the global outsourcing of production and rising need to manage currency risks provided a significant basis for the development of global derivatives markets.[148] Derivatives are financial contracts whose price is 'derived' from an underlying asset – a currency swap, for instance, is an agreement between two parties in which an initial exchange of different currencies is repaid according to terms that vary based on movements of the relative price of the two currencies. Here again, the infrastructure of tax havens produced in the aftermath of formal decolonization has played a critical role, as highly structured financial products could be more easily routed through so-called 'special purpose vehicles' – shell companies set up for the purpose of carrying out a specific transaction – which were legally and administratively much easier to set up in the context of permissive rules around incorporation and ownership in tax havens. Derivatives markets took on increasingly complex forms and invited more purely speculative uses through the 1980s and 1990s, but currency derivatives remain one of the largest markets globally, second only to interest rate derivatives.[149]

The point here is that the rapid expansion of new forms of speculative financial markets is, in fact, co-constituted with the global reorganization of production, in ways that are profoundly dependent on the reconfiguration of global financial circuits that took place in the period of formal decolonization.

Accompanying this broader managerial restructuring and the broader shift in the geography of global production in recent decades has been a radical expansion of logistical forms of capital.[150] As Martin Danyluk in particular has argued, the 'logistics revolution' – the rise of container shipping, with attendant transformations of built environments needed to accommodate new port and warehouse infrastructures, new modes of communication and coordination, third party logistics firms, and the incorporation of new business practices, notably 'just-in-time' delivery, increasingly alongside the rise of new forms of ecommerce – has accompanied and enabled the globalization of production. But while the global logistics revolution helped to restore profitability by speeding and cheapening the global circulation of capital and enabling the spatial restructuring of production in the manner described above, it also increasingly serves as a site of accumulation and for the redeployment of surplus capital in and of itself. In Danyluk's words, 'changing transportation, warehousing, and sales practices have created new opportunities for the absorption of overaccumulated capital through investments in physical and social infrastructure.'[151] As with the other developments traced in this subsection, the transformations of mid-twentieth-century-global capitalism have played a significant role in facilitating the logistics revolution. The rise of oil is particularly important in this case. As noted in the previous subsection, oil was integral to the massive expansion of global shipping networks. Global logistics also remain an important redoubt of fossil capitalism. Oil remains the source of fuel for more than 99 per cent of maritime shipping, and the steady increase in the volume of goods traded internationally (even if traded within firms or within tightly integrated global production networks) has been matched by a significant growth of oil consumption (and corresponding carbon emissions) from the shipping sector. In 2000, international maritime transport was responsible for 502 megatonnes of carbon dioxide emissions. This figure rose steadily until peaking in 2018 at 708.[152]

In short, the 'profitability' of manufacturing is increasingly an artefact of managerial strategy – whether through the deliberate deepening of the 'smile curve' in the operations of hierarchical production networks and/or, equally, through the strategic allocation of profits between different arms of transnational firms. We can already start to see how too neat a distinction between 'productive', 'commercial', and 'financial' activities would lead us to misplaced conclusions about the relative profitability of each here.[153] 'Intangible services' and financial activities remain intimately dependent on material processes of production. The contemporary restructuring of production must be understood in terms of a hierarchical and uneven redistribution of surplus value, in which finance capital is enmeshed, but which on closer inspection does not straightforwardly bear out as either the stagnation of production or as a process driven by finance capital. Not only are we dealing, then, with the distribution of total surplus value between different particular capitals (as Marx highlights), but increasingly often with a *planned* distribution of surplus value among organizationally integrated but juridically differentiated particular capitals.[154] The present global structure of production also represents, in important senses, an exacerbation of imperial and extractivist modes of productive organization which have predominated historically. Taken together, all of this suggests that the flagging productivity of manufacturing and other 'productive' sectors narrowly understood is somewhat the product of the restructuring of productive capital itself over recent decades, exaggerated by problems of measurement. Moreover, this restructuring of productive circuits is best seen as having been facilitated by the uneven restructuring of finance itself, operating on several different scales.

CONCLUSION: PUTTING FINANCE IN THE RESTRUCTURING OF PRODUCTION

Rather than the picture of stagnating production and booming finance prevalent in financialization narratives, it's best to understand the turbulent transformation of global capitalism over the last few decades as entailing the restructuring of capitalism, organizationally, technologically, and in terms of its distinct production of nature. Finance capital in various forms has played a constitutive role in the restructuring of production in recent decades. Core financial centres, under pressure from an overaccumulation crisis driven in significant part by surplus oil rents (themselves the product of the very real reconstruction of capitalized nature in the mid-century shift from coal to oil), played a vital role in the accumulation of significant debts on the part of Third World governments increasingly staggering under the contradictions of postcolonial national development projects. The subsequent financial crisis paved the way for the simultaneous renewal and expansion of a global project of agrarian capitalization and for widespread financial liberalization. This enabled a radical restructuring of global production, in which hierarchical global production networks increasingly organized through managerial techniques and complex contractual networks have restored profitability for leading segments of capital while outsourcing and suppressing profits in manufacturing. This has been made possible only through the mass dispossession of rural populations, largely through structural adjustment. The rise of the offshore world, part of the negotiation of the end of political empire, has increasingly severed the profitability of leading firms from the fiscal power of even leading states. The ongoing reconstruction of production is, itself, a story in which finance continues to play a constitutive role.

These are processes of restructuring which have generated increasingly severe social and ecological contradictions – most notably new forms of poverty in the global north and south, marked by rising precarity, deepening relations of exploitation both through work and through rents, all punctuated by crises of indebtedness, alongside and in many places exacerbated by the breakdown of the global climate. The latter in particular has begun to weigh on the productivity and profitability of capital globally, representing a deepening crisis of underproduction on a global scale, which will require massive unproductive investments of social resources in order to mitigate or manage. The deepening of uneven financial development and exacerbation of the concentration of capital makes this mobilization increasingly dependent either on the capacity to expropriate leading segments of capital or to mobilize private investment. This tension is explored further in Chapter 5. This chapter has dealt primarily with the first two premises of the financialization story – that there has been a shift from real to financial accumulation, and that this has taken place primarily since the 1970s. The alternative approach and narrative developed here both challenges the story of productive crisis and financial expansion and suggests that the lineages of the contemporary restructuring of capitalism are historically deeper than often assumed. The next chapter moves to the last premise, namely, that finance is expansionary. It does this through an engagement with what is increasingly taken as the foremost frontier of this expansionary tendency, to so-called 'financialization of nature'.

4

Finance and Nature

In September of 2020, the Chicago Mercantile Exchange (CME) launched a futures contract on Californian water. Futures are a form of derivative – they are contracts to buy some commodity in a specific volume at a specified price on a specified date in the future. The contract itself can normally then be bought and sold.[1] Commodity futures have been around in some form for centuries, particularly around agricultural commodities. They have unquestionably taken on new forms in the last few decades, and commodity derivatives markets have grown massively in volume with the entry of institutional investors and large asset managers into commodities trading.[2] If commodity futures themselves are both quite old and relatively commonplace, though, the CME contracts were the first specifically *water* futures, and they generated a good deal of controversy. As Basav Sen, climate justice project director at the Institute for Policy Studies, noted, posing water futures as a solution to climate breakdown seemed to create new avenues for financial profit on the back of a crisis from which finance had already profited enormously:

> Wall Street and its big financial institutions make loans to fossil fuel companies, or perform bond issuance to them or provide insurance underwriting ... They've profited off of the climate crisis and now they'll get a chance to profit off the solution, which, honestly, feels like a scam.[3]

The UN Special Rapporteur on the human rights to safe drinking water and sanitation raised the alarm about the futures contracts, arguing, not dissimilarly, that 'I am very concerned that water is now being treated as gold, oil and other commodities that are traded on Wall Street futures market' at the same time as water resources were increasingly under strain from climate change and (more dubiously) 'a growing population'.[4] This statement specifically about water futures was echoed roughly a year later in a wider statement by UN human rights experts, this time using the term 'financialization' explicitly to raise concerns about the 'the serious negative impact that financialization has on the enjoyment of the human rights to safe drinking water and sanitation, as well as a range of other human rights'.[5] Even some financial industry players were apprehensive, and in terms that echo 'financialization' narratives without using the term explicitly. A former senior official with the US Futures Industry Association noted to the *Financial Times* that 'We need to think now about the potential direct and indirect consequences of treating water as an asset rather than a resource'.[6]

It's hard to escape the sense, though, that worrying about the 'financialization' of water in this context is very much closing the proverbial door behind the horse that's already bolted. It's perhaps telling that the UN Special Rapporteur's comments seem to imply that financial speculation on oil, gold, and other commodities is both normal and acceptable, and only a problem when applied to water. It is also highly relevant that the CME contracts were not actually for 'water' in general, but for water *in California*. The CME contracts are built on top of an existing water infrastructure which *already* embodies relations of enclosure, commodification, and rentierization, closely entangled with histories of exterminatory settler colonialism, the hyper-exploitation of racialized labour, and ecological degradation. And indeed, these are histories which were already, in no small part, financial. In other words, for all the sound and fury they generated, water was possible to subject to financial speculation specifically because it was *already* comprehensively treated as 'an asset rather than a resource' long before the CME contracts were launched.

This case is worth dwelling on because the water futures controversy clearly reflects and draws upon a wider concern about converting nature into so many objects of financial speculation. This is a point on which a burgeoning debate on the 'financialization of nature', bridging academic, policy, and activist spheres, increasingly picks up.[7] Nature, the argument runs, is being converted into financial assets with remarkable speed, driven by an ascendant finance capital in need of continual expansion. The financialization of nature sits alongside and often bleeds into cognate debates about the financialization of land, or commodities, food, and so forth that reflect similar logics. The point I want to press in this chapter is that our understanding of the intersections of nature and finance ought to start not from the image of finance capital as a power bloc, as an inexhaustibly expansionary force, but from the contradictions already implicit in processes of commodification and the circulation of capital. The very possibility of speculation on prices for commodities, changing weather patterns, or land emerges from the spatial and temporal contradictions of underlying processes of capitalization and commodification, rather than from the articulation of a futures contract in and of itself. Finance capital cannot circulate through landscapes and ecosystems that are not already extensively enclosed and commodified – in a word, brought under the metabolic relations of capital. Indeed, it is precisely for this reason that the contemporary efforts to 'sell nature to save it' (to borrow Kathleen McAfee's phrase),[8] at the centre of debates about the financialization of nature have often proven much more 'halting, precarious, and ... largely promissory' than either their advocates or critics often imply.[9] Or, to put things in the terms introduced in the preceding chapter, finance is always part and parcel of a wider, uneven process of production of nature.

As a consequence, unfortunately, the exit of finance is not sufficient to fix things either. This latter point is where 'financialization' stories ultimately let us down most. They direct our gaze to the technical and institutional arrangements necessary to enable the trading of water or wheat as financial assets, and the ways that these arrangements ostensibly 'divorce' land, water, or wheat from their embodied form, their natural laws of reproduction, or from their status as 'resources'. Or, speaking in terms of the financialization of nature steers us towards outrage about the reduction of the basic building-blocks of life and ecosystems to financial logics, but offers few meaningful political avenues forward.

In this chapter, I want to further develop this critique and lay out some tools for thinking differently about the intersections of finance and nature(s) – or, better, of finance as part and parcel of capitalism understood as a 'way of organizing nature', in Jason Moore's felicitous phrase.[10] This discussion builds directly on the previous two chapters. If we understand finance capital as a particular kind of circulation process, then we can start to see how its intersections with the 'production of nature' under capitalism are conditioned by the core contradictions of capitalism. In the section immediately following, I trace out the debate about the financialization of nature. I show how this has often rested on narratives of 'separation' – of exchange value from use value, of value from physical commodities – most clearly encapsulated in Foster's analysis of the financialization of nature in terms of the 'metabolic rift'. The 'metabolic rift' thesis, briefly, is a concept in eco-Marxist scholarship highlighting the 'irreparable rift' introduced by the rise of capitalism between natural laws of reproduction and the expansionary drive of capital accumulation.[11] After developing an initial critique of some core tendencies of these debates, I return to the story of water futures to illustrate some of what is left out in the story of expansionary finance 'divorced' from nature. The final sections first return to Marx's discussions of ground rent and of real and formal subsumption to reconstruct an approach to finance as being imbricated in the production of nature, and then extend this perspective to a consideration of the long-run intersections of finance and land.

FINANCIALIZING NATURE?

What does it mean to talk about the financialization of nature? It is worth beginning with Marxist versions of the financialization of nature thesis, the most prominent of which are associated with the *Monthly Review* school of debates about monopoly capitalism, allied to a strong reading of the 'metabolic rift' thesis (also increasingly closely associated with the same journal). Many similar assumptions about the ontology of both 'nature' and 'finance' are more widely shared in discussions of the 'financialization of nature', though rarely spelled out quite as rigorously or extensively as in the metabolic rift thesis.

John Bellamy Foster has become a chief proponent of both the 'metabolic rift' thesis and the financialization of nature thesis in recent years. It's worth starting with the former as it very clearly informs Foster's reading of the latter. In Foster's reconstruction, there is a critical ecological dimension running through the entire corpus of Marx's thought, which reaches its fullest realization in *Capital*, particularly in Marx's discussion of labour as a 'metabolism' between 'man' and nature. This stress on labour as metabolism, in Foster's argument, allowed Marx to centre the 'irreparable rift' in these metabolic relations engendered by capitalist relations of production. Foster's initial articulation of this thesis takes inspiration from a pair of key passages of the first volume of *Capital*. As capitalist property relations simultaneously generate enclosure, concentration, and expulsion from agricultural settings, and the concomitant concentration of populations into towns, villages, and cities, Marx observes, the development of capitalism 'prevents the return to the soil of its constituent elements consumed by man in the form of food and clothing'. Human waste, rather than part of a natural metabolic cycle, becomes unproductive waste which must be disposed of. Hence, capitalist development 'destroy[s] the circumstances surrounding [the] metabolism' between producer and nature, necessitating ever-intensifying efforts to restore soil productivity. As such, 'all progress in capitalist agriculture is a progress in the art, not only of robbing the worker, but of robbing the soil'.[12] (A similar argument is also repeated in Marx's discussion of ground rent in Vol. 3, to which I'll return below.) For Foster, Marx's deployment of the 'metabolic rift' concept enabled him to 'capture the estrangement of human beings within capitalist society from the natural conditions which formed the basis of their existence';[13] and, as such, to argue that the 'nature-imposed conditions of sustainability had been violated'.[14] Against the 'natural' production according to use values, 'under the artificial regime of capital it is the search for exchange value (that is, profit) … which constitutes the object, the motive, for production'.[15]

The metabolic rift, for Foster, then, consists in the overlapping separation of producer from land, use value from exchange value, city from countryside, and the enrolment of all of the above into an 'artificial regime' of circulating values which is alien to, and as such disrupts and depletes the natural metabolisms on which they were previously based. Notably, in this framing capital is above all expansionary. Kohei Saito's recent work on 'degrowth communism', which takes considerable direct inspiration from and aims to develop the metabolic rift thesis, makes this point particularly clear. For Saito, capital's 'ever-expanding and accelerating scale of economy' brings it into ever-more intense conflict with natural limits.[16] Saito highlights a 'temporal rift' as a core component of the wider metabolic rift, insofar as capital tends continually towards the acceleration of turnover, bringing it increasingly into conflict with nature's temporal rhythms. In Saito's words, 'Productive forces can double or triple with the introduction of new machines, but nature cannot change its formation process of phosphor or fossil fuel ...'.[17]

Much of the debate about the metabolic rift has centred on a rather stale question of the difference between 'dualist' and 'monist' perspectives on the relationship between nature and the social. The primary representative of the latter is generally taken to be Jason Moore, in his insistence on a 'world-ecology' perspective emphasizing the 'double internality' and dialectical relations of nature and capitalism.[18] Moore often presents this argument for 'double internality' as a response to the bourgeois, 'Cartesian' dualism of 'society' and 'nature'. Truthfully, framed as a struggle about 'dualism' and 'monism', this is something of a non-debate. It's functionally mostly a question of emphasis and semantics, in which neither side actually holds a 'strong' version of their own position, and the more defensible 'weak' positions are more alike than the proponents of the metabolic rift thesis in particular seem to want to admit. Andreas Malm, for instance, has insisted that any capitalism-nature dualism is different from the Cartesian 'society-nature' dualism:

> Foster *et al.* would be Cartesian if they thought that labour and nature consisted of different substances or inhabited separate spheres, so that one could be analysed without reference to the other – a very common perception in the history of capitalist modernity *but precisely the opposite of what the metabolic rift school teaches.*[19]

Malm insists instead on an 'analytic' dualism rather than a 'substance' dualism – that is to say, 'capital' and 'nature' are different logics within a single totality which accordingly need to be considered separately.[20] This 'analytic dualism' is, on one hand, hard to dispute – capital's laws of reproduction are not the same as the laws of physics or those of the planet's intermingled meteorological, geological, or biophysical systems. But then this position in its most basic elements also isn't meaningfully far off Moore's 'double internality' of 'nature in capital, capital in nature'. Moore's 'double internality' position perhaps puts more of the stress on the 'substance monism', but nonetheless appears very difficult to distinguish in any practicable way, at least insofar as the very broad dualism/monism question is concerned.

But the problem with the 'metabolic rift' for present purposes is not its dualism per se, but rather with how it conceives of 'nature', on one hand, and 'capital', on the other.[21] At its core, the metabolic rift thesis conceives of nature as an ahistorical outside to capital accumulation, and capitalism as a singular expansionary logic rather than a set of contradictory historical processes.[22] The more relevant portion of Moore's critique is not that the 'metabolic rift' is 'dualist', as such, but rather that it's a perspective that 'locates accumulation crisis in one sphere, and the "crisis of the earth" in another',[23] such that we 'tend to view today's biospheric challenges as *consequences* of capitalism, rather than *constitutive* of the capitalist mode of production'.[24] The singular logic of expansion and acceleration highlighted by the metabolic rift concept underplays the contradictory and recursive dynamics of capital accumulation in practice, and the centrality of this dialectic of contradiction and displacement both to Marx's method and to the concrete history of capitalism (as highlighted in the discussion of the 'production of nature' in the previous chapter).

For now, the point is about how this matters for discussions of the 'financialization of nature'. It's worth observing that finance occupies a curious place in metabolic rift perspectives, and indeed in eco-Marxist debates generally. In fact, in Foster's original discussion of the metabolic rift, finance is almost entirely absent. This is also true of a good deal of more recent discussions on the concept. It's nonetheless useful to start the discussion of financialization of nature from the metabolic rift because similar metaphors of 'separation' and 'distancing' are widely prevalent in discussions of the financialization of nature more generally, both in the Marxist camp, as well as closely cognate discussions around the financialization of food and commodities, though not always with the same political valences. And it is clear that the concept of the metabolic rift sits at the core of Foster's more recent framing of the financialization of nature. For instance, he describes the financialization of nature as a process whose 'ultimate result ... is to impose a system geared to economic growth and debt expansion on top of natural systems, which are physically limited, and where the crucial conditions are those of reproduction and sustainability'.[25] In Foster's reading here, the creation of investible natures suitable for finance capital represents, in effect, a widening of the rift between capital and nature, and perhaps most specifically between exchange value and use value, driven by the expansionary tendencies of capital. Credit and debt relations create streams of income increasingly divorced from their physical bases, which will invariably as a result further exacerbate the degradation of nature. Finance in this guise appears to represent the apotheosis of capital's expansionary tendencies.

For Foster, the financialization of nature has accelerated considerably since 2009 – it is positioned effectively as a continuation of the monopoly capitalism-stagnation-financialization sequence posited by Magdoff and Sweezy among others in the *Monthly Review* school.[26] Foster sees the creation of assets out of ecosystems in the form of 'natural capital' as the vanguard of a process of searching out 'real' bases on which speculative accumulation might be further extended: 'This search immediately came to focus on the financialization of ecosystem services, not previously incorporated within the economy, building on global carbon markets and conservation finance, offering as the solution to the global ecological crisis the monetization of earth, constituting a new financialized ecological regime.'[27] Foster locates an intellectual movement within mainstream Economics aiming to capture and measure the value of the natural world in monetary terms, which has been increasingly embraced in leading international organizations, notably the World Bank, and after the Global Financial Crisis by finance capital itself, in search of ever-new areas that can be subjected to speculative trading.[28] The consequence of this turn, Foster emphasizes, is again in effect the widening of the metabolic rift:

> The monetization of the earth's complex biological-physical-chemical web, even in the name of conservation, will tend to replace systems of natural reproduction and evolution with reductionist, market-based criteria, for which profitable expansion is the goal ... Yet, this goes against the sustainable requirements of ecosystems, and indeed the Earth System.[29]

In this version earth's biophysical processes themselves have become the focus for a particularly intense version of the expansionary characteristics often assigned to finance capital in financialization debates, especially from 2008 onwards (recall Lapavitsas' phrase, cited in Chapter 1, that 'finance now penetrates every aspect of society').[30] The attendant separation of land and nature as use values from their status as exchange values is particularly critical for Foster, who traces what he sees as a process wherein an alliance of economists and finance capital 'have completely separated the concept of natural capital from its original use-value based critique ... conceiving natural capital instead entirely in exchange value terms, as just another form of financialized capital.'[31]

I dwell on Foster and the metabolic rift here because it's probably Foster's approach to the financialization of nature in which the 'finance' being separated from 'nature', and indeed what the 'separation' itself entails, is theorized most explicitly. It's common to talk about contemporary processes of financialization as entailing, among other things, the separation of speculative profits from the 'real' or 'material' objects being traded. Janelle Knox-Hayes, for instance, argues as such explicitly in a discussion of carbon credits, noting that in the conversion of a physical commodity into a financial asset, 'the commodity is divorced from its materiality, from its "real" space and time and abstracted as a defined certificate.'[32] Sarah Bracking somewhat similarly charts a general movement towards ever-more abstract and complex proxy calculations of climate risk, increasingly based on insurance logics, over several phases of development of the financialization of nature.[33]

One problem with this metaphor of 'rift' or 'separation' between use value and exchange value is that it often serves as a methodological justification to focus on the financial instruments themselves at the expense of the wider circuits of accumulation within which they are embedded. To invoke the financialization of nature (or what are functionally closely cognate debates about food, agriculture, etc.) is to posit the conversion of so many material commodities or biological processes into pure exchange value by the articulation of new financial instruments. The tendency is for this approach to occlude two important things: Talking in terms of 'separation' of exchange value from use value obscures the material and institutional processes involved in the production of capitalized natures which can be rendered subject to financial speculation in the first place. Martin Arboleda and Thomas Purcell make a similar critique here about the wider tendency of discussions of the financialization of food in particular to emphasize calculative devices and processes of market making over 'institutional systems of property'.[34] Equally, the emphasis on 'financialization' obscures what is often the historically quite deep role of finance capital in the production of capitalized natures in the first place.

These perspectives can still be useful in important ways, though in common with analyses elsewhere this is perhaps despite rather than because they invoke narratives of 'financialization'. Jennifer Clapp, in a highly influential contribution, describes the 'financialization' of food as producing important 'distancing' effects. Clapp uses the term 'distancing' in two discrete ways. On one hand, the entry of a growing number of financial actors into trading of key food commodities, and ownership of farmland, increases the number of actors involved in shaping global agri-food systems, widening the political 'distance' as such between producers and consumers of food. On the other, 'financialization promotes a new kind of distancing by encouraging a greater abstraction of agricultural commodities from their physical form'.[35] The latter form of 'distancing', for Clapp, reinforces the first, insofar as the very complexity and opacity of financial instruments further reduces the transparency of global agri-food regimes. Bracking's arguments about abstraction have a similar cast to them, noting that the abstraction and complexity implicit in calculating climate proxies has the ultimate effect of obscuring both historic responsibility for climate breakdown and the (limited) effects of financial solutions to the problem. She traces a series of

> innovations in risk management, wherein risk calculations in climate finance are increasingly de-linked from an actual reference to specific events, production, or exchange, and made to reside in abstract multi-variate modelling. This once-removed approach to climate governance ... generates distance between people and their management; and allows climate governance to be performative, giving the appearance if not reality of care.[36]

This discussion of 'distancing' does offer us a clear-sighted analysis of the political consequences of the undeniably growing role of finance in food production and distribution and in climate governance.[37] But it also makes particularly clear a tension in the way this discussion has been framed. There's a sense in which the forms of 'distancing' which both Bracking and Clapp describe are quite closely akin to Marx's claim (discussed previously in Chapter 2) that capital *appearing* to circulate M-M' on financial markets represents 'the capital mystification in its most flagrant form.'[38] Derivatives on food commodities, to take Clapp's focus, obscure the restructuring of nature, property, and labour relations underlying them, but at the same time depend on these articulations of corporate concentration and shifting configurations of financial investment, alongside the rise of productive relations described as 'value-chain agriculture' in the last chapter.[39] Clapp is ambivalent on this point, but 'distancing' is perhaps more usefully read as a function of obscuring or fetishizing, rather than the actually meaningful 'separation' of use value from exchange value that 'financialization' narratives often imply.

But the methodological implications of this point are important. If capital *appears* to circulate M-M' through financialized derivations of nature, the task for analysis is precisely to uncover the socio-ecological relations that such circulations obscure, but without which the circulation of finance capital cannot happen.[40] Or, we need a view of finance capital as a process rather than a power bloc. I develop this point further in the next section by returning to the Californian example with which this chapter began.

MAKING ASSETS OUT OF RESOURCES

It's hopefully clear after the last section that the debate about water futures traced in the opening paragraphs of this chapter is reflective of a wider tendency to talk about the creation of financial assets and markets as involving various means of separating value from material form, of a 'rift' between financial logics and natural reproduction. This sensibility is captured very clearly in the reference to water being treated as 'an asset rather than a resource'. Yet the Californian example already suggests some problems for this account. Rather than the financialization of an external, pre-capitalist 'nature', here we have the contradictory constitution of a speculative financial instrument out of an already thoroughly capitalized nature. Rather than the unfolding of a single expansionary logic of capital, we have a halting and contradictory process in which capital continually produces and undermines concrete historic natures. And indeed, conversely, there was ultimately no detachment of the CME water futures from the materiality of water. Quite the opposite, the financial product itself had to be designed around the physical character of water.

Futures contracts can be 'physically' or 'financially' settled. In the former, the holder of the contract has the right to take physical delivery of the commodity in question; in the latter, a 'settlement payment' of the difference between the actual spot price and the price in the futures contract is made between the issuer and holder of the future. The CME's water futures are financially settled. It may be tempting to read 'financially' settled futures as purely speculative instruments, given they don't directly involve any physical commodities transferring hands at all. Though, for a producer or a buyer of the physical product they can fill the same function of hedging against volatile prices as a physically settled contract. The cash settlement can serve as pseudo-insurance compensating the seller for an unexpectedly low price or the buyer for an unexpectedly high one. But what's critical here is that the water futures *could only be* financially settled for very prosaic reasons.

Water is a paradoxical commodity – as Karen Bakker in particular has observed.[41] Water flows, evaporates, seeps, and leaks. As such it is difficult to enclose or bound. It is also very heavy, widely if unevenly prevalent, and given its crucial importance for many different aspects of life itself, generally needs to be consumed in large volumes. Thus, it both needs to be transported in bulk to be sold profitably and is very difficult to transport in bulk. Water has proven notoriously difficult to privatize for all of these reasons. (Not that this has stopped anyone trying.) Ownership of 'water' is mediated in practice through property rights in land where streams, rivers, aquifers or other points of access to water are located, or through ownership over the infrastructure for storing and distributing water. This introduces further complications insofar as land itself also has an irreducible materiality to it that complicates its own capitalization. Stefan Ouma makes a claim very similar to Bakker's, for instance, about the materiality of farmland and its valorization as an inhibition on the financialization of land. As he puts it aptly, 'The distinctive nature of farmland as a weather-dependent, geographically variegated, socioecologically embedded, and potentially political resource makes it a very peculiar case of economization.'[42] And, indeed, as Philip Woodhouse has argued based on an overview of large-scale land transactions in Africa, the capitalist 'investibility' of land as such has long been mediated precisely by differential access to water.[43] For the moment, though, this complex interplay of land ownership, the materiality of water, and water privatization matters insofar as even if they'd wanted to, neither NASDAQ nor the CME could have warehoused physical water to allow for physical settlement. The water futures contract could only exist in financially settled form, paradoxically precisely because of the way the contracts were entangled with the physical form of water.

The material and institutional landscape of Californian water as property is also a significant reason why the water futures contracts haven't actually amounted to much of a 'market'. Marketized water systems are a historically produced 'absolute space' (to return to Smith's terms introduced in the previous chapter) within which circulations of capital can be carried out. As a number of reports noted in the aftermath of the CME contract launch, water systems (or water 'markets', where the distribution of water is organized on a market basis) are typically highly regionalized both for the material reasons and because of questions of legal jurisdiction. Having protection against fluctuating water prices *in California* is thus not likely an effective hedge against water prices for water users outside the state. From the perspective of water users, the contracts were thus, according to an agricultural consultant interviewed by the *Financial Times*, 'not a whole heck of a lot more than betting on the weather'.[44]

This case clearly gives the lie to the claims of neoliberal ideologues that the marketization and valorization of ecosystems and resources will enable their preservation. This claim, very much of a family resemblance to wider narratives about 'selling nature to save it',[45] was a crucial part of the CME's effort to legitimize the futures contracts. The information communicated to investors about the product open by noting that, in the context of water scarcity, a transparent futures market would enable more rational distribution and planning of water allocation. The rationale is worth quoting at length:

> A liquid, transparent futures market can help to create a forward curve so water users can hedge future price risk … For example, the Nasdaq Veles California Water Index Futures contract would allow an agricultural producer to plan ahead for changing costs of the water they need for large-scale irrigation. It would also allow a commercial end user, like a manufacturer, to better navigate business and financial risks when water prices fluctuate.[46]

Having liquid markets (pun not intended) for rights to water in the future, then, would ostensibly give water users greater transparency and greater ability to plan their water purchases. Insofar as the financialization of nature thesis tells us that the water futures cannot resolve the water crisis, it is correct and useful. But we should press the argument further here. The financialization narrative, stressing finance capital's need to subsume and dominate an ever-wider cross-section of life itself, is rather less helpful for understanding why speculative trading in water failed to materialize. It also unhelpfully delimits our critique here. Not only is it significant that water futures have failed to trade in the volumes hoped for by the CME group (or feared by the many critics of the project), but to focus on the financial product in question and the speculative dynamics it might have introduced to the water market in California is to write out of the picture the relations of labour, property, and ecology that underpin what was already a very real water crisis.

The water futures contract was only thinkable as a set of claims on an already privatized water system using a particular kind of 'market' mechanism to set prices. Notably, the mediation of water rights through land has proven a particularly important dynamic in the operations of this marketized framework. Agricultural uses account for the largest share of water consumption in California, an estimated 40 per cent of the total.[47] This figure is if anything an understatement – the largest category of water use in official statistics, classified as 'environmental', includes for instance water flowing through protected rivers and streams. 'Environmental' uses of this kind account for fully half of water use.[48] So agricultural water use accounts for roughly 80 per cent of what we'd normally understand as water 'consumption' in California. Californian commercial agriculture is increasingly dominated by particularly water-intensive commodities – notably dairy cattle, and increasingly almonds. The proportion of irrigated acreage devoted to perennial fruit and nut crops expanded from 22 per cent in 2000 to 48 per cent by 2018. Much of this increase was made up by expanded almond cultivation.[49] Yet, despite their prodigious consumption, agricultural owners in aggregate are also the largest sellers of water on Californian markets. The CME's own documentation for its futures contract estimates that agricultural users accounted for 67 per cent by volume of total water sold on Californian markets benchmarked by NASDAQ between 2010 and 2020. Municipalities, on the other hand, accounted for 44 per cent of purchases.[50] Some 10 per cent of the water supply of urbanized areas in southern California is leased directly from farmers, and water trading generally is taking on growing importance as a mechanism for securing water supply in urban areas.[51] Another 26 per cent of water purchases were made by 'environmental' users – government agencies and non-governmental organizations purchasing water rights, for instance, to divert it to threatened watersheds. The latter uses are an increasingly important part of environmental governance in the state more broadly. A controversial plan announced in 2022 would have seen the state government pay US$2.6 billion to water utilities in the state for rights to water which would be diverted into the Sacramento-San Juaquin River Delta.[52] Not only is the regularization of water supply through irrigation a critical part of the valorization of large-scale agriculture, but the control over water access granted by property ownership seems to have opened up a significant further stream of income for large landowners. This private control over water is not an incidental stream of revenue either, but increasingly core to the accumulation strategy of landholding capital. Julia Sizek, in a case study of Cadiz, inc. (the largest landholder in the Eastern Mojave desert), shows how the truncated valorization of water rights has become increasingly important for agricultural capital.[53] Cadiz holds the rights to extract water from aquifers lying underneath its desert landholdings (some 45,000 acres) and has sought permissions for various railway and pipeline projects to deliver water from subterranean aquifers in the desert to urban sites on the coast, 200 miles away. Although these projects have faced significant delays, the legal right to extract water and the credible (if perpetually suspended) promise of valorizing it in the future has remained a critical part of the company's strategy, and underpins the financial valuation of its assets.

In brief, water access in California was already extensively privatized and rentierized in ways that were mediated through the enclosure of agricultural land well before the launch of the futures contracts. Independent of futures trades, Californian water is already well and truly an asset rather than a resource.

Moreover, conflicts over water in California have a deep history inseparable from the longer trajectories of settler-colonial modes of dispossession and enclosure. As Theo Claire and Kevin Surprise summarize,

> The success of capitalist agriculture in California's Central Valley has required the extensive development of water resources and is predicated upon the ongoing dispossession of California's Indigenous peoples. Reclamation, which facilitated enclosure,

settlement, and agricultural development in California, simultaneously eliminated Indigenous ecologies and produced new forms of nature according to capitalist logics of accumulation.[54]

The development of commercial agriculture in California initially rested heavily on the 'reclamation' of lands in the arid Central Valley, a violent process of indigenous dispossession and enclosure. By the early twentieth century, land reclamation and agricultural capitalization had run into severe water constraints. The Central Valley Project was a massive irrigation project, through which the state government sought to build infrastructures that would allow 'moving the rain' from northern parts of the state towards agricultural settings farther south. This infrastructure has laid a significant portion of the groundwork for subsequent water problems, including a dramatic decline in salmon fisheries, vitally important for a number of indigenous communities, and the deterioration of drinking water in the Central Valley, whose impacts have been borne predominantly by migrant workers and other economically marginalized communities. These issues have been exacerbated in recent years by the acceleration of climate change and the increasing frequency of drought, and by the extensive marketization and commercialization of water access.

But what's equally important is that we can't talk about these actually existing processes of dispossession and enclosure underlying privatized water systems without talking about finance. Finance capital here as elsewhere is an integral part of this entire historical production and reproduction of nature. As George Henderson has argued, the rapid expansion of both capitalized agriculture in general and the shift towards intensive, irrigated agriculture in the early decades of the twentieth century in California were accompanied by a rapid expansion of agricultural credit, predominantly in the form of farm mortgages, but also increasingly in the form of unsecured credit to permit short-term purchases of labour, seed, fertilizer and the like necessitated by the spread of large-scale agriculture.[55] Critically, then, the conversion of land into a financial asset was part and parcel of the wider processes of production of nature both through colonial processes of dispossession and expulsion and through the transformation of watersheds and hydrological cycles. The uneven development of productive capital conditioned the uneven development of finance – Henderson notes in particular that the development of branch banking was spurred by the growing importance of rural agricultural installations for the financial system.

The point here is that there can be no speculative instruments hedging the price of water without the prior commodification of water, itself dependent on a long history of dispossession and material transformations, including the dramatic reshaping of water systems. And indeed, financial accumulation has been closely entangled with these processes from the beginning. But this does not mean that there is either a 'real' economy or a 'nature' historically or logically prior to the 'financial' one here. On this point, it's helpful to return to the point about capitalism as the contradictory production of capitalized natures developed in the previous chapter. The production of nature in this sense is always part of the expanded reproduction of capital, and as such is always already in part financial. In what remains of this chapter, I want to put forward some notes about how to put finance back into the production of nature, and how this might reframe our understandings of finance and nature away from notions of 'divorce', 'distance', and widening 'rifts'. Finance is part and parcel of the production of nature, and nature in this sense in no small part produces finance.

FINANCE AND THE PRODUCTION OF NATURE

The argument here starts from the premise – introduced in the previous chapter – that the production of nature, as such, is integral to the realization of value under capitalism.[56] There is no singular, eternal 'nature' external to historical social organization (or vice versa) in the way that the metabolic rift thesis, and the metaphors of 'separation' deployed in financialization of nature debates more widely, would imply. There were, of course, pre-capitalist natures, and things like the laws of physics do evidently have an existence external to social organization. Capital is far from omnipotent in its ability to produce natures. Capitalized natures are necessarily fragile, contradictory, and incomplete. But the point is that capital must produce and reproduce new natures in order to operate rather than divorcing itself from 'nature'. What's most important for present purposes, though, is that finance is virtually always imbricated with the production of nature. Framing the relationships between finance and nature in this way opens the way to a historically deeper and ultimately politically more productive consideration of the relationships between finance and nature. I concentrate primarily in what follows on agricultural relations, as it is arguably at the 'commodity frontier' (to borrow another of Moore's terms for the reconfiguration of space and nature in order to enable the renewed 'commodity-oriented appropriation of unpaid work/energy') where the dynamics of these processes are most plainly visible.[57] Though, to be clear, the centrality of finance to the production of nature, and vice versa, is no less significant where, say, land is capitalized in a form that allows its valorization as a mine, factory, or rental housing.

For the moment, I want to argue that a slightly different reading of Marx's discussion of ground rent – already alluded to in the section above and in many senses foundational to the metabolic rift thesis – offers some useful clues here. Marx highlights here that capitalist land relations are indeed essentially contradictory. Capitalism requires private property in land, which in turn both commands but is also fundamentally incompatible with the capitalization of agricultural production. While private property in land is 'a historical precondition for capitalist accumulation and its permanent foundation', the capitalist mode of production nonetheless does not find land in the form of landed capital. The formation of nature into capital in this way 'is only created by it [capital] itself, with the subjection of agriculture to capital'. And crucially, 'in this way feudal landed property, clan property or small peasant property with the mark community is transformed into the economic form corresponding to this mode of production, however diverse the legal forms of this may be'.[58] The capitalist mode of production simultaneously depends on the existence of landed property and generates highly variegated legal and institutional forms.

Critically, though, these highly diverse legal forms under capitalism resolve themselves into relations of rent – the right of the owner of a defined parcel of land to a stream of income derived from its use. The formation of private property in land means that, for Marx, 'ground rent is the form in which landed property is economically realized, valorized'.[59] But ground rent can only be realized with the capitalization of land. The latter refers to processes through which, in Marx's words, capital is literally 'fixed into the earth'. This happens both 'in a more transient way' (e.g., through seed or the application of fertilizer), or 'more permanently' as with drainage, irrigation, levelling. To put things in the terms I've used elsewhere in the book, ground rent depends on the production of capitalized natures. As such, 'the price of land is nothing but the capitalized and thus anticipated rent', insofar as ownership of land in and of itself 'procures a title for the purchaser to receive the annual rent, but it has absolutely nothing to do with the production of this rent'.[60] What's critical here is that the capitalization of land is, like all capital, essentially speculative in character. But the cost of acquiring access to land means that the purchaser of access (either as tenant or as owner) must both use a portion of their money capital on acquiring access to land, as a condition of being able to make further investments of capital into the production of nature necessary for carrying out production. Private property in land thus entails tying up capital in the earth well in advance of its valorization, in ways that both necessitate and serve as a brake on the production of nature required to valorize the initial purchase of land. The capitalization of nature, for these reasons, is also particularly reliant on relations of credit – as the case of California described above makes particularly clear.

In an important sense, the dynamics raised during this discussion of ground rent – private property in land both requires and inhibits the 'tying up of capital in the earth' – can be viewed as an extension to the distinction Marx draws between the 'formal' and 'real' subsumption of labour to capital in the first volume of *Capital*.[61] In cases of 'formal' subsumption, capital appropriates the products of labour without intervening directly in the labour process itself. Marx, notably, gives the example of handicraft in agriculture:

if changes occur in these traditional, established labour processes after their takeover by capital, these are nothing but the gradual consequences of that subsumption. The work may become more intensive, its duration may be extended, it may become more continuous or orderly under the eye of the interested capitalist, but in themselves these changes do not affect the actual character of the labour process, the actual mode of working.[62]

'Formal' subsumption in the above sense stands in contrast to processes of 'real' subsumption and the development of a 'specifically capitalist mode of production', in which capital *revolutionizes* the actual mode of labour and the real nature of the labour process as a whole'.[63] Critically, as Marx's later discussion of ground rent and land ownership implies, the distinction between 'formal' and 'real' subsumption is already a distinction between different modes of exploitation within capitalist relations of production, and there is no a priori reason why formal subsumption must lead to real subsumption in actual historical processes.[64] Indeed, the real subsumption of labour (and of nature) – which we might conceptualize as being fairly analogous to a move from tying up capital 'in a more transient' way to a more 'permanent' one in the terms introduced in the previous paragraph – can entail significant risks and costs for capital. In short, where social, political, and ecological conditions enable reliable rates of profit through the formal rather than the real subsumption of labour, there is no reason why capital should necessarily seek to take on the cost and risk to reorganize production directly. As Marx's caveat (emphasized in the quoted passage above) suggests, formal subsumption can nonetheless entail the intensification or other changes to the qualitative character of work. Henry Bernstein notes, in quite similar terms, that while the incorporation of peasant households in Africa into global capitalist circuits involved only 'limited technical changes in production', it nonetheless entailed 'fundamental social changes in the conditions of production and exchange in which most African producers are engaged'.[65]

For Boyd and colleagues,[66] the distinction between the real and formal subsumption of labour is mirrored in the real and formal subsumption of nature. They leave a certain degree of ambiguity about whether the subsumption of nature is a parallel process to the subsumption of labour, or whether the two are in fact mutually imbricated. If our emphasis is on exploitation as the redirection of the metabolism between labour and nature, though, the latter reading is more useful. Boyd et al. observe, for instance, that the reliance of agricultural production on seasonal rhythms often inhibits the real subsumption of the labour process, insofar as the spatial and temporal rhythms of agricultural production can only be altered so far. There is always a time lag between planting and harvest. This creates a powerful incentive for capital to externalize the costs and risks of production onto peripheral producers:

> This dependence on natural production schedules can pose serious challenges to the continuous deployment of labor and machinery, in space as well as time, and to the predictability of production. It may also give rise to nonwage and sometimes particularly repressive types of production relations, as firms pass the costs of discontinuous production schedules on to petty producers or workers.[67]

The key point here is that the labour process – as a 'metabolism' between labour and nature – is unevenly malleable.[68] Agricultural production in particular is generally bound by growing times and seasonal rhythms, such that passing the costs and risks of productive investment on to marginal producers, very often mediated through various mechanisms of indebtedness, has often appealed to capital. Or, under some social and ecological circumstances, exploitation through durable formal modes of subsumption, rather than the real subsumption of labour and nature can be functional for capital.

While capital can be 'fixed into the earth' in highly variegated forms, the fact both that capitalism as a mode of production rests on private property in land and that land in and of itself can only be valorized insofar as other capital is actually or potentially bound up in it, means that relations of credit are particularly important in the production of nature. These relations are perhaps most visible in agricultural settings,[69] but nonetheless present where land is valorized by other means (as in, say, the commodification of desert aquifers). George Henderson observes that finance capital has a particularly important role in the capitalization of agriculture specifically *because of* the limits that nature poses on the circulation of capital. Natural processes pose 'opportunities for capital precisely because it must circulate and precisely because the disunities of production and working time ... and capital's time in circulation exist'. In particular, 'if these things exist for potential capitalists as a cost to be averted, then they exist as areas of investment for capitalists looking to fund anyone who does get involved in having to cover the cost'.[70] That is to say, finance is always already particularly important for agricultural production under capitalism – and more generally for the production of capitalized natures – precisely because of the uneven materiality and temporality of capitalized natures.

MAKING LAND FINANCIAL

Speculative land purchases have emerged (or better, re-emerged) as a key flashpoint in recent debates. These have formed a major part of the debate about the financialization of nature, both through the dynamics of 'land-grabbing' and the financialization of farmland, in the context of the so-called 'global land rush' post-2008, as well as wider processes of enclosure connected to carbon trading and conservation practices connected to the financialization of nature. Land is increasingly a key touchpoint in debates about rents, assetization, and financialization – the enclosure and capitalization of land is a critical backdrop to the formation of 'natural capital' highlighted in Foster's discussion, for instance. It's notable, though, that what is probably the best analysis of the recent land rush in terms of financialization, Madeleine Fairbarn's *Fields of Gold*, lands on an ambivalent note about 'financialization', as such. Fairbarn suggests that 'we are now witnessing a "financialization" of farmland, in which farms are being targeted for financial investment and increasingly valued for their ability to produce financial profits'. However, moral contestation over the ownership of land, the 'inconvenient material attributes of its investment object', and political contestation about national sovereignty and foreign land ownership have combined such that 'Farmland may be *treated* like a financial asset class, but it is far from becoming one.'[71] It's clear, in short, that narratives of inexorable expansion of finance capital into natures are misleading. The failure of the CME's water futures is likewise notable in this respect. Finance capital seems, in fact, to struggle to make nature into so many financial assets that can meaningfully be traded.

Implicit or explicit critiques of 'financialization' narratives applied to land often stress this latter set of problems. As Marx's arguments discussed in the previous section suggest, land is not 'naturally' or inherently capital. It must be produced as such in order to render it an object of investment. Tania Li makes a series of interlinked observations about the distinctive character of land as an asset for investment:

> First, what land is for a farmer is not the same thing as for a tax collector. Land may be a source of food, a place to work, an alienable commodity or an object of taxation. Its uses and meanings are not stable and can be disputed. Second its materiality, the form of the resource, matters. Land is not like a mat. You cannot roll it up and take it away. It has presence and location. It has an especially rich and diverse array of 'affordances' – uses and values it affords to us, including the capacity to sustain human life. Third, inscription devices – the axe, the spade, the plough, the title deed, the tax register, maps, graphs, satellite images, ancestral graves, mango trees – do more than simply record the presence of land as a resource: they are integral to assembling it as a resource for different actors.[72]

A focus on the conversion of land into a financial asset, moreover, can risk obscuring the ongoing patterns of labour, property, and ecological relations that go into its valorization. As Stefan Ouma aptly observes, assets can often serve as a kind of fetish, obscuring the social relations underlying their valorization as rent-bearing or speculatively held property. As such, a focus on processes of asset-ization (of land or of nature in other forms) risks 'sidelin[ing] the fact that productive operations imbued with real labour are still key to the production of many assets'.[73] Rama Salla Dieng relatedly observes that the horticultural boom in Senegal in the context of the global land rush has depended heavily on the articulation of 'care chains' in migrant households, placing heavy burdens of social reproductive labour on women.[74] Far from separating the value of land from its materiality, then, the articulation of land as a financial asset involves the production of nature in and through the exploitation of productive and reproductive labour. These are precisely the historic relationships we risk obscuring from view by focusing on the dynamics of abstraction implicit in relations of financialization and assetization.

Here I want to build on these critiques by insisting on two things: One, reiterating a point underlined in the example of California above, is that land has a much longer history as a financial object than financialization narratives acknowledge. This is not to suggest that there is nothing new in the intersections of land and finance in the twenty-first century, but rather to insist that the significance of contemporary developments can ultimately only be adequately understood through a longer historical lens. The other is that making land financial has to, as I've insisted in other contexts throughout the book, be understood in and through the production of capitalist natures and the whole circuit of capital. A process view of finance capital, in short, calls for a much more explicitly historicized perspective on the dialectic of finance and the production of nature, and one attuned, as highlighted in the previous chapter, to the ways that the uneven development of finance and the uneven development of property and production are co-produced.

These dynamics are perhaps most evidently visible in settler-colonial contexts – notable in any case as a critical site at which, as Brenna Bhandar in particular has recently argued, historical norms and institutional forms of property relations have frequently been articulated.[75] The close entanglements between the seizure of lands for settlers, the extension of the financial system, and the transformation of ecologies in the California case discussed above clearly represent one example. But similar connections between finance and the settler production of nature are visible elsewhere. As Ouma summarizes, 'a closer look reveals that even ... petty colonialists had often tight links to (high) finance, connecting metropolitan credit, land speculation, and enclosure.'[76] These connections between settler-colonial land seizures and financial accumulation are well noted, particularly in legal and historical scholarship. K-Sue Park argues that, while the mortgage secured by a claim to land had existed for centuries in England, the mortgage backed by an unrestricted and unilateral right to the seizure of land through foreclosure was a specific invention of the British colonization of America. In her words, 'This new possibility of unilateral foreclosure allowed colonists to use land as security for credit, which in turn enabled credit transactions, real estate sales, and land conceived as real estate to become the basis of the capital market.'[77] Park notes in particular that it was primarily through predatory lending to indigenous peoples that colonial land seizures were facilitated and the alienable, monetary character of land as property was established. Catherine Comyn likewise traces the multiple intersections of financial instruments with the colonization of Aotearoa/New Zealand. Indeed, after the British Parliament had initially refused to finance the colonization of Aotearoa, colonization was in the first instance organized independently under the auspices of the joint-stock New Zealand Company. The latter's earliest earnings came from selling speculative claims on future ownership of land that had yet to be 'secured' even prior to the company's landing in Aotearoa. Finance capital, in this sense, 'not only aided but actively implemented mass colonial emigration to Aotearoa and an immense appropriation of Māori land and resources'.[78] The organization of credit for settler farmers, heavily mediated by the colonial state, played a significant role in the consolidation of settler agriculture. From 1894 onwards, the New Zealand state began borrowing funds in London and making loans to settler farms at below-market rates.[79] The way that these histories of dispossession and the articulation of land as a financial asset interlock represent, in effect, some of the most visible and ultimately consequential manifestations of the interplay between finance capital and the production of nature.

Even where settler dominance was more fragile, moreover, these relationships have had far-reaching consequences both for the uneven development of finance capital and in shaping uneven vulnerability to ecological change. To take a slightly longer example, in colonial Kenya,[80] the vast majority of settler farmers remained heavily reliant on racialized access to land ownership and the associated access this granted them to productive credit, yet at the same time were heavily indebted and increasingly subordinated to the circuits of finance capital.[81] These contradictory dynamics ultimately had significant consequences in terms of how the production of nature and exploitation of African labour took place – in effect, the articulation of Kenyan land as a financial asset came to rest on the racialized hyper-exploitation of Kenyan labour power and degradation of landscapes.

Property titles to agricultural land became a critical part of the Kenyan colonial financial system with the advent of white settlement in the early twentieth century. Transferrable property titles which could be repossessed in the event of default were the main mechanism by which banks assessed and managed credit risks. In performing this function, property titles also constituted and entrenched processes of racial and spatial differentiation. In Abreena Manji's phrase, 'Kenyan land policy was ... racialised at its inception.'[82] Titles to land in the White Highlands were reserved for 'European' settlers.[83] This racial restriction on agricultural property was retained despite the protests of Indian merchants, backed by the government of India.[84] The associated policy of segregating African populations into restrictive 'reserve' areas based on 'tribal' groupings also helped to reshape and reproduce ethnic differentiation.[85] At the same time, the enclosure of settler land required radical transformations of space and nature. It was nominally 'uninhabited' or 'unused' land which was claimed by the Crown and subsequently made available for purchase by settlers. Importantly, the question of what constituted 'vacant' land was contested – the state treated fallow land and rotating pastures as 'vacant'.[86] The allocation of land for white settlement thus disrupted existing forms of agriculture and pastoral livelihoods in favour of colonial cash crops. It was contested throughout the colonial period, particularly by Kikuyu agriculturalists living near the Highlands.[87]

Alongside their role in conjoined processes of racialized dispossession and socio-ecological transformation, the role of land titles as specifically *financial* infrastructures also strongly shaped their development. Notably, land rights were initially conditional on 'productive' use, as the state sought to minimize land speculation. This was quickly overturned as settlers complained that such restrictions inhibited their ability to use purchased land as collateral: 'the settlers are naturally anxious that the land on which they spend their labour should be a marketable and mortgageable security'.[88] Colonial officials also began to view speculation in land as a means of raising the value of farmers' collateral in land, hence enabling wider access to credit.[89] In short, while racial restrictions remained in place, other restrictions on property titles were quickly removed specifically in order to facilitate their use as means of assessing credit risk.

But the centrality of credit relations induced important contradictions. Many petty settlers were heavily indebted, particularly because banks loaned against the market value of land rather than actual or projected farm income per se.[90] As a result, petty settlers in particular struggled to service debts, becoming increasingly dependent on access to cheap labour, secured mainly through the forcible underdevelopment of reserves and restrictive laws governing the movement of African populations.[91] Financial accumulation thus depended to a considerable degree on the suppression of accumulation in reserves as a means of ensuring the super-exploitation of Kenyan labourers. Longer-term tenant farmers ('squatters'), governed by increasingly restrictive Resident Native Labour Ordinances (RNLOs), gradually increased as a proportion of the labour force. By 1937 the RNLO in force required squatters to perform 270 days of labour per year for the landowner and restricted tenant plots to 2 acres.[92] The intersection of credit infrastructures with racialized structures of property relations in this sense was also crucial. It was not simply ownership over land, but also the control this granted over access to credit – and hence over inputs and machinery – that enabled settler control over migrant and tenant labour. Indeed, the importance of uneven access to formal credit is underlined by the adoption, at the behest of settlers, of increasingly severe restrictions on credit to Africans.[93] But debts entailed important contradictions, which settlers sought the state's assistance in passing on to squatters and other migrant labourers, but could succeed in doing only up to a point. Credit/debt relations secured through the enclosure of land, in short, were both the foundation and the undoing of settler agriculture in Kenya.

As early as the 1920s, faced with growing concerns about the commercial viability of overindebted settlers, colonial banks started to restrict credit to agriculture. The British administration came under growing pressure to plug the gap, establishing a Land and Agricultural Bank (LAB) in 1931. The LAB was ostensibly meant to provide investment credit, but more than 40 per cent of loans went to bailing out existing mortgages.[94] The collapse of the settler economy spurred tentative efforts to support African agriculture from the 1930s, particularly in Kikuyu regions adjacent to the White Highlands, with the colonial state seeking both to expand its fiscal base and contain growing political threats.[95] These moves ultimately only picked up momentum in response to the intensification of the Mau Mau rebellion – an armed revolt led by the Kenya Land and Freedom Army, concentrated in Kikuyu-dominated regions, which was brutally repressed by the colonial state.[96] Critically, the reforms introduced in the aftermath of the uprising left intact both the shape of the commercial financial sector and the privatized character of land ownership – indeed, the main thrust of colonial reforms was to introduce private land titles into reserve areas in a failed effort at increasing access to credit for African smallholders. Colonial and postcolonial states unwilling or unable to directly challenge the patterns of private land ownership established under colonial rule have been faced with escalating conflict over land and access to water, exacerbated in the 1970s and 1980s and again in recent years by severe droughts.[97]

A few points about this historical narrative are worth underlining. In Kenya as in California, the early British colonization of North America more widely, and Aoteoroa/New Zealand, rendering land into a financial asset was part and parcel of its enclosure. Not only was credit important in shaping settler agriculture, but the conversion of land into a financial asset was the foundation of private property in land, full stop. Land was also the foundation of the commercial financial system in all these instances. These processes necessarily overlapped with violent expulsions constituted through the simultaneous legal construction of racial hierarchies of property ownership and of 'unoccupied' lands that could be enclosed. In Kenya the generation of land as a financial asset both made possible and depended on the production of nature. This included the spatial and ecological transformations necessary in order to make the capitalization of land possible (the construction of transport links enabling the export of cash crops, the redefinition of pastoral territories and fallow land as 'unoccupied'), as well as the violent expulsion and dispossession of African communities and their concentration into labour reserves, alongside the tying up of capital into the earth through agricultural production. These configurations of credit and production of nature have generated profound ecological contradictions and accelerating crises of underproduction. The realization of surplus value accruing to finance through the enclosure of land was always uncertain – to wit the escalating indebtedness of many farms and the ultimate need for state intervention both to create cheap labour and to provide emergency credit to relieve unpayable debts in colonial Kenya. Nonetheless, the point here is that we can see a complex dialectic of finance with the production of nature over a much longer timeframe. Farmland has always been financial, if financial returns have often only been realized from farmland at considerable difficulty and in and through the exploitation of labour and depletion of ecologies. Without glossing over the distinctive institutional and organizational features of the present-day speculative land rush, then, to treat it as an extension to wider processes of financialization both leads us to overstate the novelty of contemporary processes and to miss the more complex dynamics of labour, exploitation, and production of nature involved.

CONCLUSION: FINANCIAL RELATIONS ON A WARMING PLANET

The overarching point of the above is that, contra financialization of nature narratives, rather than finance capital prospecting for ever-new areas of nature to subject to speculative accumulation, we are better served by an understanding of finance as part and parcel of the capitalist production of nature over the long run. Seen in this light, the problem is not the presence of water derivatives, or the securitization of water user fees, but the enclosure and privatization of water, full stop. The latter parts of this chapter, drawing on Marx's discussions of ground rent and of real and formal subsumption, have sought to outline a wider historical optic, more attuned to the dialectical interplay of finance, nature, and relations of exploitation.

The core point of this is that we cannot consider the capitalization of nature without financial relations, which have always historically been integral to the production of nature. This is primarily an analytical point, but it carries important political implications. If we restrict our gaze solely to the development of novel and exotic financial instruments, we miss the much deeper-rooted and more integral role of finance in the production of nature itself. A critique of 'financialization' has a tendency to call our attention primarily to the 'dazzling form', to borrow Marx's phrase, of novel financial instruments at the expense of a consideration of the underlying dialectical transformations of labour, nature, and finance. The critique of financialization as 'distancing' helpfully points us to the kinds of obscuring and abstraction implicit in these processes, but stops there rather than interrogating the underlying relations of ownership and exploitation. Financialization of nature narratives tell us, rightly, that we ought to be concerned about futures contracts on Californian water. But in doing so they obscure how dire the settler-colonial politics of water in California already are. The latter parts of this chapter have outlined some tools, in line with the 'process' view of finance outlined in Chapter 2 and the cognate perspective on finance and the uneven restructuring of capital in Chapter 3, towards unpicking these historical processes.

But this is, in a sense, only half a critique of the 'financialization of nature'. It leaves unaddressed what is driving the unquestionably real expansion of efforts to save nature by rendering it investible or subjecting it to processes of financial valuation at the centre of, for instance, Foster or Bracking's critiques. At this point, the critique of financialization probably can't put off engaging with the relationship between finance and the state. It's to this question, then, that the following chapter turns.

5

Finance and the State

Over the last few chapters, I've laid out a sceptical take on many key aspects of the financialization narrative. But it remains the case that the financial sector as such has, objectively, grown across the board. And financial tools are widely proffered as solutions to various social problems. In this chapter I want to argue that all of this is easier to square both with a critique of financialization as a concept and with the uneven character of really existing financial expansion if we take seriously the role of the state in these processes. It might take a whole other book unto itself to fully chart out the twists and turns of Marxist state debates (of which, there are already many).[1] But we can take a few key points from these debates as a place to start – in particular, Marxist theories of the state generally emphasize the contradictory necessity of the state in fostering and facilitating capitalist accumulation. States serve to smooth out the contradictions of capital accumulation, but are constrained in their capacity to do so by their material reliance on the continuation of capital accumulation.

In a nutshell, what I'm arguing in this chapter is that states have absolutely fostered financial accumulation, but not always deliberately, and not necessarily because they are captured by financial interests. Rather, the continued recourse to fostering financial accumulation reflects the fact that in many circumstances states have few levers with which to address the social and ecological contradictions wrought by global capital accumulation. Indeed, what is perhaps most notable about various efforts to 'financialize' poverty reduction, agricultural development, climate mitigation, and the like is precisely the disinterest of finance capital (I'll develop this point further below).[2] States and other regulatory authorities have spent much of the last few decades trying and failing to coax finance capital into circulating in ways that would mitigate the contradictions of contemporary capitalism, by removing carbon dioxide from the atmosphere, conserving biodiversity, decarbonizing energy systems, building infrastructures resilient to increasingly frequent floods, storms and droughts, or enabling reductions in poverty. The resort to mobilizing private finance isn't so much a sign of the direct exercise of power by finance capital as it is of a kind of structural power enjoyed by finance capital in a context where state fiscal and organizational capacity has increasingly been undercut both by neoliberal state restructuring and by the organizational transformation of global capital traced in Chapter 3, and is hence increasingly inadequate in the face of the multifaceted breakdown of capitalist social and ecological relations. The present situation, in short, is marked by what, in Gramsci's terms, we might call 'organic crisis'.[3]

I develop these arguments in three steps. In the first section below, I outline the ways in which the state has been framed and understood in financialization debates. I highlight a general tendency to 'black-box' the state and attribute political choices to the dominance of finance capital, as well as more productive avenues developed in a few key contributions pointing to the need to situate processes of 'financialization' as such in relation to the particular contradictions of the capitalist state. In the next section, I outline a brief sketch of the capitalist state and these key dilemmas. In the final section, I aim to reframe one increasingly prominent strand of debate about contemporary 'financialization' – the 'financialization of development' – through a consideration of the tensions of capitalist statecraft amidst the crises of contemporary capitalism.

WHERE DOES THE STATE FIGURE IN DISCUSSIONS OF FINANCIALIZATION?

There is a notable tendency in financialization debates to black-box the state. Neoliberal reforms, which have notably entailed financial liberalization in the global north and global south are taken as reflections of the power of finance, understood as a 'power bloc'. I won't belabour this point here, as I recapped some foundational statements of this kind of perspective towards the end of Chapter 1 and will trace some specific more recent examples in the discussion of finance for Development below. For now, I'll simply note that, insofar as the state figures into more recent debates about the financialization of nature, financialization of development, and the like, it is again generally as a kind of medium for the interests of finance capital. The power of finance capital appears too often as a self-evident explanation for the actions of the state.

Some partial exceptions are notable in Marxist debates adjacent to 'financialization' narratives. For Magdoff and Sweezy, as noted in Chapter 3, the US state could have reined in incipient processes of financial expansion, but consistently opted not to in hopes that the financial boom would allow some kind of growth to take place.[4] Brenner, somewhat similarly, shows how American and Japanese policymakers in particular fostered stock market and real estate bubbles in the mostly vain hope that these would kick-start investment in stalling manufacturing sectors.[5] Brenner isn't entirely consistent in this; his more recent accounts of 'political capitalism' very much lean on the notion that the state is captured by leading segments of finance capital.[6] Arrighi, meanwhile, recounts the embrace of the interests of finance by US policymakers, epitomized, for him by the 'Volcker shock', in which the US Federal Reserve under chairman Paul Volcker drastically hiked interest rates. Arrighi reads this as an effort to cement the global power of the US dollar faced with declining US power globally in the 1970s: 'Working hand in hand with private high finance meant abandoning almost everything the US government had stood for, for almost half a century not just in monetary matters but in social matters as well.' The US state was faced with a situation where 'not simply [was] ... a major crisis of confidence in the US dollar ... in the making and ... an alliance with private high finance promised to add to the US armory a formidable new means of world power', but 'the US government's pursuit of power by other means was yielding rapidly decreasing returns'.[7]

Across all of these accounts, rather than states directly dominated by finance capital, in short, the embrace of finance capital was in the first instance a solution pressed on states faced with stalling economic growth and/or waning world power. Yet these perspectives still nonetheless effectively black-box the state, and render functionalist accounts of policymakers' choices. Rather than presuming the state serves the interests of finance capital, it is seen as more or less directly serving the interests of capital accumulation in general or acting to preserve a place at the peak of geopolitical hierarchy.[8]

It is more promising, I'd argue, to treat the actions of the state as an explanation for financial expansion. A few contributions to the precursor debates about 'casino capitalism' and 'financial globalization' in the 1980s and 1990s are notable for careful reconstructions of the choices and rationales of state actors in liberalizing finance. Susan Strange's *Casino Capitalism*, discussed briefly in the Introduction, is one example. Heavily influenced by Strange, Eric Helleiner's landmark *States and the Re-emergence of Global Finance* did much the same, seeking to explain the return of global financial markets after their relative suppression during the Bretton Woods period with reference to the decisions and 'non-decisions' of policymakers in leading states, predominantly in the US and UK.[9] If Strange and Helleiner sought to account for the liberalization and globalization of finance through the actions of leading states, though, they were not concerned with 'financialization' directly.

More recent works have taken a similar methodological approach to explaining financialization proper. Greta Krippner's *Capitalizing on Crisis*, primarily focused on explaining the financialization of the US economy that she'd mapped a few years previous, and Jack Copley's *Governing Financialization*, focused on the political economy of Thatcherite reforms in the UK, are particularly notable.[10] Krippner and Copley have in common an emphasis on the unintended character of 'financialization' – policymakers seeking to solve other problems inadvertently created the conditions for the drastic expansion of the financial sector.

For Krippner, the US state was faced from the late 1960s and early 1970s with three overlapping crises – a 'social crisis', 'fiscal crisis', and 'legitimation crisis'.[11] The 'social' crisis reflected growing distributional conflict amidst slowing economic growth, the fiscal crisis a widening chasm between the range of activities carried out by the state and its capacity to raise revenues sufficient to fund them, and the 'legitimation' crisis growing dissatisfaction with the state's capacity to deliver on expected improvements. The liberalization of financial markets, for Krippner, wasn't so much an effort to unleash new sources of economic growth as it was to resolve or displace the political dilemmas that followed from this 'triple crisis'. Above all, the liberalization of financial markets let policy-makers shift accountability for the allocation of resources onto an amorphous 'market'. As she describes in opening up a discussion of the liberalization of interest rates on consumer deposits,

> In a world in which capital was scarce, every attempt to allocate credit to one use meant denying it for another. Under the existing system of interest rate controls, inflation continually presented policymakers with the necessity of choosing which sector to favor in allocating credit ... Deregulation offered a way to avoid this problem: removing controls meant that *the market*, rather than state officials, could do the choosing in distributing capital between competing sectors.[12]

Liberalization did not, in fact, have the desired effect. The remainder of Krippner's book traces out the ripple effects of this liberalization of interest rates – both how they inadvertently enabled a financial boom and the ways that policymakers were left trying to grapple with the consequences. I won't repeat the entirety of Krippner's historical narrative here. What's critical for present purposes is the role of the state in this process – the state is central to the rise of finance, but the rise of finance was not an intended outcome, nor was financial liberalization carried out by a US state captured or dominated by finance capital. In Krippner's words, early on in the book, 'financialization was not a deliberate outcome sought by pol-icymakers, but rather an inadvertent result of the state's attempts to solve other problems'.[13] Financial liberalization, in short, was not driven by a coherent ideological programme, nor was it expected to produce the financial boom of the 1980s and 1990s, it was rather an effort to solve more directly political conflicts.

In its emphasis on the contingent and error-prone nature of statecraft, and more fundamentally in attempting to explain 'finan-cialization' rather than take the latter as explanation for some other social phenomenon, Krippner's account is highly useful. But Krip-pner's scope here is deliberately quite restricted. She's trying to explain the post-1970s rise of finance *in the US economy*. I noted in Chapter 1 that Krippner is explicit that the closure of the longer-run world historical scope of prior financialization arguments (especially Arrighi's, but also Phillips') is a deliberate methodological choice and Krippner is acutely aware of the trade-offs she's making. To be clear, her carefully bounded scope of analysis permits an empirically rich and zoomed-in look at particular processes in the US. Something similar happens with Krippner's treatment of the state. Hers is first and foremost an empiricist account of what US policymakers *did*. The closest we get to an explicit consideration of what the state *is* comes via a caveat in the introduction. Krippner acknowledges that she presents the state as a unitary actor throughout the book, noting that this is a necessary simplification in order to present a complex historical reality in a reasonably brief book. In reality, the state for Krippner is 'made up of multiple agencies and actors, with distinct and ... often conflicting objectives'. But critically, what this motley collection of state actors holds in common is 'the set of problems to which they were responding', and which they generally sought to displace or avoid.[14] The upshot of all of this, Copley notes (rightly I think), is that while Krippner 'puts forward an extremely convincing empirical explanation of the US state's motivations in pursuing financial liberalization, ... this is not couched in a systematic theory of the capitalist state'.[15] As a result, her account particularizes the crisis of the US economy, society, and state in the 1960s and 1970s. We wind up with a compelling and empirically rich account of US economic policymaking, but at the expense of a joined-up critique of capitalism and the capitalist state.

Copley points, I think, towards a promising direction from here. Empirically, he shares a good deal with Krippner – in tracing the role of the state in fostering financial expansion in the UK, Copley notes that 'The archives do not reveal the cunning power of financial elites, the coordinated strength of the capitalist class, nor the ideological coherence of neoliberal strategies. Instead, the state appears as an ensemble of actors desperately responding to a series of real dilemmas through haphazard and often contradictory strategic initiatives.'[16] As with Krippner, then, Copley highlights the inadvertent, error-prone, and messy character of financial liberalization. Again, the details in Copley's empirical account are extensive, but perhaps beside the point for present purposes. British financial liberalization is often attributed to the ideologically driven choices of the Thatcher government, perhaps most vividly encapsulated in the so-called 'Big Bang' reforms that radically liberalized trading on the London Stock Exchange in 1986. Copley shows convincingly that financial liberalization had in fact taken place haltingly and piecemeal, dating at least as far back as the creation of Eurodollar markets in 1957, but picking up pace in the late 1960s and 1970s under both Labour and Conservative governments. Even under Thatcher, moreover, major liberalizations (the Big Bang reforms, but also, for instance, the removal of exchange controls) were often not so much ideologically driven as they were efforts to juggle the twin compulsions facing the state to foster international competitiveness and maintain a degree of social legitimacy.

In their emphasis on inadvertency and the complex unfolding of failure, unanticipated consequences, and adaptation, Copley and Krippner's accounts share a good deal of ground. They also represent the exception that proves the rule in terms of invocations of 'financialization', insofar as they treat the latter as a contingent outcome in need of explanation (and in Krippner's case in particular, a very tightly defined outcome) rather than the ethereal and omnipresent driving force behind a host of other phenomena. Financialization for both is primarily the descriptive shorthand for the object of explanation. Perhaps needless to say at this point, I think the term might still be best avoided. Framing their arguments in terms of 'financialization' obfuscates to a degree that strictly speaking Copley and Krippner both provide close explanations of financial liberalization rather than the rise of finance per se. But both, and I think Copley in particular, point us towards a more satisfying account of the relationships between finance capital and the state which ultimately offers a more accurate and more useful picture of the political landscape of twenty-first-century capitalism. As Copley argues, the relationships between finance capital and the state must be understood within an account of the specific nature of the capitalist state, and against the backdrop of the underpinning dilemmas of capitalist statecraft. Accordingly, I move in the next section to a rough outline of the capitalist state.

THE CAPITALIST STATE: A ROUGH SKETCH

The state occupies a contradictory place in capital accumulation. It is, on one hand, absolutely necessary in order to navigate the contradiction between particular capitals and capital in general, to ensure the basic framework of law and money through which capitalist social relations can operate. At the same time, capitalist states are materially dependent for their own reproduction on the continued expansion of capital accumulation within their own territorial jurisdiction. This throws up a number of ongoing dilemmas which they must navigate. But (as Copley and Krippner's accounts suggest) states can only do so in error-prone ways, often by diffusing or displacing rather than meaningfully resolving underlying contradictions, and often with inadvertent consequences. To begin the discussion here, then, it's useful to outline these key dilemmas in general terms. This discussion is necessarily brief and schematic. The particular historical form taken by these dilemmas is likewise important. But for present purposes, three working theses about the capitalist state are important:

(1) Money is a creature of the state; the state is a creature of money. That is, the capitalist state and monetary relations are mutually constitutive, and as such mutually binding. The state makes possible capital accumulation, but in so doing comes to depend existentially on the continuation of capital accumulation and on its capacity to maintain monetary stability. Monetary and financial relations are a particularly crucial aspect of these dynamics.

(2) The core function of the capitalist state is to mitigate or displace the contradictions of capitalist relations of production in order to enable the continued reproduction of capital accumulation. States must do this, because as noted in (1), their own reproduction is intrinsically bound up with capital accumulation.

(3) The state is inherently territorialized, but this territorialization is uneven and unstable, and itself generates important contradictions which must be continually managed. The functions

of the capitalist state are increasingly distributed across different scalar levels in a contested process of continual rescaling.

I develop each of these points further in turn.

Money Is a Creature of the State; the State Is a Creature of Money

The state is always already a monetary and financial thing. Geoff Mann helpfully argues that money forms 'the common skeleton of the state and of civil society [i.e., markets]' and functions 'as the principal "material" basis upon which the relation between the two operates in capitalism.'[17] Money, in short, is at once (as argued elsewhere in this book) the embodiment of capitalist relations of value and a crucial material infrastructure through which modern states are constituted and operate. Monetary relations are thus critical to the articulation of state power and at the same time powerfully and materially bind the state to the valorization of land and labour within its territory through ongoing capital accumulation.

National currencies have historically been central to the production of statehood.[18] Michael Mann describes the development of standardized currencies 'allowing commodities to be exchanged under the ultimate guarantee of value by the state' as one of the key techniques by which the 'infrastructural' power of the state has been expanded since the nineteenth century.[19] This relationship has, if anything, deepened in recent decades. As Daniela Gabor in particular has argued, the role of the state as an issuer of debt in the form of bonds has become increasingly central to the operations of market-based finance.[20] In short, money is undergirded by state power, and the stability and pervasiveness of state power is predicated in large part on its role in the production of the background features of daily life, of which the role of money is particularly important.

But the centrality of money to the production and reproduction of the state is also a powerful constraint on state action in some ways. One important dimension of this is that states become dependent on the maintenance of monetary stability. Rapid appreciation or depreciation of the value of monetary issue poses significant material problems for the state and threatens a core basis of the state's 'infrastructural power'. This in turn is an important reason why state action can tend to favour finance capital, even without the latter having to operate as a coherent 'power bloc'. At the same time, states are compelled to foster continued capital accumulation more generally. Carolina Alves, in a detailed reconstruction of Marx's category of 'fictitious capital', notes a critical corollary of this – namely, that if fictitious capital in the form of government bonds has become increasingly central to the operation of financial markets, then this only amplifies the state's reliance on ongoing capital accumulation. Hence: 'government bonds underpin both the capitalist state and the credit system, and both are based on a mode of production predicated on exploitation, social exclusion and inequality'.[21] The key point is that the tension between abstract and concrete labour embodied in money creates continual pressures for the ongoing valorization of land and labour, on one hand, and for monetary and financial stability, on the other. Thus, while money is a key mechanism through which the capitalist state is produced and reproduced, this also means that the reproduction of state power is inextricably bound up with capital accumulation.[22] As Copley puts it,

> in constructing the fabric of capitalist society, states unconsciously produce a competitive logic that imposes itself back upon them as a seemingly external economic imperative ... States are forced by the global monetary relations of their own making to continually augment the competitiveness of their territory ...[23]

In short, the mutual entanglement of the state and capital accumulation, expressed through money and financial relations in the first instance, means that quite independently of the direct power exercised by finance capital or any other segment of the capitalist class over the state, capitalist states will be compelled to foster the conditions for capital accumulation. There is a critical territorial dimension to this tension. The modern, liberal state is by definition territorially bounded and hence in actual or potential scalar tension with capital. As Simon Clarke rightly notes:

... the capitalist state is constituted on a national basis. The concern of the state is not with the global accumulation of capital, but with securing the accumulation of domestic productive capital at a pace sufficient to absorb the surplus population, provide stable or rising wages, and growing public revenues.[24]

The operation of what Marx calls 'world money' in this sense compels not only continued capital accumulation, but the continual valorization of land and labour at rates of profit approximating those that can be achieved elsewhere. 'It is in the world market', Marx notes, 'that money first functions to its full extent as the commodity whose natural form is also the directly social form of realization of human labour in the abstract.'[25] The 'world market' in this sense serves in Maria Ivanova's words as the 'fundamental framework of global capitalism where profit rates are equalized'.[26]

As noted in Chapter 3, the competitive dynamics of capital accumulation have historically produced an uneven patchwork of 'growth' in some places and 'stagnation' and extractive depletion in others. For Marx the uneven realization of sufficient rates of profit in practice is reflected in continual fluctuations in rates of exchange and balance of payments: 'Gold and silver continually flow backwards and forwards between different spheres of circulation, and this movement follows the unceasing fluctuations of the rate of exchange.'[27] If circulations of money constitute national space, the fact that money also circulates unevenly between territories simultaneously amplifies pressures towards the continued exploitation of land and labour, and binds state action towards activities that foster this exploitation.[28] Global movements of money are one of the primary mechanisms, in short, by which states are bound to reassert and reinforce relations of class dominance. In Ilias Alami's words,

the asymmetric movement of money and financial capital between uneven spaces in perpetual search of higher profit opportunities is precisely the way through which class power (re)asserts itself: financial capital leaves those locations and sectors of activities which do not conform to capitalist value disciplines and flows into those locations and sectors with better prospects of labour exploitation and domination.[29]

Moreover, as intimated in Chapter 3, these pressures are not evenly distributed. Finance capital, as Alami again neatly puts it, 'does not flow in a void'.[30] As a range of authors note, national moneys have always existed in a hierarchy.[31] The precise institutional arrangements through which this hierarchy is articulated have varied historically, but currency hierarchies very much hinge on the degree to which national currencies can perform the functions of money internationally – on the liquidity, stability, and convertibility of currencies in international transactions. The 'exorbitant privileges' afforded to states issuing core currencies – especially the US dollar, which increasingly stands in for 'world money' in practice[32] – are well documented.[33] Growing attention is being paid to the inverse; that is, to the 'implications of being on the lower level of the hierarchy', in Annina Kaltenbrunner and Juan Pablo Paincera's words.[34] For peripheral states, which issue currencies that do not readily circulate beyond their own borders, the costs and constraints imposed by circulations of world money are borne particularly heavily. As Koddenbrock notes, 'for societies whose currencies are hardly considered valuable monetary dependency ... severely limits the space for self-determination'.[35] In particular, this means persistent restricted policy space, heightened exposure to financial volatility, and challenges in mobilizing resources. Maintaining the value and credibility of the domestic currency represents a significant policy challenge that must be managed actively and is prone to failing, including for reasons entirely beyond the control of peripheral states. One example of this was the global debt crisis prompted by the Volcker shocks discussed in Chapter 3. It also means an embedded compulsion to facilitate the production of export commodities, at rates of productivity matching the socially necessary averages embedded in the world market.[36]

The upshot is that the capitalist state is necessary for accumulation to take place but is by the same token bound to foster the continual expansion of capital accumulation, a compulsion felt with particular force in states occupying subordinated positions in global monetary and financial hierarchies. One crucial implication of this is that, while individual capitalists can and do cultivate influence over particular policymakers, this kind of direct influence is not the only reason why states tend to act in the interest of capital accumulation. Capitalist states find themselves needing to maintain the conditions for capital accumulation and the money power of capital even without the direct intervention of particular capitalists. As Peter Burnham neatly puts it, the state is 'an integral aspect of the set of social relations whose overall form is determined by the manner in which the extraction of surplus value from the immediate producer is secured'.[37]

Coping with Contradictions

If the state is necessarily an integral part of the wider complex of social relations of exploitation and valorization that make up the process of accumulation under capitalism, that perhaps leaves open the question of what, precisely, it is that the state *does*. This is evidently a question with many possible concrete answers insofar as actually existing historical statecraft is concerned. But, on a very fundamental level, seeking means of addressing the pervasive tension between the interests of particular capitals and the conditions of reproduction for capitalism as a whole, as Simon Clarke in particular argues very effectively, is the primary *raison d'être* of the capitalist state.[38] For Clarke, this tension is manifest most clearly in the need to maintain the subjection of all particular capitals to the discipline of the market. Though critically, the state does this in practice only imperfectly, as 'capital-in-general only exists in the form of particular capitals'.[39] State action in practice thus necessarily entails contested choices that prioritize the interests of some particular capitals over others – and state action in this sense is often speculative and anticipatory in nature. The result of this is that, while the state

> secures the general interest of capital in the first instance not by overriding the rule of the market, but by enforcing the rule of money and the law, which are the alienated forms through which the rule of the market is imposed ... However, the rule of

the market does not resolve the contradiction between the individual and social interests of particular capitals, but gives rise to periodic crises which call for the substantive intervention of the state.[40]

These substantive interventions are moreover complicated by the fact that, while the state is bound primarily to foster accumulation by a particular class, it can only do so as an expression of the 'general' interest. In Clarke's words, 'the substance of state power, as the power of a particular class, contradicts its form, as an expression of the general interest'.[41]

One particularly important manifestation of this basic contradiction is the tendency of capital to externalize and degrade its conditions of production, discussed in Chapter 3 in particular. As O'Connor argues at length in introducing the 'second contradiction' and crises of underproduction, this often puts the state in the position of managing capital's social and ecological spillovers.[42] Yet states are not always particularly good at doing this, precisely because states do not confront capital in general directly, but rather via the aggregate of particular capitals unevenly territorialized within their own territory, and subject to the need to foster accumulation within those constraints. It might make sense for states to foster the interests of particular capitals which are primarily territorialized within their jurisdiction (and hence are at least potentially a source of jobs and public revenues), even at the expense of the long-run conditions for global capital accumulation in general.[43]

Commodity exports of all kinds, as discussed in Chapter 3, are often good examples of this dynamic. It has created particular dilemmas for oil-exporting states in the context of the intensification of climate breakdown. Kyla Tienhaara and Jeremy Walker, for instance, describe the peculiar case of the 'neoliberal nationalization' of the Trans-Mountain Pipeline (TMP) in Canada.[44] In 2012, Kinder Morgan, then-owner of the pipeline, which carries diluted bitumen more than 1,000km from the oil sands in northern Alberta through the Rocky Mountains to the coast of British Columbia, proposed a major project expanding the capacity of the TMP. The expansion project has remained stalled amidst resistance, especially from First Nations and other communities in the way of the pipeline, with Kinder Morgan publicly threatening to withdraw from the project in 2018. Despite the federal government under Justin Trudeau having renewed commitments to cut carbon emissions, the Canadian government ultimately bought the pipeline from Kinder Morgan the following year, framing the nationalization as a temporary measure to 'de-risk' the project (mainly by forcing through its construction). This tension is perhaps only amplified where the state functions as an owner of capital in some industries.

Aside from mitigating ecological destruction, capitalist states are confronted with the fact that wages in and of themselves tend to be inadequate for the reproduction of labour – both because all else being equal particular capitals will try to force down wages to the lowest level they can get away with paying while still securing access to sufficient labour power, and because the continual restructuring of capital requires that individual workers very often cycle between active employment and various modes of relative surplus population.[45] The contradiction here is not so much that capital produces relative surplus populations which must be managed as it is that capital accumulation needs a relative surplus population in order to reproduce itself, but the latter cannot be produced and reproduced through market means alone. States are as a rule less concerned with avoiding the formation of relative surplus populations than with juggling between maintaining market discipline over them while ensuring (most) people have minimal subsistence needs met and operating within the limits of the state's fiscal capacity and monetary discipline. De Brunhoff rightly observes that capital systematically evades paying the full cost of the reproduction of labour:

> While capitalists require a regular supply of 'always available, always exploitable human material', they absolve themselves of responsibility for the upkeep of the workers by the payment of wages. If the worker is to remain exploitable and available, the wage has to cover daily maintenance; if it did more, by guaranteeing reproduction, it would exceed its capitalist function and lose its necessary (although fallacious) appearance as the

'price of labour' ... The commodity form, when it is extended to labour-power, submits it to a law of value which must be upheld, but which cannot be entirely upheld within the confines of capitalist production alone.[46]

This dynamic is, in many instances, a basis for state action. De Brunhoff goes as far as to note that 'the main task of the state's management of labour-power is to assume responsibility for that part of its value which capitalists do not directly remunerate'.[47] It requires both the longer-term management of the reproduction of the labour force (e.g., through the organization of education and healthcare), as well as securing the shorter-term reproduction of an available and exploitable labour force. One way of doing this would be through welfarist policies (redistributive social transfers, social security, etc.). But it is far from universally the case that the state makes up for the inadequacy of wages with transfers of resources or by providing services directly. Understanding quite how the capitalist state might pursue the basic aims of maintaining the discipline of the market and the conditions of production in any given place and time is a problem requiring a kind of conjunctural analysis.

Stuart Hall's argument in *Policing the Crisis* and subsequent pieces – that the rise of media discourses about petty crime, and ultimately the assertion of a forceful escalation of authoritarian state action directed at predominantly Black Britons, were a response to the profound crises of accumulation and political legitimacy of the 1970s and ultimately paved the way for 'Thatcherism' as a political formation – is relevant here.[48] Readers may recall from the discussion of Kevin Phillips and *Boiling Point* in Chapter 1 that much the same can be said of the 'southern strategy' pursued by the Republican Party in the US. As Ruth Wilson Gilmore in particular has argued at length, in this context, prisons have served as mechanisms for the simultaneous management of surpluses of labour, land, capital, and state capacity through the state-backed mobilization of racist violence in the US.[49] Indeed, the neoliberal restructuring of the state has entailed in no small part a shift from limited forms of redistributive state transfers towards making the disproportionately racialized populations surplussed by capital available for exploitation in renewed forms through the application of state violence. In short, the availability of 'always available, always exploitable' labour can be secured through the application of state violence, often operating through constructions of race, just as much as through welfarist means.

Borders and bordering practices likewise operate both to (re) produce supplies of cheap labour below the cost of reproduction by mediating the movement of labour. Michael Burawoy, in a classic article, makes a useful distinction between functions of 'maintenance' and 'renewal' – the former referring to the day-to-day survival of the workforce, the latter to the mechanisms by which a continued supply of available labour is reproduced. The border functions, in Burowoy's argument, precisely to maintain the physical and legal separation of the sites where maintenance and renewal take place, with the latter confined to sites where it can be externalized onto households and communities in peripheral social formations and performed more cheaply.[50] As Rafeef Ziadah and Adam Hanieh put it, 'borders mediate how the various aspects of a globally constituted capitalism manifest themselves, concretely *fixing* the distribution of surplus populations – and the ways that they interlock – across various national spaces'.[51] These processes are, like carceral responses, inextricably tied, they rightly insist, to the construction of race and racial difference.

We might also note that neoliberal responses to the dilemma that de Brunhoff identifies increasingly rely on the fantasy that private financial practices will plug the gaps. Susanne Soederberg's analysis of 'debtfarism', already noted in Chapters 2 and 3, is helpful here. Soederberg maps the global development of strategies of governance aiming to plug the gaps created by the retrenchment of social protection schemes and the wider insecurities engendered by processes of neoliberalization, while creating new sites for financial accumulation, through the state-backed promotion of new forms of debt relations. Debtfarism takes variegated form, often drawing on new techniques of securitization, ranging from subprime mortgages, the marketization of student debt, to microcredit.[52] Ali Bhagat and Rachel Phillips, relatedly, map the more recent rise of a 'techfare state', most prominently in the US, where the redeployment of digital technologies, both through the extension of debt and credit instruments and through the extension of law enforcement, serve as mechanisms for locking a growing relative surplus population into capitalist value relations.[53]

Lest this discussion drag on, the point is that the capitalist state works to manage the contradictions of capital accumulation – at core, by maintaining the discipline of the market over particular capitals and by maintaining the social and ecological conditions for production by means welfarist and directly coercive (or both, simultaneously). These governance strategies in practice play out through the complex unfolding of the overarching dilemmas of capitalist statecraft through particular conjunctural dynamics.

Scaling the State

To this point, I've somewhat narrowly and artificially focused on 'national' states. However, as the discussion of 'world money' above has already intimated, states do not exist in isolation. Individual nation-states exist in hierarchical relation to global circuits of capital, as noted above, but also in relation to each other and with various multilateral organizations. In Burnham's words, 'National states ... founded on the rule of money and law (as the source of their revenue and claim to legitimacy) are at the same time confined within limits imposed by the accumulation of capital on a world scale.'[54] They also coexist with various subnational and international political authorities. The functions of the capitalist state are unevenly distributed across local, national, and international scales.[55] The fragmentation of the political under capitalist social relations into so many national units also necessarily means that inter-state relations play a significant role in shaping state action. International coordination is needed to secure conditions for the reproduction of capital on a global scale, but the global needs of capital in general do not always align neatly with the accumulation strategies pursued by individual states shaped by the particular constellations of relations of force prevailing within their own jurisdiction. As Burnham puts it, 'The dilemma facing national states is that while participation in multilateral trade rounds and financial summits is necessary to enhance accumulation of capital on the global level, such participation is also a potential source of disadvantage which can seriously undermine a particular national state's economic strategy.'[56]

It's also worth noting that as a matter of historical fact, the majority of states in the contemporary world were formed through histories of colonialism and the negotiation of formal decolonization. As I noted in the discussion of formal decolonization in Chapter 3, the fact that peripheral states remain capitalist states, and hence bound to foster continued capital accumulation, means that they have often struggled to confront or challenge monetary discipline. Equally, governance in peripheral states has historically been closely entangled with the multilateral sphere, particularly through 'Development' interventions. In referring to 'Development' with a capital 'D', I'm following Gillian Hart's useful distinction between 'big-D' 'Development' – the formal apparatus of 'developmental' intervention in the global south – and 'small-d' 'development' – the systemically uneven development of global capitalism.[57] In Hart's reading, 'Big-D' development is part and parcel of how 'the conditions for global capital accumulation must be actively created and constantly reworked' – a continual process of papering over contradictions of capitalist development necessary in order to enable its continuation.[58] Or, in other words, a particular phenomenal form of the function served by the capitalist state in the broadest sense.

The point here is that contradictory scalar strategies are part and parcel of how the state operates. State functions are unevenly distributed across and beyond jurisdictional territory, and continually rescaled through the concrete operations of statecraft. Critically, this means that we cannot attribute a more directly functional role in serving the interests of capital to multilateral organizations than we can to national states. Institutions like the World Bank and IMF are in important senses extensions of the functions of capitalist states – and as such very often engaged in failure-prone efforts to maintain the conditions for capital accumulation. Indeed, we can read the turn to neoliberal approaches at the Bank in terms not far off those used by Krippner or Copley to describe financial liberalization in the US and UK.[59] The growing embrace of financial liberalization at the World Bank, for instance, was driven in no small part by operational failures of programmes for agricultural and housing credit. By the same token, while the structural adjustment packages embraced at the Bank and the IMF in the 1980s were undoubtedly imposed on some states, they also in many instances provided a kind of political cover for national policymakers seeking to impose programmes of austerity, privatization, and financial liberalization in hopes of re-establishing the bases for renewed capital accumulation.[60] The mechanisms of 'global governance', in short, need to be viewed as extensions of the same contradictions facing the capitalist state generally, refracted through conjunctural struggles over the scalar form of governance.

Capitalist States in Organic Crisis

Taken together, these general points about the capitalist state give us some worthwhile leverage to think about the relationship between states and more recent transformations in global finance. We usefully understand the turn to financial solutionism against the backdrop of the contradictory situation facing capitalist states and multilateral institutions called on to manage accelerating social and ecological crises. Chapter 3 has already given some sense of the roots of the current crisis: We are faced with an accelerating crisis of underproduction on an unprecedentedly global scale through the accumulation of carbon emissions. This has exacerbated myriad more localized dynamics of underproduction. At the same time, the profitability of leading capitals is increasingly decoupled from accumulation in general, exacerbating the uneven yet tightening constraints on state action posed by the structure of liberal, capitalist states. The advent of managerial modes of control and concomitant proliferation of 'tax optimized' organizational structures has also brought about, as Clair Quentin puts it, a 'crisis of the tax state'.[61] The restructuring of global capitalism in recent decades has generated social and ecological contradictions which plausibly call into question the very survival of human life on earth, and yet this crisis presents itself in a way that capitalist states are unable to meaningfully confront.

This situation can helpfully be described in Gramsci's terms as one of 'organic crisis'. Neither crises of accumulation nor the social and ecological crises provoked by the intensification of capitalist contradictions, for Gramsci, are sufficient in and of themselves to call into being a new social order. Historic change, Gramsci notes, 'can come about ... because hardship has become intolerable and no force is visible in the old society capable of mitigating it'. But crucially this depends on a configuration of the wider 'relations of force' capable of installing that new order.[62] Gramsci suggests that

> If this process of development from one moment to the next is missing ... the situation is not taken advantage of, and contradictory outcomes are possible: either the old society resists and ensures itself a breathing space, by physically exterminating the élite of the rival class and terrorising its mass reserves; or a reciprocal destruction of the conflicting forces occurs, and peace of the graveyard is established.[63]

We could do worse for a description of the current global predicament. We approach, or indeed for the global majority we passed some time ago, the point where the hardships imposed by contemporary capital accumulation have become intolerable. And there is indeed as of yet no force in the current political-economic order capable of mitigating it. Capitalist state forms are increasingly inadequate, but there remains no social force or combination of social forces yet capable of inaugurating an alternative.

We are thus living through so many efforts on the part of capitalist states to secure some form of 'breathing room'. In part this has been accomplished through the direct application of violence. The broader intensification of carceral and authoritarian forms of statecraft in the context of the growing failure of neoliberal governance, both in the core and in peripheral countries, is notable.[64] Here it's also worth highlighting that the notion that state forms might be shifting under the aegis of contemporary contradictions is increasingly central to debates about the political economy/ecology of climate breakdown. Kai Heron notes the emergence of a 'capitalist catastrophism' marked by a growing gulf between the articulation of post-capitalist futures and the capacity of movements to realize them, the increasingly intense foreclosure of human and non-human futures, and 'cascading and mutually amplifying socio-ecological crises that outrun the capacities of states and capital to contain them'.[65] One emergent response to this bundle of contradictions, Heron argues, is a regime of eco-apartheid, in which core states act to mitigate some of the worst harms of climate breakdown in ways that intensify the exposure of working classes in the global periphery. Alami and colleagues argue compellingly that the intersection of intensifying climate breakdown on a global scale, coupled with dynamics of overaccumulation and the contradictions of managing growing relative surplus populations, have rendered liberal modes of governance increasingly 'anachronistic'.[66] Focusing on the dynamics of solar-photovoltaic electricity production in particular, they note the dependence of non-fossil energy on the emergence of a complex and contradictory mix of both repressive measures required to maintain and discipline cheap labour with various forms of subsidy, protectionist measures, and state ownership. Joel Wainwright and Geoff Mann trace the first shoots of what they see as an emergent global 'climate leviathan' – technocratic, authoritarian modes of governance articulated on a global scale necessary to reconcile the reproduction of capitalism with the management of climate change.[67]

But 'breathing room' in Gramsci's terms can also be accomplished through so many efforts at what Gramsci elsewhere calls 'transformism' or 'passive revolution'. Gramsci defines 'passive revolution' as a process of 'molecular changes which in fact progressively modify the pre-existing composition of forces, and hence become the matrix of new changes'.[68] Or he describes a process in which states and powerful actors attempt to shore up their fragile position through reforms. In this vein it's perhaps worth pointing to the increasingly direct role that states have been compelled to take on in responding to the intensifying social and ecological crises they are faced with. We might point to the example of the reluctant nationalization of the Trans-Mountain Pipeline, discussed above. Alami and Adam Dixon more widely note the increased diffusion of the direct role of the state as a 'promoter, supervisor, and owner of capital' through the uneven rise of various 'state capitalist' institutional forms – for example, sovereign wealth funds, development banks, state enterprises, industrial policy – arguing that these form responses to the intensifying contradictions of twenty-first-century capitalism.[69] For present purposes, the more important point is that it's in the light of these dynamics of organic crisis and truncated restoration that we must also read the continued resort to financial solutions to myriad social and ecological problems. Nudging and steering overaccumulated private capital, unless and until there is a sufficient array of self-conscious social forces able to compel more radical expropriation and democratization of social investment, remains the path of least resistance for many states and their multilateral appendages confronted with accelerating contradictions. In the following section I take up these dynamics in more detail.

SOLVING PROBLEMS WITH FINANCE?

Perhaps the leading edge of the phenomenon described at the end of the previous section is what's often called the 'private turn' in global Development.[70] In distinguishing 'Big-D' Development from development (introduced above), Gillian Hart takes as her task to analyze 'how instabilities and constant redefinitions of official discourses and practices of Development since the 1940s shed light on the current conjuncture'.[71] The point is that 'big-D' Development, insofar as it turns on some of the sites where the contradictions of global capitalism in the postcolonial world are felt most acutely, and where ostensibly innovative 'financial solutions' are being offered up with the most consistency, offers a particularly important window into the uneven development of capital accumulation and the mechanisms available to capitalist states. Hart's injunction to take the contortions of Development as a window on the shifting terrain of uneven development, in short, is particularly useful with respect to what is often called the 'private turn' in Development finance. It is also an area of growing emphasis for studies of 'financialization'.

The Private Turn in Development[72]

UN Secretary General Antonio Guterres' foreword to the UN's Inter-agency Task Force on Financing for Development's 2021 *Financing for Sustainable Development* report, speaks to a prevalent piece of common sense in global Development:

Financing for sustainable development is at a crossroads. Either we close the yawning gap between political ambition and development financing, or we will fail to deliver the Sustainable Development Goals (SDGs) ...[73]

Public resources are presumed insufficient to bridge this gap. As such, developing countries 'require a boost in private investment if they are to achieve sustainable development goals'.[74] This 'finance gap', and the consequent need for expanded private investment, is an increasingly prominent focus for development practice across a range of areas, following on the heels of similar high-profile initiatives like the World Bank's 'Billions to Trillions' agenda and subsequent 'Mobilizing Finance for Development' (MF4D) framework.

Preparatory discussions for the post-2015 Sustainable Development Goals (SDGs) identified 'enormous unmet financing needs', and a concomitant need to 'un[lock] the transformative potential of people and the private sector' in order to address that gap.[75] On this basis, the World Bank and other multilateral development banks (MDBs) laid out what was initially called the 'Billions to Trillions' agenda in 2015. The 'ambitious' 2030 SDGs 'demand equal ambition in using the "billions" in ODA [official development aid] and in available development resources to attract, leverage, and mobilize "trillions" in investments of all kinds'.[76] The *Billions to Trillions* report emphasizes a wide range of interventions aimed at improving the 'environment' for private investment:

> Governments play a critical role in providing a conducive investment climate through supportive governance structures, competition policy, hard and soft infrastructure and instruments that foster healthy, commercially sustainable markets.[77]

In practice, this included a key role for MDBs and national governments in providing 'credit enhancement and risk mitigation' facilities to private investors – including developing public-private partnerships alongside guarantees and various structured finance and 'blended finance' instruments.[78] The G20 agreed shortly after on the 'Hamburg Principles' for MDBs, reinforcing commitments to developing both de-risking facilities, including 'guarantees, insurance products, blended finance, equity investment, and liquidity backup facilities' and changes to the broad 'policy environments' of developing countries.[79] The Bank subsequently dropped the 'billions to trillions' slogan for MF4D, and subsequently the so-called 'Evolution Roadmap' but in each case has redoubled the commitment to mobilizing private finance.[80] Indeed, recent statements from Bank president Ajay Banga seem to redefine the mobilization of private finance from a means of achieving development aims amidst fiscal constraints to an end in and of itself. In an op-ed shortly after assuming office, Banga would describe his vision for the Bank in terms of a renewed focus on 'results': 'incentivizing output, not input, and ensuring our focus is not limited to money out the door but how many girls are in school, how many jobs are created, how many tons of carbon dioxide emissions are avoided, and *how many private-sector dollars are mobilized*'.[81] Mobilizing private finance, in short, is increasingly identified as perhaps the core aim of the World Bank's programming.

There is a growing critical literature engaging with this push in terms of the 'financialization of development'.[82] In different ways, authors have emphasized the ways that this private turn in development finance empowers financial capital at the expense of exposing states, ecosystems, and people in the global south to new risks, as well as restricting policy space for development. Daniela Gabor compellingly describes these developments as epitomizing the rise of a 'Wall Street Consensus' – a new 'development mantra' aiming 'to create investible development projects that can attract global investors'.[83] Gabor's account highlights both the growing power of institutional investors and the central role of macro-financial policies. The 'Wall Street Consensus' in a related co-authored article is taken to 'reflec[t] attempts by global finance to expand in the Global South and policy initiatives that aim to facilitate that expansion'.[84] In this sense, the 'Wall Street Consensus' represents a hegemonic framing of Development articulated around what we could usefully call a 'power bloc' centred on finance capital. The 'Wall Street Consensus' 'successfully articulated a new development narrative shared by G20 governments, multilateral development banks and private financial actors from institutional investors and their asset managers to global and local banks'.[85] For Gabor, the 'Wall Street Consensus' is thus Development 'designed by finance capital seeking to expand into new areas'.[86] The state in development is increasingly oriented towards a role radically subordinated to the needs to global finance capital. While Gabor's account is particularly influential among recent engagements, similar readings are reflected, notwithstanding important differences of emphasis, across much of the literature on the financialization of development.[87] These existing critiques are broadly correct about the dangers of the 'private turn'.[88] Yet, insofar as the causes of the 'private turn' are explicitly considered, there is a frequent presumption – very much in common with the wider framing of financialization – that the turn to private finance reflects the interests of finance capital in carving out new spaces for the profitable deployment of speculative capital.[89]

The financialization narrative in this way closes off a set of questions that needs to be investigated. Emma Mawdsley rightly notes that 'converting the "mundane" into investible objects and tradeable commodities (whether risk, the weather, the control of infectious diseases, girls' education or Tanzanian government pensions) requires work'.[90] What needs to be unpicked more explicitly is *who* is undertaking these kinds of work, *why*, and *with what implications*? Gabor's argument – and more generally, in many cases, the concept of 'financialization' – provides an intuitive, and prima facie compelling, answer: This is action for and on behalf of finance capital. But it's not clear this is an entirely satisfactory diagnosis, not least precisely because (as I'll show further in what follows) finance capital in itself has been demonstrably uninterested in many of these projects. As Jessica Dempsey and Daniel Chiu Suarez aptly argue of efforts to promote investment in biodiversity:

> profit-seeking capital remains mostly indifferent to biodiversity conservation. If the proliferation of such schemes cannot be appropriately characterized as the outcome of a class project propelled by the accumulative drive of elites ... we are left with difficult but important questions regarding how to interpret their

emergence, how to understand their specific consequences, and how we might intervene in their potential trajectories.[91]

For Dempsey and Suarez, the primary effects of efforts to render biodiversity investible are *political*: these initiatives reinforce depoliticized and technical visions of conservation, reinforce and reiterate neoliberal rationalities, and foreclose more radical, reparative or redistributive possibilities. Though, they rightly stop short of seeking to *explain* the persistent private turn from those political effects in any straightforwardly functionalist way. More recently, some critical engagements with the 'Wall Street Consensus' have helpfully raised questions about the role of states in fostering the turn to private capital. Schindler and colleagues note that peripheral states have increasingly sought to facilitate the pursuit of strategic objectives through engagements with 'Wall Street Consensus' forms of de-risking.[92] De-risking strategies, then, are not as starkly determined by finance capital as the accounts of Gabor and others would imply. Alami and colleagues somewhat similarly point to a wider shift in the place of the state in Development, with a cautious embrace of a more active role for the state in directing, even owning, capital in response to wider ideological and geopolitical shifts.[93] These pieces, in different ways, suggest that the political underpinnings of the private turn lie in the ways that capitalist states seek to navigate the complex of dilemmas currently facing them.

The global restructuring of capital in recent decades has severely restricted the means by which states and multilateral agencies are able to respond to the contradictions it throws up. It has created the conditions for recurrent debt crises and deepened quasi-permanent conditions of austerity in the global north and (especially) south. Restructured global financial systems have tightened persistent restrictions on resources available to developing country governments.[94] Private investment in peripheral countries is thus increasingly determined by global market conditions over which they have little control.[95] We can see a fairly clear illustration of this 'big picture' in Figure 5.1, which shows the total volume of 'Development Flows', as measured by the OECD, into Development Assistance Committee (DAC)-recipient countries. The volatility of private investment, moreover, accounts for a good deal of the overall volatility of investment and capital inflows – as is clear from how closely total flows (including official development aid) track private inflows. These pressures have been exacerbated by political imperatives to privatize key industries and assets and to restrict public spending, especially for social purposes.[96] Neoliberal development has, in short, generated a conjuncture marked by what we could call organic crisis. The climate crisis and other accelerating contradictions call for the mobilization of social resources on a global scale, at the same time as the concentration of capital, entrenchment of financial subordination, and weakening of state institutions has stripped away many of the mechanisms by which public responses to these might be asserted.

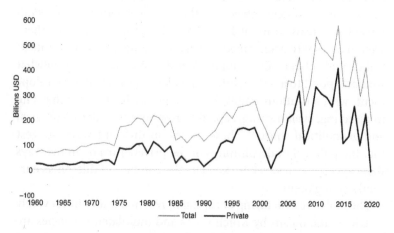

Figure 5.1   Total and private 'Development Flows' to Development Assistance Committee (DAC) countries, 1960–2020, in US$ billions
Source: OECD.

The work being undertaken under the rubric of mobilizing private finance for Development is fundamentally *anticipatory* and uncertain. The turn to finance capital is often, or even largely, about states and multilateral institutions with restricted means trying to coax finance capital into circulating in ways the latter is reluctant to do. This connection between the growing concentration of capital, deepening deprivation, and the 'private turn' is made explicit both by its critics and its promoters. Kate Bayliss and Elise Van Waeyenberge – writing about the revival of public-private partnerships (PPPs) in particular, but making a point of wider relevance – note a substantive shift in the ways that public-private partnerships are understood: 'PPP policy is now driven far more by the availability of global finance than by the previously perceived potential for efficiency gains through privatisation.'[97] This is a critical distinction – the promotion of PPPs is a means of attracting overaccumulated capital into involvement in formal Development, not necessarily something being done at the behest of finance capital. It is a state-backed effort to resolve simultaneous crisis of overaccumulation and underproduction by directing the former towards the 'unproductive' expenses needed to resolve the latter. For advocates of private financing, precisely the point is often that we simply have no choice but to try to steer the largest pools of capital available. In the words of one *Financial Times* columnist, writing about the challenges facing the development of ESG (Environmental, Social and Governance) ratings for financial markets: 'Regardless of your view on the power large companies wield, harnessing it still seems one of the most promising ways to address our greatest collective challenges.'[98]

The speculative, anticipatory positioning of these initiatives is evident in some major multilateral and donor discussions of the role of private finance. Private investment – particularly held in institutional funds and asset management – is framed as a potentially extensive pool of untapped capital. Meanwhile, a USAID-commissioned guide to MF4D, produced by Deloitte, notes that 'Private capital is abundantly available and seeking investment in ... developing economies. Thus, development agencies can play a critical role in facilitating that investment.'[99] A World Bank report on infrastructure and urban 'resilience' notes that

> There is large funding potential among traditional as well as non-traditional investors for urban infrastructure. Long-term-investors such as pension funds and insurance companies have expressed willingness to increase their allocation to this asset class ... And USD 106 trillion of institutional capital,

in the form of pension and sovereign-wealth funds, is available for potential investment.[100]

Development agencies clearly increasingly seek to position social outcomes ranging from poverty reduction to the construction of green infrastructures as frontiers for overaccumulated capital. Yet, as noted above, there has been relatively little concrete interest on the part of capital in practice. In the revealing words of one OECD report on blended finance, 'Institutional investors are estimated to manage over USD 200 trillion ... but just over 1 percent is allocated to alternative investment classes in developing countries.'[101]

Finance capital likely cannot be made to circulate in ways that will resolve these contradictions. Patrick Bigger and Sophie Weber hit on an important aspect of the problem here in describing the rise of 'green structural adjustment' in the World Bank's urban infrastructure programming. The Bank, they argue, seeks to produce cities as sites of investment through policy conditionalities, describing this as a 'preparatory program for creating "surfaces" to which spatially fixing capital *might* adhere.'[102] Crucially, though, 'not all frontiers are equally investable, nor do they all promise lucrative returns.'[103] There is, undoubtedly, a glut of finance capital which exists alongside a desperate need for resources and investment in many areas. What is perhaps less clear is whether and how far the holders of finance capital are actually much interested in carving investable assets out of the needs of Development. In aggregate, the answer seems to be that they're not. Perhaps this shouldn't surprise us since, as noted in the preceding section and in Chapter 3, the uneven circulation of finance capital is part and parcel of the operation of capitalist value relations.[104]

To take one high-profile example, when the 21st Conference of Parties to the UN Framework Convention on Climate Change renewed the target of mobilizing US$100 billion per year in climate finance for developing countries, it was projected that a third of this would be delivered through the mobilization of private investment. Between 2016 and 2019 – as Table 5.1 shows – less than half of this private finance target has been met.[105] Indeed, while public and multilateral climate financing has increased marginally since the 2015 pledge (albeit remaining significantly below promised levels), there has been little notable change in private 'climate-linked' financing to developing countries. Not only has private finance fallen short of targets, then, it has hardly responded at all to the initiatives adopted in the aftermath of the Paris Agreement. Even setting aside the (no doubt very important) question of the compatibility of private finance with principles of climate justice or actually effective climate mitigation, on a very basic level efforts to mobilize private finance for the climate have failed on their own terms.

Table 5.1   Climate finance provided or mobilized by donor countries, 2013–19

	2013	*2014*	*2015*	*2016*	*2017*	*2018*	*2019*
Public bilateral (in US$ billion)	22.5	23.1	25.9	28.0	27.0	32.0	28.8
Public multilateral (in US$ billion)	15.5	20.4	16.2	18.9	27.5	29.6	34.1
Climate-related export credits	1.6	1.6	2.5	1.5	2.1	2.1	2.6
Private finance (in US$ billion)	12.8	16.7	N/A	10.1	14.5	14.6	14.9
Total	52.2	61.8	N/A	58.6	71.2	78.3	79.6
Private finance as per cent of total	**24.5**	**27.0**	**N/A**	**17.1**	**20.4**	**18.6**	**18.7**

Note: No private sector data for 2015, as OECD implemented new measurement criteria, private finance figures from 2013 to 2014 are not directly comparable to 2016–19.
Source: Adapted from OECD, *Climate Finance.*

We see similar patterns in the activities of the largest asset managers, which could be taken as the foremost institutional manifestations of global finance capital.[106] As Adrienne Buller and Benjamin Braun note, in 2021 the two largest such firms globally (BlackRock and Vanguard) managed roughly US$9 trillion and US$8 trillion worth of assets, respectively – enough for each to buy all the listings on the London Stock Exchange twice over.[107]

Alongside pensions and mutual funds, these make up a considerable portion of the pools of institutional capital which MF4D and the like seek to attract. Some significant pools of capital are increasingly under the control of a handful of states through sovereign wealth funds and other state-owned investment vehicles,[108] but these are neither exempt from the wider pressure to ensure returns, nor generally controlled by peripheral states. BlackRock has also increasingly positioned itself publicly as a leading face of the 'Wall Street Consensus'. During COP 26 in Glasgow in 2021, BlackRock launched its 'Climate Finance Partnership' (CFP) to considerable fanfare. CFP – a blended finance vehicle dedicated to climate-themed investments in developing countries – is a quintessential 'Wall Street Consensus' project in many ways. The activities of the major private asset managers in relation to d/Development are thus especially worth unpacking more directly.

It is, in this respect, worth noting to begin that CFP, despite the accompanying fuss, is relatively minuscule next to BlackRock's overall portfolio of assets under management. It raised an initial US$673 million.[109] CFP thus represented approximately 0.007 per cent of BlackRock's total assets under management at the time. In 2021, BlackRock spent more than triple this amount (US$2.17 billion) on new real estate acquisitions alone.[110] More generally, tailored 'alternative' investments of this kind are unquestionably peripheral to BlackRock's overall asset management strategy. The firm's assets under management are heavily concentrated in equities and fixed income securities (e.g., corporate and sovereign bonds) – see Table 5.2. Or, put slightly differently, major asset managers continue to prefer investments predominantly in highly liquid financial securities. By some distance BlackRock's largest 'impact' funds consist of a series of green bond indices predominantly made up of European sovereign green bonds. In total, these manage roughly US$10 billion,[111] about 0.1 per cent of BlackRock's total assets under management. Moreover, if there is a crisis of capitalist profitability in general, it has left BlackRock largely unscathed. BlackRock's returns remain high amidst concerted state action across leading economies to maintain and boost asset prices – itself increasingly necessitated by the fact that retirement and broader risk management for remaining salaried workers are increasingly mediated through housing markets and financial investments in the context of decades of retrenchment of social transfers.[112] BlackRock itself, equally, reports operating margins of 35 per cent or higher over the years 2017–21, over 38 per cent in every year except 2020.[113] While this figure represents fee income to the company itself and not directly returns on assets under management, it does suggest that the firm is not in dire need of new outlets for investment beyond the already deep and liquid core financial markets.

Table 5.2   BlackRock long-term assets under management, 2017–21, in US$ billions

	2017	2018	2019	2020	2021
Equity	3,371.6	3,085.8	3,820.3	4,419.8	5,342.4
Fixed income	1,855.5	1,884.4	2,315.4	2,674.5	2,822.0
Multi-asset	480.3	461.9	568.1	658.7	816.5
Alternatives	129.3	143.4	178.1	235.0	264.9
Total AUM	6,288.2	5,975.8	7,429.6	8,676.7	10,010.1

Note: Total AUM (assets under management) include cash reserves not included in chart, and may not add precisely due to rounding.
Source: Adapted from *BlackRock 2021 Annual Report.*

The crucial point here is that, across the board, it is not at all clear that either finance capital in aggregate or its chief organizational manifestations are actually particularly interested in 'maximizing' their opportunities to invest in Development projects. All of this suggests that the role of finance capital in driving these shifts in Development strategy is less direct than many accounts of the financialization of development often suggest. MF4D may prioritize the interests of the financial circuits of capital, but does not do so at the behest of finance capital.

The point here is that, with increasingly limited means by which to 'steer' capital directly, and faced with volatile movements of capital, Development is increasingly framed in terms of laying the groundwork in anticipation of attracting spatially fixing capital.

Here Harvey's distinction between 'finance capital' as a power bloc and finance capital as a particular kind of circulation process is particularly helpful. The growing concentration of capital and intensification of uneven development have amplified this tension and rendered it particularly acute while restricting the available means by which it can be addressed. State and multilateral managers are increasingly oriented towards navigating this tension, and barring widespread political support for outright expropriation, appealing to the interests of asset managers in hopes of aligning the circulation of finance capital with the needs of Development is one of few remaining alternatives.

Critically, framing the 'private turn' as an error-prone effort to grapple with a deepening crisis of overaccumulation and uneven development casts the power of finance capital in general, and of its concrete form as major global asset managers differently. The concentration of capital generates crucial social and ecological contradictions, while also simultaneously posing barriers to their resolution. State institutional structures have in many cases been hollowed out, and fiscal constraints in the global south in particular have been progressively tightened. In this context we should read the turn to efforts to coax private capital into investing in Development as efforts by state and multilateral governing institutions to reshape flows of capital in ways that will mitigate these contradictions without requiring radical changes to existing structures of accumulation.

CONCLUSION

The point of the preceding is two-fold. The growing turn of states and multilateral governors to the promotion of financial accumulation is less the result of any direct capture by finance capital operating as a power bloc, or of the straightforward unfolding of the interests of finance capital. It is rather an increasingly prevalent modality of governance for states faced with organic crisis – accelerating socio-ecological crises amidst the radically uneven distribution of control over resources. The redeployment of social resources on the scale needed is impossible to achieve absent large-scale expropriation, for which a sufficiently self-conscious and organized class base does not currently exist. The promotion of financial accumulation needs to be understood less in terms of the direct power of finance and more in terms of the contradictory position of the capitalist state.

The wider political significance of this point in terms of financialization debates is that there can be no straightforward 'confronting' finance capital, or 'recapturing' the state. The relationship of capitalist states to finance needs to be understood in terms of the core contradictions of statecraft amidst capitalist relations of production. It's to these questions, and what they mean politically, that I turn in the following, and final, chapter.

6

Conclusion:
Revolutionizing Finance

Global capitalism is in severe and deepening crisis. The previous chapters of this book have sketched some of the contours of this crisis – the acceleration of climate breakdown and the collapse of secure livelihoods, traced in Chapters 3 and 5 in particular, alongside slower-burning crises of localized ecosystems under strain through the longer-run depredations of colonial capitalism traced in Chapter 4. The upshot is that global capitalism is increasingly incompatible with the survival of most of us, and the capitalist states through which we are governed are constitutionally incapable of responding in the ways and on the scale necessary. But that capitalism is in crisis doesn't necessarily portend its end. As Gramsci puts it eloquently, 'A crisis cannot give the attacking forces the ability to organise with lightning speed in time and in space; still less can it endow them with fighting spirit.'[1] There's a tendency for Marxist books to end on a kind of note – either we really get the revolution this time or the present crisis will be the end. Arrighi's conclusion to the *Long Twentieth Century*, discussed in Chapter 1, is one example. And much of what I've written in this book, not least in the preceding chapter, does seem to point in a similar direction. It is socialism or barbarism, and the path towards the former isn't so clear.

I don't want to close things by vaguely gesturing at our impending doom, though. By way of conclusion here, I want to talk about what the preceding chapters and the wider critique of 'financialization' narratives this book has outlined tell us about the place of finance in the present conjuncture and why that matters. Rather than recapping the turns of the arguments outlined in the preceding chapters, I aim to extend some of what I've argued to take up the question of what the reframing of finance and its place in the wider circuits of capital accumulation I've sought to make in this book means politically. While I don't have a fully fleshed out revolutionary programme to offer here, much less any 'recipes for the cook-shops of the future', I do want to suggest that the kind of perspective articulated here can at least help us spot some of the traps we're setting ourselves at the moment when we think about finance in contemporary capitalism, and gesture towards the kinds of questions we ought to be asking.

For Hilferding, who we encountered in Chapter 2 as the classical standard-bearer for the 'power bloc' view of finance, the accelerating concentration of finance capital would ultimately lay the groundwork for socialism. Insofar as finance capital centralized control over capital, it would also 'facilitate enormously the task of overcoming capitalism'.[2] The expropriation of capital had already taken place to a considerable extent, all that remained was to seize the banks. Indeed, Hilferding went as far as to insist that 'the victory of the proletariat is bound up with the concentration of economic power in the hands of a few capitalist magnates ... and with their domination of the state'.[3] The structural changes wrought by the rise of finance capital, Hilferding thought, both held out the promise of facilitating the seizure of the means of production insofar as they concentrated control over capital in a few places, and increasingly necessitated that seizure. In the closing words of *Finance Capital*, he suggested that the rise of finance capital would create a mass of people 'exploited by finance capital but also summoned into battle against it', concluding that 'in the violent clash of these hostile interests the dictatorship of the magnates of capital will finally be transformed into the dictatorship of the proletariat'.[4] Finance capital would ultimately, despite itself, create the bases for the democratic organization of the whole economy.

With hindsight, it's easy enough to conclude that Hilferding was wrong about this, at least as far as late nineteenth- and early twentieth-century Germany went. But what's perhaps more salient is the political direction implied by his perspective on finance. Hilferding would drift towards the right wing of the German Social Democrats over the decades that followed the publication of *Finance Capital*, eventually serving as finance minister during the Weimar Republic. The ambivalent conclusions he drew about the tendencies of finance capital are often seen as having laid the basis for a turn towards the theory of 'organized capitalism' in the 1920s, in which state planning would replace the anarchy of the market, greatly facilitated by the increasingly planned form taken by monopoly capitalism dominated by interlocking ownership. As Chris Harman neatly summarizes:

> *Finance Capital* contains the germs of two quite different appreciations of the course of capitalism. One sees the drive to accumulate surplus-value as necessarily leading to ever-greater clashes between rival capitalist groups, to repeated social disruption, and to an era of wars and revolutions. The other sees the larger units of capital able to take greater control of their own destiny until they escape the dynamics of capitalism as analysed by Marx, whether this takes the benign form of the social-democratic or Keynesian welfare state, or the malignant form of 'totalitarian' or 'bureaucratic' 'collectivism'.[5]

Hilferding's analysis of finance capital seems to have predisposed him towards a kind of reformism (or, perhaps vice versa). As Harman notes, Hilferding ultimately 'opted to urge people to put their faith in the reform of a system that was, in its essence, not amenable to serious reform and which would take its eventual vengeance on those who tried to undertake it'.[6] The latter illustrated perhaps no more clearly than by the fact that Hilferding himself died in a Nazi prison in occupied France in 1940.

I don't wish to press the analogy too far here. Hilferding wrote, of course, about a very different context, and for the most part retains a loose influence at best on present financialization debates. But he is perhaps one of the clearest historical progenitors of the 'power bloc' view of finance capital. And we can make out the outlines of arguments not entirely alien to Hilferding's about the routes to transformation within and alongside debates about financialization – including the ideas that the current centralization of economic power in the financial sector might make possible the articulation of more democratic forms of social and economic organization. There are two themes of particular importance on which the ambivalences of Hilferding's work presage contemporary debates – on the extent to which contemporary financial relations, most notably indebtedness, might pave the way for new forms of class politics; and on the role of the state, paradoxically now seized by finance capital but holding the potential to be redeployed towards emancipatory ends.

What I will insist is that Hilferding's example hints that the financialization narrative steers us into a political cul-de-sac. It offers up a tempting and superficially compelling shortcut to our analyses: this or that phenomenon is down to the rising power of finance capital and the latter's continual, compulsive quest for new spaces to be mined for speculative profit. Critically, this is also a narrative that seems to hold out some clear political implications: The route to a better world runs through confronting finance, whether through what we might call 'de-financialization' or by democratizing finance itself. Relatedly, some arguments assert that it is through experiences of indebtedness, assetization and investment, rather than exploitation through work, that people are most meaningfully incorporated into the global capitalist system and (by extension) through which they might best resist.

DE-FINANCIALIZATION?

As a first cut, we might note that one of the implications of the arguments presented in the preceding chapters is that the answer to our present challenges cannot lie in reining in finance in and of itself. Any 'rebalancing' of 'productive' and 'financial' capital has profound limits. To insist that 'finance' and 'productive' capital need to be seen as integrally linked moments in the full circuit of capital, or that financial relations do very much help to produce and reproduce relations of value is, of course, not in any sense to rehabilitate the bankers. It is arguably the core point of a Marxist critique that capitalist productive relations are exploitative, socially and ecologically destructive, and inhibit our collective and individual freedom and flourishing. Finance capital is intrinsic to capitalist value relations. This is precisely the problem with finance capital!

Insofar as Marxist perspectives assert that 'financialization' is a secular and structural change in capitalist relations of production, they do militate against any claims that reeling in the power of finance is sufficient. This is not necessarily a new insight. For all that *The Class Struggles in France* represent (as noted in Chapter 2) a Marx with an as yet relatively underdeveloped understanding of the place and power of finance capital in the circuits of capital accumulation, Marx does nonetheless aptly note that the presentation of 'socialism' as a revolt against finance as such ultimately handicapped the achievements of the 1848 revolution. He contrasted the 'petty bourgeois socialism' that sought to regulate finance and reduce its sway over the state with a more thoroughgoing communism which would abolish class society altogether.[7] As Stefan Eich has recently compellingly argued, Marx's thinking about capital and capitalism more broadly developed in no small part in a critical dialogue with Proudhonian proposals for the 'democratization' or 'republicanization' of money and credit.[8] Reforming money and credit was not sufficient, for Marx, to overturn the contradictions of capitalist social relations.

Something like this insistence is shared in most Marxist commentary on financialization – overturning the power of finance is not enough. Yet, as with Hilferding, the logic of financialization arguments themselves seem sometimes to undercut this insistence, or at least to leave us with few clues as to the route towards a deeper-rooted transformation of capitalist societies. Lapavitsas' conclusion to *Profiting without Producing* is perhaps the case in point. Here he insists that regulatory reforms would be inadequate to confront the deep-seated secular change in the nature of capital accumulation that is financialization, and that processes of financialization themselves have made the reimposition of meaningful regulatory controls difficult. While public ownership of financial institutions might offer a platform from which to 'control finance and to reverse financialization', confronting financialization would nonetheless 'be far more complex than merely introducing public banking on a large scale'.[9] This confrontation, for Lapavitsas, requires the public provision of basic goods and services, and a more general confrontation with the ideological apparatus of neoliberalism.

In the most general terms, Lapavitsas is correct in this insistence. Public ownership of finance capital in and of itself, by states still beholden to logics of capital accumulation, will offer no panaceas. At best, we might read public financial institutions as being more open to contestation and more adaptable to genuinely public ends.[10] However, pitching this argument in terms of financialization ultimately leads him down something of a dead end. He insists that financial re-regulation or the introduction of public banks in and of themselves are insufficient, because 'confronting financialization would ultimately lead to confronting the capitalist character of society as a whole'.[11] Yet, after a detailed discussion of the barriers to meaningfully regulating financial capital as it exists post-2008, Lapavitsas returns to a brief discussion of de-financialization, duly reframed as the first step to socialism. This necessarily includes the development of public banks and a 'Tobin Tax' on financial transactions to slow the churn of speculative financial trading, as well as a 'reassertion' of the rights to public health, education, housing, and the like. The logic here is that confronting financialization, because it leads in the direction of 'anti-capitalist ideas, policies and practices', should thus 'for this reason ... be a part of the struggle for socialism'.[12]

But then, some questions immediately pose themselves: From whence would these changes come? And who would carry them out? Implicitly the answer to the latter seems to be the state, recaptured from neoliberal dogmas and from the power of finance. Some of the problems with this have been discussed elsewhere, notably in Chapter 5. In short, capitalist states are materially, institutionally unable to dismantle the bases of capitalist accumulation. So, a state which would 'rein in' finance would necessarily be a radically transformed state. Lapavitsas offers little insight as to what social forces might lead this process of state transformation, which itself suggests further questions: Must the 'struggle for socialism' pass through a confrontation with financialization? Does 'confronting financialization' provide a meaningful guide to the way forward? Or, does framing the struggle for 'socialism' around the confrontation with financialization pave the way for an analogue to what Marx called 'petty bourgeois socialism' in France?

DEMOCRATIZING FINANCE

For a range of authors, rather than reining in finance capital, processes of financialization call for efforts, largely beyond the state, to
transform and 'democratize' finance itself. The phrase 'democratization of finance' is often associated with economics 'Nobel' laureate
Robert Shiller. In the 2003 book *The New Financial Order*, Shiller
makes the central claim that 'we need to democratize finance and
bring the advantages enjoyed by clients of Wall Street to the customers of Wal-Mart'.[13] By this, Shiller means giving them access to
a fleet of (digitally enabled) risk management tools. As examples of
what this might mean, Shiller discusses new forms of insurance for
'livelihood loss' and home equity, or loan contracts where repay-
ments are recalculated when income falls below expected levels.
In his later book *Finance and the Good Society*,[14] Shiller makes the
political terms of this democratization especially clear, introducing the term in what he imagines as a rebuke to Marx. There's a
slight shift away from Shiller's earlier emphasis on risk management towards the provision of entrepreneurial opportunities.
The 'central argument for public ownership of capital' in Marx's
writing, according to Shiller, is that it would enable the breaking
of a 'vicious cycle of poverty'.[15] Here, Shiller cites as evidence a
passage from Marx's discussion of primitive accumulation, where
the latter notes that 'the process ... that clears the way for the capitalist system, can be none other than the process which takes away
from the labourer his means of production'.[16] In Shiller's reading
of this passage, Marx is arguing that 'under capitalism the goals of
society are set by those at the top', on the 'unstated' and unexplained
assumption that 'a poor labourer could never start a business by
getting credit from a bank or capital from wealthy investors'.[17] If
you've read the preceding chapters, never mind Marx's writing or
any other Marxist scholarship, it is hopefully clear that this is a
questionable interpretation of Marx. For Shiller, setting aside the
small matter that capitalism has in practice failed to ever actually
empower 'poor labourers' to do this, a truly 'democratic' financial
system would allow everyone access to credit to start their own
business: 'Our capitalist institutions do not yet fully live up to this
ideal, but throughout history there has been a long trend toward

the democratization of finance, the opening of financial opportunities to everyone.[18] This imaginary of 'democratization' through access to credit is increasingly taken up by promoters of new financial technologies.[19] This sort of view is, above all, premised on a profoundly naive and impoverished conception of 'democracy' itself, reduced to equalizing access to financial products.

The idea of 'democratizing finance' has nonetheless increasingly been reclaimed in recent years, and taken up in much more intellectually and politically serious projects. Fred Block, introducing a recent edited collection on the democratization of finance, notes that the phrase 'democratizing finance' comes bundled with a wide range of meanings – from expanding access to formal credit to people traditionally reliant on loan sharks and pawnshops, to opening up new forms of savings and investment.[20] Block notes that the phrase is 'politically ambiguous' when used in this way, insofar as extending credit or investment opportunities to the poor can be 'either a project of egalitarian reform, a cover for new forms of exploitation, or a complicated combination that benefits some and hurts others'.[21] But for Block, a meaningful democratization of finance cannot stop with access to affordable credit for poor and middle-class households. It must include weakening the dominance of major financial firms, as well as establishing meaningful collective democratic control over the investment functions currently dominated by large corporations. This nonetheless leaves hanging the critical question of how a meaningfully democratized finance in this sense would be brought about.

Michael McCarthy argues that progressive visions of 'democratized finance' generally have tended to skirt engagement with explicitly political questions – most of all with how democratized financial structures might be protected against efforts to erode democracy and accountability on the part of incumbent financial elites.[22] He argues ultimately that community- or public-controlled financial structures cannot coexist with private ones organized along capitalist lines. The nationalization of banks is thus a necessary (though not sufficient) condition for a genuinely democratic financial system, insofar as 'leaving capitalist financial institutions intact and private fails to confront the basic source of their structural power in politics: their control over the allocation of finance'.[23]

A genuinely democratic financial system, for McCarthy, would depend on public control, but also means of 'activating and reproducing' direct public engagement in the governance and operation of publicly owned banks. Stefan Eich similarly talks about a need for 'an improved public understanding of the power of money, its political possibilities, and how these are currently unfulfilled'.[24] These perspectives echo, with slightly different points of emphasis, Lapavitsas' claim that confronting financialization offers a route towards building the ideological and political bases for socialism. Here building a kind of counter-hegemonic public capable of engaging actively and directly in the governance of finance and money is a prerequisite to a successful confrontation with finance. Though there is a certain ambiguity here about whether the aim is to democratize finance or, again, whether this is (as in Lapavitsas' framing) only a stepping-stone towards the wider socialization of the economy. McCarthy's argument here has the merit of taking seriously the political question of building a meaningful class politics around a more democratic financial system. But it remains somewhat hampered by an understanding of finance as a power bloc. The key locus of politics here remains the state – which must, on one hand, be recaptured and, on the other, protected from finance capital.

In a slightly different vein, some authors have suggested that the increasingly widespread experience of indebtedness might itself be a basis for the exercise of collective power over the way the economy is governed. 'Mass indebtedness', notes *Can't Pay Won't Pay*, a collaborative manifesto from the US-based Debt Collective, 'connects those of us living in the US with millions of others around the world – it connects Ferguson to Greece, Puerto Rico to Bolivia'. Debt in this sense is 'a non-violent weapon we all have access to – if we can leverage it in concert'.[25] Collective refusal to pay, through 'debt strikes' organized locally, regionally, nationally, and even transnationally, the authors hold, represents not just a way of challenging unjust relationships of indebtedness but also a meaningful way to exert 'people power' over the terms on which the economy is organized and run. Claiming collective control over our debts, then, might well be a means of exerting collective control over finance, and ultimately over the economy more widely.

Carolyn Hardin's work, also discussed in Chapter 2, is one of a number of recent contributions to argue that the axes of vulnerability, stratification, and power in contemporary capitalism have less to do with 'work' than they may have used to. Her claim here is that a progressive politics able to deal with the real operations of finance will need to be articulated on the terrain of 'risk'. In concrete terms, she raises a pair of examples: efforts to address the specific ways that credit risks are calculated with an eye to redressing racialized disparities, and through 'household unions' in which contractual payment streams (debt service, along with, e.g., utility payments) are organized collectively. Instead of making payments directly to service providers, a 'union' might enable the strategic withholding of payments. The latter proposal draws from the work of Dick Bryan and Michael Rafferty.[26] These perspectives, much like the Debt Collective proposals, perform a useful service in opening up the question of how the work of organizing subaltern social forces might take place under contemporary capitalism. They do point to real enough strategic chokepoints – financial accumulation and rentier capitalism more generally depend on the everyday maintenance of streams of payments. Debts need to be, in Johnna Montgomerie and Daniela Tepe-Belfrage's words, 'cared for'.[27]

Can refusing indebtedness, or the collective control of other securitized payment streams offer leverage to reformist or anti-capitalist movements in this context? The short answer is probably yes, under some circumstances. A debt strike is, in the end, much like a conventional strike: It is an expression of labour's power to disrupt the accumulation of capital, as such it is a weapon that can extract concessions, but it is not in and of itself the basis for revolutionary change. Moreover, it is hard to see how a concerted withholding of payments would not be very much contingent on the messy and difficult work of organizing and mobilizing solidarities on a wide enough scale to enable mass refusals. The common experience of indebtedness operates on a wider scale than any concrete workplace, but is nonetheless no more a guarantee of automatic solidarity and capacity for collective movement than the common experience of exploitation in the workplace. Indeed, the former arguably presents an additionally difficult task because secondary forms of exploitation are almost by definition more individualizing, more obfuscating, more isolating forms of exploitation when compared to direct exploitation through work. Not for nothing does Marx describe the financial circuit appearing as M-M' 'the capital mystification in its most flagrant form' (as quoted previously in Chapter 2).[28] As Cédric Durand puts it, 'household indebtedness feeds an immediately antagonistic relation between creditors and wage-earners/borrowers. However, this relation struggles to express itself, since unlike the wage relation it a priori sets each individual household against its creditors in an isolated and not collective manner.'[29] The refusal of indebtedness is no shortcut to what Gramsci would allude to as the 'integral autonomy' of the global proletariat, but rather depends on the prior construction of the latter.

In Chapter 2, I noted that the argument that labour was no longer as relevant to capital accumulation rested on what Dianne Elson helpfully describes as the 'misplaced concreteness' of labour in orthodox readings of Marx's theory of value. A reframing of labour on the order that Elson and others propose has important implications. Namely: there is no such thing as the 'working class' in and of itself as a ready-made political subject.[30] Class solidarities need to be assembled, not just mobilized. Gramsci helpfully distinguishes between the 'relations of force' at three interrelated levels: 'objective' class relations in the process of production; the 'relation of political forces', or the degree to which various social classes have developed a 'homogeneity, self-awareness, and organization'; and the relations of 'military force', both in the sense of control over means of repression and the 'politico-military' capacity of subaltern groups to blunt, weaken, sabotage, etc. the military capacities of dominant classes.[31] All of this, as Stuart Hall among others has highlighted, is shot through with articulations of racial and gendered social difference.[32] On the other hand, we need to consider not just exploitation at the point of production, but the wider suite of social conditions that explain why labour takes the alienated form it does under capitalism. Debt is often critical in this respect. As argued in Chapters 2 and 3, relations of indebtedness both emerge out of the spatial and temporal contradictions implicit in the commodification of labour power and in turn amplify the 'mute compulsion' to sell one's labour power.

There is, to be fair, a real argument to be made, quite apart from financialization debates, that the workplace can no longer serve as the sole political centre of working-class lives amidst globally rising precarity. In any case, stable, formal, unionized jobs have always made up the minority of the global working class.[33] Irregular forms of work are undoubtedly widely prevalent, and perhaps the majority of the global working class are not engaged in formal waged work. This is hardly unique to contemporary capitalism. Many people now and historically have found themselves living as some part of the relative surplus population at certain points in time. We must, then, be cautious of attributing this development to any periodized process of 'financialization'. Nonetheless, it remains the case that our starting point must be the necessary plurality of exploitation under capitalism. As Alessandra Mezzadri argues, a recognition of the multiplicity of capitalist exploitation 'allows us to recuperate ... a broader capitalist history of the wageless across the colonial and postcolonial world, where petty commodity production, non-wage and disguised-wage labour, including forms of slave, indentured, unfree and bonded labour are the norm'.[34]

The fact remains that debts and rents are important sites of accumulation as well as critical relations through which the 'mute compulsion' of capital over labour is articulated. Streams of payment are a potential pinch point that can be used to apply pressure to capital, but there's no reason to expect that this might serve as an alternative to other forms of class struggle, or that the refusal of debt can be the main lever of resistance to contemporary capitalism. The central point must be that 'primary' exploitation through labour and 'secondary' exploitation through debt, rent, and the like are inextricably interlinked. Whether one or the other is felt more directly or acutely at any given time is dependent on a whole host of conjunctural factors, mediated through complex layers of social difference, and subject to a heavy dose of contingency. But in the final analysis, working classes, broadly understood, are almost always 'exploit[ed] in two directions at once'.[35]

The latter phrase is Marx's. He uses it in Chapter 25 of the first volume of *Capital*, in a discussion of the 'nomadic' population engaged in mining and railway construction in nineteenth-century England, which he considers a specific fraction of the wider relative surplus population. Marx is here talking specifically about the reliance of these workers, necessarily highly mobile and often working in relatively remote locations, on their employers for the provision of housing. This condition ultimately often positioned mining capitalists as *both* boss and landlord. I'm admittedly taking some liberty here in using the phrase out of context. The specific experience Marx is describing in the full passage is an unusual one (if not entirely unique, it's a common experience for temporary migrant workers). Many of us encounter our employers, landlords, and creditors as separate particular capitals rather than folded into the same individual. But the fact of simultaneous and mutually reinforcing exploitation through debts and work, which the phrase neatly captures, is typical. Of course, there's much at stake in the particular configurations of these simultaneous exploitations. One clear example here might be the rise and fall of the compound labour system in South African gold and platinum mining, discussed briefly in Chapter 3. But the formal separation there of employer and landlord, if anything, intensified the exploitation of mining workers by both. Indebtedness, in short, is not the basis for a new kind of class relationship in which the compulsion to labour is sidelined, but rather a phenomenal form of the wider impersonal compulsions through which capitalist value relations operate.

But in any case, what's crucial is that if we grasp these dynamics in the context of the whole circuit of capital, it seems necessary to strike at the common root of both – the subjection of survival needs to processes of commodification. This is, as Søren Mau aptly notes, ultimately the core of the 'mute compulsion' of capital – the separation of people from the social and biological requirements for material reproduction, and the mediation of access to these through money.[36] Bryan and Rafferty grasped this with particular acuity in an earlier piece. Against the commodification of risks through ever-more complex financial instruments, 'the alternative politics is conceived in resistance to risk-shifting: a struggle for public housing, public pensions and public education; not better practices in the process of lending and securitization of mortgages and tuition fees, or greater prudence in the investment of workers' savings'.[37] It is perhaps beside the (theoretical) point being made here, but there is the added benefit here that we are scarcely starting from scratch in this respect. There is a plethora of ongoing struggles globally against the privatization and commodification of water, of housing, of education, of land, of transport, and more broadly for climate justice and reparations for the entwined damages of colonial exploitation and climate breakdown.

From the perspective articulated here, then, more democratic control over money, reining in finance capital through regulation, or the development of public financial institutions, ought to be considered mainly insofar as they might contribute to weakening the multifaceted compulsions through which capitalist relations of exploitation operate. They cannot, however, be sufficient for those purposes. We are indeed confronted by a choice between socialism and barbarism, but there are no financial shortcuts to the former. We are left with the difficult work of building a self-aware and organized working class on a global scale.

Notes

INTRODUCTION

1. Leonard Silk, 'The peril behind the takeover boom', *New York Times*, 29 December 1985, available at: www.nytimes.com/1985/12/29/business/the-peril-behind-the-takeover-boom.html.

2. There is a long history of legal and regulatory efforts to differentiate finance from gambling, suffice to say that the boundary is necessarily blurry. Marieke de Goede's *Virtue, fortune and faith* (Minneapolis: University of Minnesota Press, 2005) remains an essential account.

3. A. Bianco, 'The casino society: Playing with fire', *BusinessWeek*, 16 September 1985, p. 83.

4. J.M. Keynes, *General theory of employment, interest and money* (London: Macmillan and Co., 1936), p. 158.

5. W. Buffett, 'How to tame the casino society', *Washington Post*, 4 December 1986.

6. S. Strange, *Casino capitalism* (Oxford: Basil Blackwell, 1986).

7. N. Costello, J. Michie and S. Milne, *Beyond the casino economy: Planning for the 1990s* (London: Verso, 1989), p. 125.

8. Eventually collected as H. Magdoff and P. Sweezy, *Stagnation and the financial explosion* (New York: Monthly Review Press, 1987).

9. Ibid., 143.

10. For an excellent overview and research agenda, see I. Alami, C. Alves, B. Bonizzi, A. Kaltenbrunner, K. Koddenbrock, I. Kvangraven and J. Powell, 'International financial subordination: A critical research agenda', *Review of International Political Economy* 30, no. 4 (2023), 1360–86. Related pieces include I. Alami, *Money power and financial capital in emerging markets: Facing the liquidity tsunami* (London: Routledge, 2020); A. Kaltenbrunner and J.P. Paincera, 'Subordinated financial integration and financialization in emerging capitalist economies: The Brazilian experience', *New Political Economy* 23, no. 3 (2018), 290–313; I. Kvangraven, K. Koddenbrock and N.S. Sylla, 'Financial subordination and uneven development in 21st century Africa', *Community Development Journal* 56, no. 1 (2021), 119–40; I.A. Akolgo, 'Collapsing banks and the cost of finance capitalism

in Ghana', *Review of African Political Economy* 49, no. 174 (2022), 624–33.

11. See J. Gort and A. Brooks, 'Africa's next debt crisis: A relational comparison of Chinese and Western lending in Zambia', *Antipode* 55, no. 3 (2023), 830–52; Debt Justice, *Colonialism and debt: How debt is used to exploit and control* (London: Debt Justice, 2022).

12. The list of potential references on this point is extensive, so with apologies for the inevitable omissions, see J. Montgomerie and D. Tepe-Belfrage, 'Caring for debts: How the household economy exposes the limits of financialization', *Critical Sociology* 43, no. 4–5 (2017), 653–68; A. Roberts, 'Household debt and the financialization of social reproduction: Theorizing the UK housing and hunger crises', *Research in Political Economy* 31, 135–61; S. Soederberg, *Debtfare states and the poverty industry: Money, discipline and the surplus population* (London: Routledge, 2014); I. Guerin and G. Venkatasubramanian, 'The socio-economy of debt: Revisiting debt bondage in times of financialization', *Geoforum* 137 (2022), 174–84; L. Cavallero and V. Gago, *A feminist reading of debt* (London: Pluto Press, 2021); Debt Collective, *Can't pay won't pay: The case for economic disobedience and debt abolition* (Chicago: Haymarket Books, 2020).

13. See B. Bonizzi and A. Kaltenbrunner, 'Liability driven investment and pension fund exposure to emerging markets: A Minskyian analysis', *Environment and Planning A: Economy and Space* 51, no. 2 (2019), 420–39.

14. B. Christophers, *Our lives in their portfolios: Why asset managers own the world* (London: Verso, 2023); A. Buller and B. Braun, *Under new management: Share ownership and the rise of UK asset manager capitalism* (London: Common Wealth, 2021); A. Gibadullina, 'Who owns and controls global capital? Uneven geographies of asset manager capitalism', *Environment and Planning A: Economy and Space* 56, no. 2 (2024), 558–85.

15. See D. Gabor, 'The Wall Street Consensus', *Development and Change* 52, no. 3 (2021), 429–52; E. Mawdsley, 'Development geography II: Financialization', *Progress in Human Geography* 42, no. 2 (2018), 264–74; A. Buller, *The value of a whale: On the illusions of green capitalism* (Manchester: Manchester University Press); D. Cohen and E. Rosenman, 'From the schoolyard to the conservation area: Impact investment across the nature/social divide', *Antipode* 52, no. 5, 1259–85.

16. See P. Mader, 'Contesting financial inclusion', *Development and Change* 49, no. 2 (2018), 461–83; N. Bernards, *A critical history of poverty finance: Colonial roots and neoliberal failures* (London: Pluto Press, 2022).

17. On the grim outcomes of these measures in early-adopter South Africa, see E. Torkelson, 'Sophia's choice: Debt, social welfare, and racial finance capitalism', *Environment and Planning D: Society and Space* 39, no. 1 (2021), 67–84.

18. See J. Fairhead, M. Leach and I. Scoones, 'Green grabbing: A new appropriation of nature?', *Journal of Peasant Studies* 39 (2), 237–61; C. Hesketh, 'Clean development or the development of dispossession? The political economy of wind parks in Southern Mexico', *Environment and Planning E: Environment and Space* 5, no. 2 (2021), 543–65.

19. See J. Dempsey and D.C. Suarez, 'Arrested development? The promises and paradoxes of "selling nature to save it"', *Annals of the American Association of Geographers* 106, no. 3 (2016), 653–71; N. Bernards, 'Where is finance in the financialization of development?', *Globalizations* 24, no. 1 (2024), 88–102.

20. See, for instance, the essays collected in F. Block, ed., *Democratizing finance: Restructuring credit to transform society* (London: Verso, 2022).

21. K. Phillips, *Boiling point: Democrats, Republicans, and the decline of middle-class prosperity* (New York: Random House, 1993). Or, at least, Phillips was probably the first to use the term in the sense with which it is now most commonly associated. A World Bank Working Paper from 1989 is probably the actual first use of the term. However, 'financialization' here is used in a discussion of interest rate liberalization and financial depth, arguing that the 'financialization of savings' – when savings are intermediated through the formal financial system – was a mechanism linking interest rate liberalization to economic growth. This argument is questionable for a number of reasons, but this use of the term never really took off. A.H. Gelb, 'Financial policies, growth, and efficiency', *Policy, Planning and Research Working Papers, WPS 202* (Washington: World Bank, 1989).

22. G. Arrighi, *The long twentieth century: Money, power and the origins of our times* (London: Verso, 1994).

23. M. Collins, 'Wall Street and the financialization of the economy', *Forbes*, 4 February 2015, available at: www.forbes.com/sites/mikecollins/2015/02/04/wall-street-and-the-financialization-of-

the-economy/?sh=23088c355783; R. Hockett, 'Liquidity reserves and commodity reserves: A marriage proposal', *Forbes* 13 June 2022, available at: www.forbes.com/sites/rhockett/2022/06/13/liquidity-reserves-and-commodity-reserves-a-marriage-proposal/?sh=13c470bb3a2c; R. Woodbury, 'What happens when you're the investment', *The Atlantic*, 29 November 2021, available at: www.theatlantic.com/ideas/archive/2021/11/financialization-everything-investment-system-token/620804/; N. Shaxson, 'The finance curse: How the outsized power of the City of London makes Britain poorer', *Guardian*, 5 October 2018, available at: www.theguardian.com/news/2018/oct/05/the-finance-curse-how-the-outsized-power-of-the-city-of-london-makes-britain-poorer.

24. E.g., G. Blakeley, *Stolen: How to save the world from financialization* (London: Repeater Books, 2019).

25. E.g., J. Kay, *Other people's money: Masters of the universe or servants of the people?* (London: Profile Books, 2016).

26. United Nations Conference on Trade and Development, *Trade and Development Report, 2015: Making the international financial architecture work for development* (New York: UNCTAD, 2015).

27. S. Ouma, 'From financialization to operations of capital: Historicizing and disentangling the finance-farmland nexus', *Geoforum* 72 (2016), 82–93, p. 82.

28. See especially B. Christophers, 'Anaemic geographies of financialization', *New Political Economy* 17, no. 3 (2012), 271–91; 'The limits to financialisation', *Dialogues in Human Geography* 5, no. 2 (2015), 183–200; *Rentier capitalism: Who owns the economy, and who pays for it?* (London: Verso, 2020).

29. S. Soederberg, *Debtfare states and the poverty industry: Money, discipline and the surplus population* (New York: Routledge, 2014).

30. K. Koddenbrock, I.H. Kvangraven and N.S. Sylla, 'Beyond financialisation: The longue durée of finance and production in the global south', *Cambridge Journal of Economics* 46, no. 4 (2022), 703–33.

31. B. Best, 'Political economy through the looking glass: Imagining six impossible things about finance before breakfast', *Historical Materialism* 25, no. 3 (2017), 76–100.

32. J. Montgomerie and D. Tepe-Belfrage, 'Caring for debts: How the household economy exposes the limits of financialization', *Critical Sociology* 43, no. 4–5 (2017), 653–68.

33. Christophers, 'Anaemic geographics' and B. Christophers, 'The limits to financialization', *Dialogues in Human Geography*, 5, no. 2

(2015), 183–200 are notable exceptions, as is Ouma, 'Financialization', to a degree.

34. K. Marx, *Capital, Vol. 3* (London: Penguin, 1991).

35. G. Ingham, *The nature of money* (Cambridge: Polity, 2004), p. 62. As will become clear in Chapter 2, Ingham is (to put it kindly) wrong about Marx, money, and abstraction.

36. A. Leyshon and N. Thrift, *Money/Space: Geographies of monetary transformation* (London: Routledge, 1997).

37. See B. Christophers, 'Follow the thing: Money', *Environment and Planning D* 29, no. 6 (2011), 1068–84; G. Mann, 'Time, space, and money in capitalism and communism', *Human Geography* 1, no. 2 (2008), 4–12; 'Value after Lehman', *Historical Materialism* 18 (1), 172–88.

38. K. Marx, *Capital, Vol. 1* (London: Penguin, 1990), p. 169.

39. See esp. Soederberg, *Debtfare*; W. Bonefeld, 'Capital *par excellence*: On money as an obscure thing', *Estudios de Filosofía* 62 (2020), 33–56.

40. S. de Brunhoff, *Marx on money* (London: Verso, 2015); D. Harvey, *The limits to capital* (London: Verso, 2006); W. Bonefeld, 'Money, equality, and exploitation: An interpretation of Marx's treatment of money', in W. Bonefeld and J. Holloway, eds., *Global Capital, National State and the Politics of Money* (New York: Palgrave Macmillan, 1996).

41. D. Harvey, 'From managerialism to entrepreneurialism: The transformation in urban governance in late capitalism', *Geografiska Annaler B: Human Geography* 71, no. 1 (1989), 3–17, p. 16.

42. This point is made very clearly in Bonefeld, 'Capital *par excellence*'; Best, 'Political economy'.

43. Harvey, *Limits*.

CHAPTER 1

1. N. van der Zwan (2014) 'Making sense of financialization', *Socio-Economic Review* 12, no 1 (2014), 99–129.

2. Ben Fine for instance, includes a four-page appendix listing his specific areas of disagreement with fellow Marxist (and then-departmental colleague) Costas Lapavitsas over different aspects of financialization in a 2013 article outlining a Marxist approach to financialization. B. Fine, 'Financialization from a Marxist perspective', *International Journal of Political Economy* 42, no. 4 (2013), 47–66.

3. R. Lee, G.L. Clark, J. Pollard and A. Leyshon, 'The remit of financial geography – before and after the crisis', *Journal of Economic Geography* 9, no. 5 (2009), 723–47.

4. Some notable contributions include J. Clapp, 'Financialization, distance, and global food politics', *Journal of Peasant Studies* 41, no. 5 (2014), 797–814; D. Gabor, 'The Wall Street Consensus', *Development and Change* 52, no. 3 (2021), 429–52; J.B. Foster, 'The defense of nature: Resisting the financialization of the earth', *Monthly Review*, 73, no. 11 (2022).

5. B. Christophers, 'The limits to financialization', *Dialogues in Human Geography*, 5, no. 2 (2015), 183–200, p. 184.

6. For instance, R. Venugopal, 'Neoliberalism as concept', *Economy and Society* 44, no. 2 (2015), 165–87.

7. Christophers, 'Limits', pp. 186–7.

8. C. Lapavitsas, 'Financialised capitalism: Crisis and financial expropriation', *Historical Materialism* 17, no. 1 (2009), 114–48, p. 126.

9. E.g., B. Fine and A. Saad-Filho, 'Thirteen things you need to know about neoliberalism', *Critical Sociology* 43, no. 4–5 (2017), 685–706.

10. J.A. Hobson, *Imperialism: A study* (London: Allen and Unwin, 1902/1938); V.I. Lenin, *Imperialism: The highest stage of capitalism* (New York: International Publishers, 1917/1988); R. Hilferding, *Finance capital: A study of the latest phase of capitalist development* (London: Routledge, 1910/1981); N. Bukharin, *Imperialism and world economy* (London: Martin Lawrence, 1929).

11. A. Mezzadra and B. Neilson, 'Operations of capital', *South Atlantic Quarterly* 114, no. 1 (2015), 1–9, p. 2.

12. A. Leyshon and N. Thrift, 'The capitalization of almost everything: The Future of finance and capitalism', *Theory, Culture, and Society* 24, no. 7–8 (2007), 97–115.

13. There are important differences, again, between Magdoff and Sweezy's diagnosis of the stagnation of productive capital and Brenner's – I discuss these further in Chapter 3. Both nonetheless hang a good deal on the notion of falling profits in productive sectors and a growing reliance on finance. See R. Brenner, *The economics of global turbulence: The advanced capitalist economies from long boom to long downturn, 1945–2005* (London: Verso, 2006); 'The economics of global turbulence', *New Left Review* I/229 (1998); *The boom and the bubble: The US in the world economy* (London: Verso, 2003).

14. S. Strange, *States and markets: An introduction to international political economy* (London: Pinter, 1988).

15. See also E. Helleiner, 'Political determinants of international currencies: What future for the US dollar?', *Review of International Political Economy* 15, no. 3 (2008), 354–78.

16. M. Ali, 'Acute dollar dominance', *Phenomenal World*, 3 February 2022, available at: www.phenomenalworld.org/analysis/acute-dollar-dominance/; H. Thompson, *Disorder: Hard times in the twenty-first century* (Oxford: Oxford University Press, 2022); M. Beck, 'Extroverted financialization: How US finance shapes European banking', *Review of International Political Economy* 29, no. 5 (2022): 1723–45.

17. G. Arrighi 'A crisis of hegemony', in S. Amin, G. Arrighi, A.G. Frank and I. Wallerstein, eds., *Dynamics of global crises* (London: Macmillan, 1982), pp. 55–108; see also *The Geometry of Imperialism* (London: Verso, 1983).

18. K.P. Phillips, *The emerging Republican majority* (New Rochelle, NY: Arlington House, 1969).

19. J. Boyd, 'Nixon's Southern Strategy: "It's all in the charts"', *New York Times*, 17 May 1970.

20. See R.W. Gilmore, 'Globalisation and US prison growth: From military Keynesianism to post-Keynesian militarism', *Race & Class* 40, no. 2–3 (1999), 171–88; J. Inwood, 'Neoliberal racism: The "Southern Strategy" and the expanding geographies of white supremacy', *Social and Cultural Geography* 16, no. 4 (2015), 407–23; R. Nonye Ndubuizu, 'Reagan's austerity bureaucrats: Examining the racial and gender bias of Ronald Reagan's housing vouchers', *Du Bois Review* 16, no. 2 (2020), 535–54; for a wider perspective on the role of race in the establishment of neoliberalism, see A. Kundnani, 'The racial constitution of neoliberalism', *Race & Class* 63, no. 1 (2021), 51–69.

21. Phillips, *Boiling point*, xx.

22. Ibid., xxi.

23. Ibid., 3, my emphasis.

24. For a detailed critical discussion of the myth of 'standard employment', see L. Vosko, *Managing the margins: Gender, citizenship, and the international regulation of precarious employment* (Oxford: Oxford University Press, 2011).

25. On the family and the articulation of neoliberalism and resistance to it, see M. Cooper, *Family values: Between neoliberalism and the new social conservatism* (New York: Zone Books, 2017).

26. C. Maier, 'The politics of productivity: American international economic policy after World War II', *International Organization* 31, no. 4 (1977), 607–33.

27. Phillips, *Boiling point*, 168–9.

28. For sharp critiques of these narratives, see J. Narayan, 'The wages of whiteness in the absence of wages: Racial capitalism, reactionary intercommunalism and the rise of Trumpism', *Third World Quarterly* 38 no. 11 (2017), 2482–500; R. Shilliam, *Race and the undeserving poor: From abolition to Brexit* (Newcastle: Agenda, 2018).

29. G. Standing, *The precariat: The new dangerous class* (London: Bloomsbury, 2011), p. 14. For an incisive critique of Standing's concept and argument, see J. Breman, 'A bogus concept?', *New Left Review* 84 (2013), 130–8.

30. Standing, *Precariat*, p. 25.

31. Phillips' main touchstones are F. Braudel, *Civilization and capitalism, 15th–18th century, Vol. 3: The perspective of the world* (New York: Harper and Row, 1984) and E. Hobsbawm, *Industry and empire: The birth of the industrial revolution* (London: Weidenfield & Nicholson, 1964).

32. Phillips, *Boiling point*, 193–4, emphasis in original.

33. Arrighi, *Long twentieth century*, 315.

34. Ibid., 27. Arrighi is in a dialogue of sorts here with Robert W. Cox, Stephen Gill and others in 'neo-Gramscian' international political economy, likewise stretching Gramsci's concept of 'hegemony' to inter-state relations, e.g., R. Cox, *Production, power and world order: Social forces and the making of history* (New York: Columbia University Press, 1987); S. Gill, *American hegemony and the Trilateral Commission* (Cambridge: Cambridge University Press, 1991). Indeed, an earlier version of one of the chapters from the *Long twentieth century* is published in a collection edited by Gill on Gramsci and International Relations: G. Arrighi, 'The three hegemonies of global capitalism', in S. Gill, ed., *Gramsci, historical materialism and international relations* (Cambridge: Cambridge University Press, 1993), 148–85.

35. Arrighi, 'Crisis of hegemony', 78.

36. Arrighi, *Long twentieth century*, ix.

37. Ibid., x.

38. Braudel, *Civilization and capitalism, Vol. 3*, 245.

39. Arrighi, *Long twentieth century*, 6.

40. Braudel, *Civilization and capitalism, Vol. 3*, 246.

41. Arrighi, *Long twentieth century*, 4.

42. F. Braudel, *Civilization and capitalism, 15th–18th century, Volume II: The wheels of commerce* (Berkeley: University of California Press, 1982), p. 433, emphasis in original.

43. Ibid., 248. There are well-rehearsed critiques of this understanding of capital and capitalism. Ellen Meiksins Woods, in a notable argument, positions both Braudel and the World-Systems Analysis tradition in which Arrighi is situated as examples of the 'commercialization thesis', in which the rise of capitalism is treated as merely a generalization of age-old mercantile practices, or the extension of capital beyond its habitual realms of commerce into production. E.M. Wood, *The origin of capitalism: A longer view* (London: Verso, 2002), p. 17. I don't know that straying too far into the weeds of this debate would be helpful here, so I'll just say that the 'commercialization' critique is apt in Braudel's case, and largely in Arrighi's as well.

44. I'll discuss the 'general formula' further in Chapter 2.

45. Arrighi, *Long twentieth century*, 5.

46. Ibid., 5.

47. Ibid., 6.

48. I discuss Marx's use of M-M' as shorthand and its implications further in Chapter 2.

49. Arrighi, 'Crisis of hegemony'.

50. Arrighi, *Long twentieth century*, 1.

51. Ibid., x.

52. Ibid., 81.

53. Ibid., 341.

54. Ibid., 370. Though it's perhaps less directly relevant to the present task, it is perhaps worth noting that Arrighi's sequel of sorts to the *Long twentieth century*, published 13 years later on, sees something like this 'East Asian material expansion' scenario coming to pass, albeit much more squarely focused on China, see G. Arrighi, *Adam Smith in Beijing: Lineages of the twenty-first century* (London: Verso, 2007).

55. Arrighi, *Long twentieth century*, 370.

56. S. Amin, 'The challenge of globalization', *Review of International Political Economy* 3, no. 2 (1996), 217.

57. On the 'law of value' and its relation to finance, see Chapter 2.

58. Amin, 'The challenge of globalization', 242.

59. See especially G. Krippner, 'The financialization of the American economy', *Socio-Economic Review* 3, no. 2 (2005), 173–208. Also discussed further below.

60. N. van der Zwan, 'Making sense'.

61. Arrighi, *Long twentieth century*, 1.
62. Krippner, 'The financialization of the American economy'.
63. G. Krippner, *Capitalizing on crisis: The political origins of the rise of finance* (Cambridge, MA: Harvard University Press, 2011), p. 51.
64. G. Epstein, ed., *Financialization and the world economy* (Cheltenham: Edward Elgar, 2005).
65. G. Epstein and A. Jayadev, 'The rise of rentier incomes in OECD countries: Financialization, central bank independence, and labor solidarity', in ibid., 46.
66. Ibid., 47.
67. D. Harvey, 'The "new" imperialism: Accumulation by dispossession', *Socialist Register* 40 (2004), 63–87, pp. 77–8.
68. G. Duménil and D. Levy, *Capital resurgent: Roots of the neoliberal revolution* (Cambridge, MA: Harvard University Press, 2004), pp. 1–2.
69. Krippner, *Capitalizing*, 13–14.
70. The Marxist criticisms of World Systems and Braudelian analyses mentioned in fn 43 above suggest that these are not unambiguously analogous perspectives. Equally, Marxist and adjacent analyses do very much manage to produce more detailed accounts of the error-prone activities of state and firm managers, e.g., J. Copley, *Governing financialization: The tangled politics of financial liberalization in Britain* (Oxford: Oxford University Press, 2021); S. Knafo and S.J. Dutta, 'The myth of the shareholder revolution and the financialization of the firm', *Review of International Political Economy* 27 no. 3 (2020), 476–99; Brenner, *The boom and the bubble*.
71. W. Lazonick and M. O'Sullivan, 'Maximizing shareholder value: A new ideology for corporate governance', *Economy and Society* 29, no. 1 (2000), 13–35.
72. Ibid., 14–15.
73. Ibid., 19.
74. P. Gibbon, 'At the cutting edge? Financialisation and UK clothing retailers' global sourcing patterns and practices', *Competition and Change* 6, no. 3 (2002), 289–308; A. Pike, '"Shareholder value" versus the regions: The closure of Vaux Brewery in Sunderland', *Journal of Economic Geography* 6, no. 2 (2006), 201–22; J. Froud, C. Haslem, S. Johal and K. Williams, 'Cars after financialisation: A case study in financial under-performance, constraints, and consequences', *Competition and Change* 6 no. 1 (2002), 13–41.
75. J. Froud, C. Haslam, S. Johal and K. Williams, 'Restructuring for shareholder value and its implications for labour', *Cambridge Journal*

of Economics 24, no. 6 (2000), 771–96; W. Milberg, 'Shifting sources and uses of profits: Sustaining US financialization with global value chains', *Economy and Society* 37 no. 3 (2008), 420–51.

76. J. Rabinovich, 'The financialization of the non-financial corporation: A critique of the *financial turn of accumulation* hypothesis', *Metroeconomica* 70, no. 4 (2019), 738–75. I will have more to say about the restructuring of production and the 'offshoring' of capitalist profits in Chapter 3.

77. G. Liagouras, 'Beyond corporate financialization: From global value chains to the conundrum of intangible investments', *Competition and Change* 27, no. 5 (2023), 685–706.

78. R. Martin, *The financialization of daily life* (Philadelphia: Temple University Press, 2002).

79. P. Langley, *The everyday life of global finance: Saving and borrowing in Anglo-America* (Oxford: Oxford University Press, 2008), p. 47.

80. S. Hall, 'Geographies of money and finance II: Financialization and financial subjects', *Progress in Human Geography* 36, no. 3 (2012), 403–11, p. 407.

81. See, e.g., A. Agunsoye, '"Locked in the rat race": Variegated financial subjectivities in the United Kingdom', *Environment and Planning A: Economy and Space* 53, no. 7 (2020), 1828–48; L. Pellandini-Simanyi, F. Hammer and Z. Vargha 'The financialization of everyday life or the domestication of finance?', *Cultural Studies* 29, no. 5–6 (2015), 733–59; T. Samec, 'Performing housing debt attachments: Forming semi-financialised subjects', *Journal of Cultural Economy* 11, no. 6 (2018), 549–64.

82. P. Langley, 'Everyday investor subjects and global financial change: The rise of Anglo-American mass investment', in J. Hobson and L. Seabrooke, eds., *Everyday politics of the world economy* (Cambridge: Cambridge University Press, 2007), p. 103.

83. Christophers, 'Limits', 188.

84. See R. Aitken, '"An economics of capital": Genealogies of everyday financial conduct', *Journal of Historical Sociology* 31, no. 1 (2018), 213–35.

85. See N. Bernards, *A critical history of poverty finance: Colonial roots and neoliberal failures* (London: Pluto Press, 2022).

86. S. Soederberg, *Debtfare states and the poverty industry: Money, discipline and the surplus population* (London: Routledge, 2014), p. 25.

87. J. Montgomerie and K. Williams, 'Financialised capitalism: After the crisis and before neoliberalism', *Competition and Change* 13, no. 2, 100.

88. E. Engelen, 'The case for financialization', *Competition and Change* 13, no. 2, 113.

89. Scopus is a large database of academic publications. The data in this chart was obtained in January 2023. The pattern and trajectory, if not the specific numbers, are largely the same if a similar exercise is repeated with, e.g., Google N-Gram, which scans a large corpus of book publications for mentions of a term.

90. Christophers, 'Limits'.

91. Ibid., 192.

92. Ibid., 194.

93. K. Koddenbrock, I.H. Kvangraven and N.S. Sylla, 'Beyond financialisation: The longue durée of finance and production in the global south', *Cambridge Journal of Economics* 46, no. 4 (2022), 703–33.

94. S. Amin, *Accumulation on a world scale: A critique of the theory of underdevelopment* (New York: Monthly Review Press, 1974), p. 438; see also N.S. Sylla, 'Fighting monetary colonialism in West Africa: Samir Amin's contribution', *Review of African Political Economy* 48, no. 167 (2021), 32–49.

95. On the latter, 'failed' cases, see N. Bernards, 'Child labour, cobalt, and the London Metal Exchange: Fetish, fixing and the limits of financialization', *Economy and Society* 50, no. 4 (2021), 542–64; 'Where is finance in the financialization of development', *Globalizations* 24, no. 1 (2024), 88–102; J. Dempsey and D.C. Suarez, 'Arrested development? The promises and paradoxes of "selling nature to save it"', *Annals of the American Association of Geographers* 106, no. 3 (2016), 653–71. See also the example of water futures discussed in Chapter 4.

96. Knafo and Dutta, 'Shareholder revolution', p. 478, emphasis in original.

97. The LBO boom was discussed in the first pages of the Introduction.

98. Ibid., 487.

99. Ibid., 490.

CHAPTER 2

1. D. Harvey, *Limits to capital* (London: Verso, 2006), p. 283.

2. 'Fictitious capital' has a very specific, but often somewhat underdeveloped and misunderstood, meaning in Marx's usage. It refers to tradeable claims over future flows of income – stocks and bonds are the 'typical' examples. 'Fictitious' capital differs from the more general category of 'interest-bearing' capital (which is all oriented to

future income) insofar as it is tradeable on a secondary market. But, returns on 'fictitious' forms of capital must nonetheless be realized through the whole circuit of capital. For excellent recent overviews, see C. Alves 'Fictitious capital, the credit system, and the particular case of government bonds in Marx', *New Political Economy* 28, no. 3 (2023), 398–415; A.W.A. Palludeto and P. Rossi, 'Marx's fictitious capital: A misrepresented category revisited', *Cambridge Journal of Economics* 46, no. 3 (2022), 545–60.

3. Lapavitsas, for one, is to his credit quick to insist that finance is not, in fact, parasitic: C. Lapavitsas, *Profiting without producing: How finance exploits us all* (London: Verso, 2013). But, as we'll see further below, the logic of his argument tends to undermine this insistence.

4. Harvey, *Limits*, 88.

5. For a similar argument, see W. Bonefeld, 'Capital *par excellence*: On money as an obscure thing', *Estudios de Filosofía* 62 (2020), 33–56.

6. For a detailed reconstruction of this approach and an effort to apply it to contemporary capitalism, see G. Carchedi and M. Roberts, *Capitalism in the twenty-first century through the prism of value* (London: Pluto Press, 2023).

7. K. Marx, *Capital, Vol. 1* (London: Penguin, 1990), pp. 300–1.

8. C. Lapavitsas, 'Financialised capitalism: Crisis and financial expropriation', *Historical Materialism* 17, no. 1 (2009), 114–48, p. 128.

9. Ibid., 131. Marx's own use of the term 'exploitation' is ironically much more flexible than this.

10. Lapavitsas, *Profiting* and 'The financialization of capitalism: "Profiting without producing"', *City* 17, no. 6 (2013), 792–805.

11. Lapavitsas, 'Financialization of capitalism', 793.

12. C. Durand, *Fictitious capital: How finance is appropriating our future* (London: Verso, 2017), p. 72.

13. Lapavitsas, 'Financialization of capitalism', 798.

14. C. Lapavitsas and I. Martinez-Muñoz, 'Financialization at a watershed in the United States', *Competition and Change* 22, no. 5 (2018), 488–509.

15. D. Bryan, M. Rafferty and C. Jefferis, 'Risk and value: Finance, labor, and production', *South Atlantic Quarterly* 114, 307–29, p. 309; cf. B. Christophers, 'Risking value theory in the political economy of finance and nature', *Progress in Human Geography* 42, no. 3 (2018), 330–49.

16. For a similar critique of this tendency to dismiss Marxist value theory, see B. Best, 'Political economy through the looking glass:

Imagining six impossible things about finance before breakfast', *Historical Materialism* 25, no. 3 (2017), 76–100.

17. 'Value form' Marxism refers to a loose amalgamation of different strands of recent Marxist thought. Aside from Postone, these notably include Michael Heinrich: *An introduction to the three volumes of Marx's Capital* (New York: Monthly Review Press, 2012), and others in the German *Neue Marx Lektüre*; the British-centred Open Marxism (e.g., S. Clarke, *Marx, marginalism and modern sociology: From Adam Smith to Max Weber* (Basingstoke: Macmillan, 1991); W. Bonefeld, R. Gunn and K. Psychopedis, eds., *Open Marxism 1: Dialectics and history* (London: Pluto Press, 1992)); and some Latin American approaches (e.g., G. Starosta, *Marx's Capital, method and revolutionary subjectivity* (Leiden: Brill, 2016); M. Arboleda, *Planetary mine: Territories of extraction under late capitalism* (London: Verso, 2020)). Generally, these authors share a critique of the 'orthodox' Marxist reading of value as relying on, in Dianne Elson's useful phrase, a kind of 'misplaced concreteness' and an emphasis on the character of value under capitalism as abstract, alienated social labour: 'The value theory of labour', in D. Elson, ed., *Value: The representation of labour in capitalism* (London: Verso, 1979/2015). The Open Marxist tradition in particular has produced a lot of brilliant work on finance, especially on the relations between finance and the state, e.g., S. Clarke, *Keynesianism, monetarism, and the crisis of the state* (Aldershot: Edward Elgar, 1988); W. Bonefeld and John Holloway, eds., *Global Capital, National State and the Politics of Money* (New York: Palgrave Macmillan, 1997), or, more recently, I. Alami, *Money power and financial capital in emerging markets: Facing the liquidity tsunami* (London: Routledge, 2020); J. Copley, *Governing financialization: The tangled politics of financial liberalization in Britain* (Oxford: Oxford University Press, 2021). The arguments that follow in this chapter chime quite closely with, and draw on, many of these perspectives.

18. M. Postone, *Time, labour and social domination: A reinterpretation of Marx's critical theory* (Cambridge: Cambridge University Press, 1993).

19. Ibid., 3–4.

20. Ibid., 161.

21. G. Mann, 'Value after Lehman', *Historical Materialism* 18, no. 1 (2010), 172–88.

22. Ibid., 177.

23. Ibid., 177.

24. C. Hardin, *Capturing Finance: Arbitrage and Social Domination* (Durham, NC: Duke University Press, 2021).
25. Ibid., 75.
26. Ibid., 75.
27. See Christophers, 'Risking'; Bryan et al., 'Risk and value'.
28. Christophers, 'Risking', 336.
29. See also L. Adkins, M. Cooper and M. Konings, *The asset economy* (Cambridge: Polity, 2021).
30. A similar argument is made compellingly in S. Soederberg, *Debtfare states and the poverty industry: Debt, discipline and the surplus population* (London: Routledge, 2014).
31. This is noted by a range of recent research in very different contexts. Steven Campbell notes, e.g., that debts serve as a form of 'labour discipline' in squatter settlements inhabited predominantly by people in 'informal' forms of employment in Myanmar: 'Debt collection as labour discipline: The work of finance in a Myanmar squatter settlement', *Social Anthropology* 28, no. 3 (2020), 729–45. Giorgios Gouzoulis, in a large-scale econometric study covering Japan, Korea, the UK and Sweden, notes that rising household debt correlates strongly with a decline in strike activity: 'What do indebted employees do? Financialisation and the decline of industrial action', *Industrial Relations Journal* 54, no. 1 (2023), 71–94. The role of indebtedness in disciplining migrant workers in particular is also frequently noted, see G. LeBaron, 'Reconceptualizing debt bondage: Debt as a class-based form of labour discipline', *Critical Sociology* 40, no. 5 (2014), 763–80.
32. S. Mau, *Mute compulsion: A Marxist theory of the economic power of capital* (London: Verso, 2023), p. 135.
33. M. Postone, 'The current crisis and the anachronism of value: A Marxian reading', *Continental Thought and Theory* 1, no. 4 (2017), 38–54.
34. Ibid., 51.
35. Ibid., 52.
36. Ibid., 52.
37. I'm not principally concerned with whether what follows is a more scripturally 'accurate' reading of Marx than either the 'traditional' reading of exploitation or the 'value form' version (I'd consider the following a close cousin of the latter anyway). I think there's a plausible claim that it is more in keeping with Marx's overall method. But Marx's writing on finance and the credit system in particular is inarguably unfinished and sometimes terminologically inconsistent.

Marx also changes his mind over time. So, inevitably, Marx opens himself to multiple plausible interpretations with respect to finance. In the end, this book is not an exercise in Marxology, but an effort to reframe the way we think about the political economy/ecology of finance in what I think are more useful directions. I hope readers will take the latter as a more suitable test.

38. F.H. Knight, *Risk, uncertainty and profit* (Boston: Houghton Mifflin, 1921), p. 129. See also C. Clarke, 'The legacy of Frank H. Knight for the politics of financial governance', *Journal of Institutional Economics* 17, no. 6 (2021), 973–87.
39. Marx, *Capital, Vol. 1*, 256.
40. Ibid., 256.
41. K. Marx, *Capital, Vol. 2* (London: Penguin, 1992), p. 496.
42. For a useful discussion on this point, see Harvey, *Limits*, 88.
43. Marx, *Capital, Vol. 2*, 496–7.
44. This point is made particularly clearly in S. de Brunhoff, *Marx on money* (London: Verso, 1976), as well as R. Bellofiore and R. Realfonzo, 'Finance and the labour theory of value', *International Journal of Political Economy* 27, no. 2 (1997), 97–118.
45. S. Clarke, *Marx, marginalism, and modern sociology: From Adam Smith to Max Weber* (New York: St Martin's Press, 1991), p. 307.
46. D. Elson, 'The value theory of labour', in D. Elson, ed., *Value: The representation of labour in capitalism* (London: Verso, 1979), 115–80.
47. Clarke, *Marx*, 101.
48. Elson, 'The value theory'.
49. Ibid., 132.
50. Marx, *Capital, Vol. 1*, 150.
51. K. Marx, *A contribution to the critique of political economy*, trans. N.I. Stone (Chicago: Charles H. Kerr, 1859/1904), pp. 104–5.
52. Marx, *Capital, Vol. 1*, 196.
53. Ibid., 196.
54. Ibid., 196.
55. Marx, *Critique*, 81.
56. D. Harvey, 'From managerialism to entrepreneurialism: The transformation in urban governance in late capitalism', *Geografiska Annaler B: Human Geography* 71, no. 1 (1989), 3–17, p. 16.
57. I return to this point further in the next chapter, but it is at the core of James O'Connor's 'second contradiction' thesis. See J. O'Connor, 'Capitalism, nature, socialism: A theoretical introduction', *Capitalism, Nature, Socialism* 1, no. 1 (1988), 11–38.
58. Elson, 'The value theory', 128.

59. Marx, *Capital, Vol. 1*, 440–1.
60. See, e.g., writing about very different time periods and contexts: S.J. Gunawardana, "'To finish, we must finish'": Everyday practices of depletion in Sri Lankan export processing zones', *Globalizations* 13, no. 6 (2016), 861–75; N. Holdren, *Injury impoverished: Workplace accidents, capitalism and law in the Progressive Era* (Cambridge: Cambridge University Press, 2020).
61. S. Hall, 'Gramsci's relevance for the study of race and ethnicity', *Journal of Communication Inquiry* 10, no. 2 (1986), 5–27, p. 24.
62. There is little space to get into 'transition' debates here. They are variously touched on (or evaded) by a number of the other pieces referenced elsewhere in this book, including notably, e.g., G. Arrighi, *The long twentieth century: Money, power and the origins of our times* (London: Verso, 1994); E.M. Wood, *The origin of capitalism: The longer view* (London: Verso, 2006); J.M. Moore, *Capitalism in the web of life: Ecology and the accumulation of capital* (London: Verso, 2015). I'd argue, largely in line with Moore, that the rise of global capitalism represents a set of transformations in labour processes induced the collision of a number of different historical tendencies that took place within a global matrix of exchange networks and relations of imperialism. Trading relations are not in and of themselves 'capitalism', but neither does the concrete history of capitalism as a mode of production make sense without them.
63. L. Paulani, 'Money in contemporary capitalism and the autonomisation of capitalist forms in Marx's theory', *Cambridge Journal of Economics* 38, no. 4 (2014), 779–95, p. 789.
64. S. Clarke, 'The value of value', *Capital and Class* 10, no. 1 (1979), 1–17, pp. 8–9, emphasis in original.
65. K. Marx, *Capital, Vol. 3* (London: Penguin, 1991).
66. K. Marx, *The class struggles in France: 1848 to 1850* (Moscow: Progress Publishers, 1960), p. 43.
67. It also reaches important limits in the political analysis of concrete historical situations, which I'll discuss further in Chapters 5 and 6.
68. Harvey, *Limits*, 283.
69. Ibid., 283.
70. Ibid., 283.
71. Notably, Alami, *Money power*.
72. De Brunhoff, *Marx*.
73. R. Hilferding, *Finance capital: A study of the latest phase of capitalist development* (London: Routledge, 1981), p. 21.
74. Cf. Lapavitsas, *Profiting*.

75. Hilferding, *Finance capital*, 225–6.
76. Ibid., 226.
77. De Brunhoff, *Marx*, 26.
78. Marx, *Capital*, Vol. 3, 640.
79. De Brunhoff, *Marx*, 74–5; Marx, *Capital*, Vol. 2, 420–1.
80. Marx, *Capital*, Vol. 2, 329.
81. Marx, *Contribution*, 190.
82. See Mau, *Mute compulsion*.
83. Marx, *Capital*, Vol. 1, 278.
84. Ibid., 278–9 n.14.
85. Ibid., 785.
86. Ibid., 794.
87. Ibid., 812.
88. Ibid., 840.
89. Ibid., 849.
90. Marx, *Capital*, Vol. 3, 461.
91. Ibid., 467.
92. W. Bonefeld, 'Money, equality, and exploitation: An interpretation of Marx's treatment of money', in W. Bonefeld and John Holloway, eds., *Global capital, national state and the politics of money* (New York: Palgrave Macmillan, 1997), p. 183; see also Paulani, 'Money'.
93. Marx, *Capital*, Vol. 3, 471.
94. Ibid., 516. See also Bonefeld, 'Capital *par excellence*'.
95. Harvey, *Limits*, 286, citing K. Marx, *Grundrisse* (London: Penguin, 1993), p. 623.
96. Harvey, *Limits*, 286.
97. G. Mann, 'Time, space, and money in capitalism and communism', *Human Geography* 1, no. 2 (2008), 4–12, p. 9.
98. Marx, *Grundrisse*, 623.
99. Cf. Paulani, 'Money'.
100. Bonefeld, 'Money', 193.
101. See Durand, *Fictitious capital*.

CHAPTER 3

1. On falling labour shares, see UNCTAD, *Trade and Development Report, 2022 - development prospects in a fractured world: Global disorder and regional responses* (Geneva: United Nations Conference on Trade and Development, 2022), p. 6.

2. See S. Schindler, T. Gillespie, N. Banks, M.K. Bayirbag, H. Burte, J.M. Kanai and N. Sami, 'Deindustrialization in cities of the global south', *Area Development and Policy* 5, no. 3 (2020), 283–304.

3. J. Green and S. Lavery, 'The regressive recovery: Distribution, inequality and state power in Britain's post-crisis political economy', *New Political Economy* 20, no. 6 (2015), 894–923.

4. H. Magdoff and P. Sweezy, *Stagnation and the financial explosion* (New York: Monthly Review Press, 1987); G. Arrighi *The long twentieth century: Money, power and the origins of our times* (London: Verso, 1994). See also Introduction and Chapter 1.

5. Brenner has been prolific with this argument, but it's most clearly articulated in R. Brenner, *The economics of global turbulence: The advanced capitalist economies from long boom to long downturn, 1945-2005* (London: Verso, 2006); an expanded version of a book-length article initially appearing in *New Left Review*, R. Brenner, 'The economics of global turbulence', *New Left Review* I/229 (1998); in the intervening years, Brenner makes a cognate argument, more focused on the US, in *The boom and the bubble: The US in the world economy* (London: Verso, 2003).

6. R. Brenner, 'Escalating plunder', *New Left Review* 123 (2020), 5–22.

7. I will come back to the role of the state in Chapter 5.

8. S.G. Cecchetti and E. Kharroubi, 'Reassessing the impact of finance on growth', *BIS Working Papers no. 381* (Basel: Bank for International Settlements, 2012).

9. E. Bengtussen and M. Ryner 'The (international) political economy of falling wage shares: Situating working class agency', *New Political Economy* 20 no. 3 (2015), 406–30; K.H. Lin and D. Tomaskevic-Devey, 'Financialization and US income inequality, 1970–2008', *American Journal of Sociology* 118, no. 5 (2013), 1284–329.

10. There is a growing parallel literature on the 'financialization' of peripheral economies, which tends to emphasize somewhat different dynamics. Lapavitsas emphasizes enforced financial liberalization, net capital flight, and accumulation of dollar reserves by central banks in developing countries in C. Lapavitsas, *Profiting without producing: How finance exploits us all* (London: Verso, 2013), pp. 245–7. This is not to imply that the picture is static or uniform. Ewa Karwowski, e.g., writes in detail about the variegated character of 'financialization' in emerging economies, see E. Karwowski, 'The regional distinctiveness and variegation of financialisation in emerging economies', *Cambridge Journal of Economics* 45, no. 5, 931–54. It's arguable that these dynamics are better understood in

terms of a longer-run dynamic of 'international financial subordination' rather than a contemporary trend of 'financialization', see K. Koddenbrock, I.H. Kvangraven and N.S. Sylla, 'Beyond financialisation: The longue durée of finance and production in the global south', *Cambridge Journal of Economics* 46, no. 4 (2022), 703–33; I. Alami, C. Alves, B. Bonizzi, A. Kaltenbrunner, K. Koddenbrock, I. Kvangraven and J. Powell 'International financial subordination: A critical research agenda', *Review of International Political Economy* 30, no. 4 (2023), 1360–86.

11. See especially G. Krippner, 'The financialization of the American economy', *Socio-Economic Review* 3, no. 2 (2005), 173–208.

12. On this point, see Koddenbrock et al., 'Beyond Financialisation'.

13. This point is a core finding and premise of frankly too much scholarship in various feminist, Third World Marxist, anti-imperialist and anti-racist traditions to cite adequately in one endnote. For foundational statements, notwithstanding different points of emphasis, it may be worth pointing readers to S. Amin, *Accumulation on a world scale* (New York: Monthly Review Press, 1974); M. Mies, *Patriarchy and accumulation on a world scale* (London: Zed Books, 1986); U. Patnaik and P. Patnaik, *A theory of imperialism* (New York: Columbia University Press, 2016); S. Hall, 'Race, articulation, and societies structured in domination', in *Sociological Theories: Race and Colonialism* (Paris: UNESCO, 1980), pp. 305–43. Some recent work emphasizes the ways that relations of racialization have also made possible the global extension of financial operations past and present, notably: P. Hudson, *Bankers and Empire: How Wall Street colonized the Caribbean* (Chicago: University of Chicago Press); L. Tilley, 'Extractive investibility in historical colonial perspective: The emerging market and its antecedents in Indonesia', *Review of International Political Economy* 28, no. 5 (2021), 1099–118; I. Alami and V. Guermond, 'The colour of money at the financial frontier', *Review of International Political Economy* 30, no. 3 (2023), 1073–97.

14. See especially J. Moore, *Capitalism in the web of life: Ecology and the accumulation of capital* (London: Verso, 2015).

15. Arrighi, *Long twentieth century*, 239.

16. Ibid., 239–41.

17. Ibid, cf. G. Arrighi, 'A crisis of hegemony', in S. Amin, G. Arrighi, A.G. Frank and I. Wallerstein, eds., *Dynamics of global crises* (London: Macmillan, 1982), pp. 55–108.

18. Magdoff and Sweezy, *Stagnation*, 145.

19. Ibid., 143.

20. P. Baran and P. Sweezy, *Monopoly capital: An essay on the American economic and social order* (New York: Monthly Review Press, 1966).
21. Magdoff and Sweezy, *Stagnation*, 147.
22. Ibid., 147.
23. Most notably, J.B. Foster, 'The financialization of capitalism', *Monthly Review*, 58 no. 11 (2007). Foster has also become one of the leading proponents of arguments about the 'financialization of nature', building very much on this vein of argument about finan-cialization and monopoly capitalism, e.g., Foster, 'The defense of nature: Resisting the financialization of the earth', *Monthly Review* 73, no. 11 (2022). I deal with this strand of argument further in the next chapter.
24. Brenner, *The boom and the bubble*, 10.
25. Ibid., 12.
26. Ibid., 17.
27. See especially Endnotes, 'Misery and debt: On the logic and history of surplus populations and surplus capital', *Endnotes 2: Misery and the value form* (London: Endnotes, 2010), p. 46; also A. Benanav, *Automation and the future of work* (London: Verso, 2020).
28. C. Durand, *Fictitious capital: How finance is appropriating our future* (London: Verso, 2014), p. 12. We could also point to, e.g., Postone's arguments about the crisis of value production discussed in the previous chapter, where the crisis of productive capital is likewise assumed rather than established; see M. Postone, 'The current crisis and the anachronism of value': A Marxian reading', *Continental Thought and Theory* 1, no. 4 (2017), 38–54.
29. This is less true of Endnotes, who do gesture towards a more genu-inely global analysis.
30. S. Clarke, *Keynesianism, monetarism and the crisis of the state* (Alder-shot: Edward Elgar, 1988), p. 122.
31. D. McNally, 'From financial crisis to global slump: Accumulation, financialization, and the global slowdown', *Historical Materialism* 17 (2009), 44.
32. See B. Christophers, *Banking across boundaries: Placing finance in capitalism* (Oxford: Wiley-Blackwell, 2013); D. Bryan, 'Global accu-mulation and accounting in national economic identity', *Review of Radical Political Economics* 33, no. 1 (2001), 57–77; I. Alami, *Money power and financial capital in emerging economies: Facing the liquid-ity tsunami* (London: Routledge, 2020); J. Smith, 'The GDP illusion: Value added versus value capture', *Monthly Review* 64, no. 3–4 (2012).

33. Parenthetically, this point is often well made by advocates of 'degrowth' – see M. Schmelzer, A. Vetter and A. Vansintjan, *The future is degrowth: A guide to a world beyond capitalism* (London: Verso, 2022), pp. 39–43 – but not carried through to the logical conclusion that 'growth' as such is also a poor explanation of capitalist socio-ecological degradation and destruction.

34. Christophers, *Banking*, 246. See also Alami, *Money power*.

35. Christophers, *Banking*; see also B. Christophers, 'Anaemic geographies of financialization', *New Political Economy* 17, no. 3 (2012), 271–91.

36. See Bryan, 'Global accumulation'; L. Linsi and D. Mügge, 'Globalization and the growing defects of international economic statistics', *Review of International Political Economy* 26, no. 3 (2019), 361–83.

37. See further discussion below. For excellent general discussions, see G. Starosta, 'Global commodity chains and the Marxian law of value', *Antipode* 42 no. 2 (2010), 433–65; B. Selwyn, 'Poverty chains and global capitalism', *Competition and Change* 23, no. 1 (2019), 71–97; K. Meagher, 'The scramble for Africans: Demography, globalisation and Africa's informal labour markers', *Journal of Development Studies* 52, no. 4 (2016), 483–97; N. Phillips, 'Labour in global production: Reflections on Coxian insights in a world of global value chains', *Globalizations* 13, no. 5 (2016), 594–607.

38. L. Seabrooke and D. Wigan, 'Global wealth chains in the international political economy', *Review of International Political Economy* 21, no. 1 (2014), 257–63; J. Bair, S. Ponte, L. Seabrooke and D. Wigan, 'Entangled chains of value and wealth', *Review of International Political Economy* (2023), doi:10.1080/09692290.2023.2220268.

39. Especially in Brenner, *The boom and the bubble*.

40. J. Copley, *Governing financialization: The tangled politics of financial liberalization in Britain* (Oxford: Oxford University Press, 2021). Discussed further in Chapter 5.

41. See S. Clarke, 'The value of value', *Capital and Class* 10, no. 1 (1979), 1–17.

42. N. Smith, *Uneven development: Nature, capital, and the production of space* (Oxford: Basil Blackwell, 1990).

43. K. Marx, *Capital, Vol. 1* (London: Penguin, 1990), p. 283. I return to a discussion of the ecological dimensions of this 'metabolism' and the production of capitalist natures in the next chapter. For now, the important point is that capitalist production is self-undermining and thus requires constant restructuring.

44. Smith, *Uneven development*, 92.

45. Ibid., 196.
46. See International Energy Agency, *Renewables 2023* (Paris: IEA, 2024), p. 71.
47. D. Harvey, *Limits to capital* (London: Verso, 2006), p. 427.
48. Marx, *Capital*, Vol. 1, Chapter 25.
49. See N. Bernards and S. Soederberg, 'Relative surplus populations and the crises of contemporary capitalism: Reviving, revisiting, recasting', *Geoforum* 126 (2021), 412–19.
50. J. O'Connor, 'Capitalism, nature, socialism: A theoretical introduction', *Capitalism, Nature, Socialism*, 1, no. 1 (1988), 11–38, p. 17. As Rudy notes, O'Connor is somewhat ambiguous here about whether the conditions of production, as such, are internal or external to capitalist relations of production: A.P. Rudy, 'On misunderstanding the second contradiction thesis', *Capitalism, Nature, Socialism* 30, no. 4 (2019), 17–35.
51. Rudy, 'Misunderstanding', 18.
52. O'Connor, 'Capitalism', 25.
53. Moore, *Capitalism*, 277–8.
54. Ibid., 25.
55. Ibid., 109.
56. Ibid., 3.
57. O'Connor, 'Capitalism', 26.
58. Smith, *Uneven development*, 150.
59. See Harvey, *Limits*, 415.
60. Most notably, P. Bond, *Uneven Zimbabwe: A study of finance, development, and underdevelopment* (Trenton: Africa World Press, 1998).
61. Moore, *Capital*, 104–5.
62. O'Connor, 'Capitalism', 27.
63. This point is developed at greater length in Bernards and Soederberg, 'Relative surplus populations'; cf. S. Soederberg, *Debtfare states and the poverty industry: Money, discipline and the surplus population* (London: Routledge, 2014).
64. See N. Bernards, *A critical history of poverty finance: Colonial roots and neoliberal failures* (London: Pluto Press, 2022), pp. 9–12.
65. Donald MacKenzie and colleagues' work on high-frequency trading is a particularly prominent example, which has paid special attention to the materiality of financial trading, see e.g., D. MacKenzie, 'A material political economy: Automated trading desk and price prediction in high-frequency trading', *Social Studies of Science* 47, no. 2 (2017), 172–94; D. MacKenzie, D. Buenza, Y. Millo and J. Pardo-Guerra, 'Drilling through the Allegheny Mountains: Liquidity,

materiality, and high frequency trading', *Journal of Cultural Economy* 5 no. 3 (2012), 279–96.

66. This point is made in N. Bernards and M. Campbell-Verduyn, 'Understanding technological change in global finance through infrastructures', *Review of International Political Economy* 26, no. 5 (2019), 773–89; B. Christophers, 'From Marx to market and back: Performing the economy', *Geoforum* 57 (2014), 12–20.

67. On the concept of financial infrastructures, see Bernards and Campbell-Verduyn, 'Understanding technological change'; Marieke de Goede, 'Finance/security infrastructures', *Review of International Political Economy* 28, no. (2021), 351–68.

68. One of the arguments in Brett Christophers' effort to reconsider Marxian value theory in light of finance (discussed in the last chapter) is that these kinds of labour are important to the production of financial value. As is probably clear from the last chapter I don't buy the entirety of the argument Christophers makes, but on this point he is correct. See B. Christophers, 'Risking value theory in the political economy of finance and nature', *Progress in Human Geography* 42, no. 3 (2018), 330–49.

69. See N. Bernards, "Colonial financial infrastructures and Kenya's uneven fintech boom', *Antipode* 54, no. 3 (2022), 708–28.

70. Alami et al., 'International financial subordination'.

71. The latter dynamic is examined brilliantly in Alami, *Money power*.

72. B. Bonizzi, A. Kaltenbrunner and J. Powell, 'Financialised capitalism and the subordination of emerging capitalist economies', *Cambridge Journal of Economics* 46, no. 4 (2022), 651–78; Starosta, 'Global commodity chains'.

73. See V. Smil, *Energy transitions: Global and national perspectives*, 2nd edn (Santa Barbara: Praeger, 2017), pp. 42–7; see also T. Mitchell, *Carbon democracy: Political power in the age of oil* (London: Verso, 2013); H. Thompson, *Disorder: Hard times in the twenty-first century* (Oxford: Oxford University Press, 2022).

74. This shift did not just happen, and must itself be understood as the product of the restructuring of capital accumulation, mediated though state action and geopolitical relations, not least the unfolding of late colonial imperialism. Andreas Malm has famously argued about the rise of coal at the expense of water power in preceding centuries, it was not that coal was necessarily a cheaper or more efficient source of energy than water, but rather that burning coal allowed capital far greater discipline over labour and greater control over the production process; see A. Malm, *Fossil capital: The rise of steam*

power and the roots of global warming (London: Verso, 2016). Coal aligned with the needs of capital for concentration and control over the labour process. We might say something very similar about oil, which was not necessarily cheaper or more efficient than coal, but could be transported over longer distances, and enabled the replacement of natural materials produced according to seasonal cycles with synthetic ones. But we have to start somewhere, and the consequences of the global oil boom are perhaps more important than its causes for present purposes.

75. Smil, *Energy transitions*, Appendix A.

76. A. Hanieh, 'Petrochemical empire: The geopolitics of fossil-fuelled production', *New Left Review* 130 (2021), 25–51.

77. Author calculation based on UNCTAD, *Review of Maritime Transport – 2007* (Geneva: United Nations Conference on Trade and Development, 2007), p. 7, table 3; cf. T. Mitchell, 'Carbon democracy', *Economy and Society* 38, no. 3 (2009), 399–432; p. 407.

78. See M. Huber, 'Oil, life, and the fetishism of geopolitics', *Capitalism Nature Socialism* 22, no. 3 (2011), 32–48.

79. Brett Christophers makes this point very clearly about the role of North Sea oil in enabling the Thatcherite experiment in privatization and financial deregulation in the UK. See B. Christophers, *Rentier capitalism: Who owns the economy and who pays for it?* (London: Verso, 2020), Chapter 2.

80. Yet another meaning frequently attached to 'financialization' is the tendency for mineral and agricultural commodity prices, not least oil, to be set by financial markets. This has been driven in no small part by the increased entry of institutional investors into trading in commodities. Though we can debate whether we should describe this as 'financialization', and should acknowledge that this is a more contested and failure-prone process than is often assumed, a substantial literature has shown that, as a result, commodity prices are both increasingly volatile and increasingly intercorrelated. See I.H. Cheng and W. Xiong, 'Financialisation of commodity markets', *Annual Review of Financial Economics* 6, no. 1 (2014), 419–41. On the limits to these processes, see N. Bernards, 'Child labour, cobalt, and the London Metal Exchange: Fetishes, fixing, and the limits of financialization', *Economy and Society* 50, no. 4 (2021), 542–64.

81. G. Bridge, 'Global production networks and the extractive sector: Governing resource-based development', *Journal of Economic Geography* 8 (2008), 402.

82. See especially P. Burnham, 'Capital, crisis and the international state system', in W. Bonefeld and J. Holloway, eds., *Global capital, national state, and the politics of money* (London: Macmillan, 1996), 92–116.

83. Adom Getachew reconstructs this connected critique of colonialism and project of 'worldmaking', with all its attendant contradictions, in great detail. See A. Getachew, *Worldmaking after empire: The rise and fall of self-determination* (Princeton: Princeton University Press, 2019).

84. F. Cooper, *Africa in the world: Capitalism, empire, nation-state* (Cambridge, MA: Harvard University Press), p. 91.

85. On the colonial state as a distinct form of capitalist state, see B. Berman, 'Structure and process in the bureaucratic states of colonial Africa', *Development and Change* 15, no. 1 (1984), 161–202; G. Capps, 'Custom and exploitation: Rethinking the origins of the modern African chieftancy in the political economy of colonialism', *Journal of Peasant Studies* 45, no. 5–6 (2018), 969–93.

86. Amin, *Accumulation on a world scale*, p. 438; see also N.S. Sylla, 'Fighting monetary colonialism in West Africa: Samir Amin's contribution', *Review of African Political Economy* 48, no. 167 (2021), 32–49.

87. V. Ogle, '"Funk money": The end of empires, the expansion of tax havens, and decolonization as an economic and financial event', *Past & Present* 249 (2020), 213–49, p. 214. For a more general theorization of the role of race in shaping global flows of finance capital, see Alami and Guermond, 'The colour of money'.

88. Ogle, 'Funk money', 227–30.

89. See N. Bernards, 'States, money and the persistence of colonial financial hierarchies in British West Africa', *Development and Change* 54, no. 1 (2023), 64–86.

90. Republic of Kenya, *African socialism and its application to planning in Kenya* (Nairobi: Government Printer, 1965), p. 19.

91. K. Currie and L. Ray, 'The Kenyan state, agribusiness and the peasantry', *Review of African Political Economy* 14 no. 38 (1987), 89–96, p. 90.

92. This history is traced out in more detail in Bernards, 'Colonial financial hierarchies'.

93. See A. Acker, 'A different story of the Anthropocene: Brazil's post-colonial quest for oil (1930–1975)', *Past & Present* 249 (2020), 167–211; M. Schutzer, 'Oil, money and decolonization in South Asia', *Past & Present* 258 (2023), 212–45; F. Dafe, 'Fuelled power: Oil,

financiers and central bank policy in Nigeria', *New Political Economy* 24, no. 5 (2019), 641–58.

94. Schutzer, 'Oil', 216.

95. S. Amin, 'After the New International Economic Order: The future of international economic relations', *Journal of Contemporary Asia* 12, no. 4 (1982), 432–50, p. 423.

96. On the wider history and significance of the Eurodollar markets, see E. Helleiner, *States and the re-emergence of global finance: From Bretton Woods to the 1990s* (Ithaca: Cornell University Press, 1994).

97. M. Campbell-Verduyn, M. Goguen and T. Porter, 'Finding fault-lines in long chains of financial information', *Review of International Political Economy* 26, no. 5, 911–37, p. 919.

98. Y. Altunbas, B. Gadanecz and A. Kara, 'The evolution of syndicated loan markets', *Service Industries Journal* 26, no. 6, 689–707.

99. The phrase 'ground clearing' here is Saskia Sassen's, from: 'A savage sorting of winners and losers: Contemporary versions of primitive accumulation', *Globalizations* 7, no. 1–2 (2010), 23–50.

100. C. Callahan and J.S. Mankin, 'Globally unequal effect of extreme heat on economic growth', *Science Advances* 8, no. 43 (2022), eadd3726.

101. See N. Bernards, '"Latent" surplus populations and colonial histories of drought, groundnuts and finance in Senegal', *Geoforum* 126 (2021), 441–50; N. Tousignant, 'Residual unprotection: Aflatoxin research and regulation in Senegal's postcolonial peanut infrastructures', *Globalizations* 20, no. 6 (2023), 932–49.

102. See R.L. Naylor, 'The Bryson synthesis: The forging of climate change narratives during the World Food Crisis', *Science in Context* 34 (2021), 375–91.

103. See M. Mackintosh, *Gender, class, and rural transition: Agribusiness and the food crisis in Senegal* (London: Zed Books, 1989).

104. This is also true of structural adjustment more generally, see N. Bernards, 'The World Bank, agricultural credit and the rise of neo-liberalism in global development', *New Political Economy* 27, no. 1 (2022), 116–31.

105. McNally, 'Financial crisis', 43.

106. M. Arboleda, *Planetary mine: Territories of extraction under late capitalism* (London: Verso, 2020).

107. His account draws heavily on R. Bevaqua, 'Whither the Japanese model? The Asian economic crisis and the continuation of Cold War politics in the Pacific Rim', *Review of International Political Economy* 5, no. 3 (1998), 410–23 and M. Bernard and J. Ravenhill, 'Beyond product cycles and flying geese: Regionalization, hierarchy, and

the industrialization of East Asia', *World Politics* 47, no. 2 (1995), 171–209.

108. Brenner, *The boom and the bubble*, 159.
109. Endnotes, 'Misery'.
110. G. Arrighi, *Adam Smith in Beijing: Lineages of the twenty-first century* (London: Verso, 2007).
111. I. Weber, *How China escaped shock therapy: The market reform debate* (London: Routledge, 2021). See also C. Muelbroek, 'Gillian Hart in Beijing: Negotiating capitalist models at the World Bank-China nexus', *Environment and Planning A: Economy and Space* 55, no. 5 (2023), 1218–38.
112. N. Pun and J. Chan, 'The spatial politics of labor in China: Life, labor, and a new generation of migrant workers', *South Atlantic Quarterly* 112, no. 1 (2013), 179–90.
113. Smil, *Energy transitions*, 42.
114. Starosta, 'Global commodity chains', 450–1.
115. This rapid urbanization is traced in vivid fashion in M. Davis, *Planet of slums* (London: Verso, 2007). See also T.M. Li, 'To make live or let die? Rural dispossession and the protection of surplus populations', *Antipode* 41 no. s1 (2009), 66–93.
116. C. Quentin and L. Campling, 'Global inequality chains: Integrating mechanisms of value distribution into analyses of global production', *Global Networks* 18, no. 1 (2018), 33–56, p. 43.
117. K.L. Kraemer, G. Linden and J. Dedrick, *Capturing value in global networks: Apple's iPad and iPhone* (University of California, Irvine, 2011).
118. J. Kollewe, 'Samsung to cut chip production as profits plunge by 96%', *Guardian*, 7 April 2023, available at: www.theguardian.com/technology/2023/apr/07/samsung-to-cut-chip-production-as-profits-plunge. 14 trillion won is slightly more than US$10 billion, 600 billion won is equivalent to under US$500 million.
119. See B. Selwyn and D. Leyden, 'World development under monopoly capitalism', *Monthly Review* 73, no. 6 (2021).
120. On concentrated corporate control of staple crops, see J. Clapp and J. Purugannan, 'Contextualizing corporate control in the agrifood and extractive sectors', *Globalizations* 17, no. 7 (2020), 1265–75; J. Clapp, 'Concentration and crises: Exploring the deep roots of vulnerability in the global industrial food system', *Journal of Peasant Studies* 50, no. 1 (2023), 1–25. There is a vast literature on the depredations of contract agriculture, e.g.: J. Guthman, 'Life itself under contract: Rent-seeking and biopolitical devolution in California's strawberry

industry', *Journal of Peasant Studies* 44, no. 1 (2017), 100–17; A.Y. Iddrisu, S. Ouma and J.A. Yaro, 'When agricultural commercialization fails: "Re-visiting" value-chain agriculture and its ruins in Northern Ghana', *Globalizations* (2022), doi:10.1080/14747731.202 2.2135423; F. Mazwi, *The political economy of contract farming in Zimbabwe* (Cape Town: HSRC Press, 2022). A classic collection is P. Little and M. Watts, eds., *Living under contract: Contract farming and agrarian transformation in sub-Saharan Africa* (Madison: University of Wisconsin Press, 1994).

121. P. McMichael, 'Value chain agriculture and debt relations: Contradictory outcomes', *Third World Quarterly* 34, no. 4 (2013), 671–90.

122. On the intersections of waged work, informal labour, and social reproduction, see A. Mezzadri, 'A value theory of inclusion: Informal labour, the homeworker, and the social reproduction of value', *Antipode* 53, no. 4 (2021), 1186–205.

123. Selwyn, 'Poverty chains and global capitalism'.

124. E. Baglioni, 'The making of cheap labour across production and reproduction: Control and resistance in the Senegalese horticultural value chain', *Work, Employment and Society* 36, no. 3 (2021), 445–64.

125. See J.F. Gerber, 'The role of rural indebtedness in the evolution of capitalism', *Journal of Peasant Studies* 41, no. 5 (2014), 729–47. Jairus Banaji has also made similar arguments, emphasizing the long-run role of relations of indebtedness in structuring the incorporation of peasant production into global circuits of commercial capitalism. See J. Banaji, 'Capitalist domination of the small peasantry: Deccan districts in the late nineteenth-century', *Economic and Political Weekly* 12 no. 33/34 (1977), 1375–404 and 'Merchant capitalism, peasant households and industrial accumulation: Integration of a model', *Journal of Agrarian Change* 16 no. 3 (2016), 410–31.

126. See McMicheal, 'Value-chain agriculture'.

127. K. Brickell, S. Lawreniuk, T. Chhom, R. Mony, H. So and L. McCarthy, '"Worn out": Debt discipline, hunger, and the gendered contingencies of the COVID-19 pandemic amongst Cambodian garment workers', *Social and Cultural Geography* 24, no. 3–4 (2023), 600–19.

128. D. James and D. Rajak, 'Credit apartheid, migrants, mines, and money', *African Studies* 73, no. 3 (2014), 455–76.

129. J. Schräten, 'The transformation of the South African credit market', *Transformation* 85 (2014), 1–20.

130. See P. Bond, 'Debt, uneven development and capitalist crisis in South Africa: From Moody's macroeconomic monitoring to Marikana

microfinance *Mashonisas*, *Third World Quarterly* 34, no. 4 (2013), 569–92.

131. G. Moncur and S. Jones, 'The South African mining industry in the 1970s', *South African Journal of Economic History* 14, no. 1–2 (1999), 114–42, p. 118.

132. A. Bowman, 'Financialization and the extractive industries: The case of South African platinum mining', *Competition and Change* 22, no. 4 (2018), 388–412.

133. B. Kenny and A. Bezuidenhout, 'Contracting, complexity, and control: An overview of the changing nature of subcontracting in the South African mining industry', *Journal of the South African Institute of Mining and Metallurgy* (1999) (July/August), 185–91.

134. K. Forrest, 'Rustenburg's labour recruitment regime: Shifts and new meanings', *Review of African Political Economy* 42 no. 146 (2015), 508–25.

135. Ibid., 515.

136. C. Chinguno, *Marikana and the Post-Apartheid Workplace Order* (Johannesburg: Society, Work, and Development Institute, 2013), p. 10.

137. A. Bezuidenhout and S. Buhlungu, 'Enclave Rustenburg: Platinum mining and the post-Apartheid social order', *Review of African Political Economy* 42 no. 146 (2015), 526–44.

138. L. Steyn, 'Marikana miners in debt sinkhole', *Mail & Guardian*, 7 September 2012, available at: https://mg.co.za/article/2012-09-07-00-marikana-miners-in-debt-sinkhole.

139. E. Baglioni, L. Campling and G. Hanlon, 'Global value chains as entrepreneurial capture: Insights from management theory', *Review of International Political Economy* 27, no. 4 (2020), 903–25, p. 906.

140. Starosta, 'Global commodity chains', 451.

141. See C. Quentin, 'Global production and the crisis of the tax state', *Environment and Planning A: Economy and Space* (2022), doi:10.1177/0308518X221105083; M. Ylönen and T. Teivainen, 'Politics of intra-firm trade: Corporate price planning and the double role of the arm's-length principle', *New Political Economy* 23, no. 4 (2018), 441–57; Quentin and Campling, 'Global inequality chains'; Bair et al., 'Entangled chains'.

142. R. Lanz and S. Miroudot, 'Intra-firm trade: Patterns, determinants, and policy implications', *OECD Trade Policy Papers no. 114* (Paris: OECD, 2011), p. 47.

143. M. Brulhart, 'An account of global intra-industry trade, 1962–2006', *The World Economy* 32, no. 3 (2009), 401–59.

144. Ibid., 426. Brulhart defines industries based on the UN's 'Standard International Trade Classification' – which assigns numerical codes to different categories of trade products. The codes work on a branching basis, so that a 'three-digit' code refers to a general category of product, and a 'five-digit' code to a more specific item. For instance, in the most recent revision, the three-digit code 841 refers to men's clothing, while 841.51 refers to 'Shirts of cotton' and 841.59 to 'Shirts of textile materials other than cotton'. The figure reported in the text above is for the more restrictive 'five-digit' codes; the more expansive figure based on three-digit codes – probably a more realistic measure of how firms are actually organized in most cases – shows a more-than-doubling from 20.3 per cent of goods traded 'intra-industry' in 1962 and 43.7 per cent in 2006.

145. D. Bryan, M. Rafferty and D. Wigan, 'Capital unchained: Finance, intangible assets and the double life of capital in the offshore world', *Review of International Political Economy* 24, no. 1 (2017), 56–86, p. 61.

146. K.A. Clausing, 'The effect of profit shifting on the corporate tax base in the United States and beyond', *National Tax Journal* 69, no. 4 (2016), 905–34.

147. L. Wier and G. Zucman, 'Global profit shifting, 1975–2019', UNU-WIDER Working Paper 2022/21 (Helsinki: United Nations University World Institute for Development Economics Research, 2022).

148. E. LiPuma and B. Lee, 'Financial derivatives and the rise of circulation', *Economy and Society* 34, no. 3 (2005), 404–27.

149. See Bank for International Settlements, *OTC derivatives statistics at end-December 2022* (Basel: BIS, 2023).

150. See D. Cowen, 'A geography of logistics: Market authority and the security of supply chains', *Annals of the American Association of Geographers* 100, no. 3 (2010), 600–20; M. Arboleda and T. Purcell, 'The turbulent circulation of rent: Towards a political economy of property and ownership in supply chain capitalism', *Antipode* 53, no. 6 (2021), 1599–618.

151. M. Danyluk, 'Capital's logistical fix: Accumulation, globalization and the survival of capitalism', *Environment and Planning D: Society and Space*, 36, no. 4 (2018), 630–47, p. 640; cf. Arboleda and Purcell, 'Turbulent circulation'.

152. These figures are all from International Energy Agency, *International Shipping* (Paris: IEA, 2022).

153. On this point, see also Bonizzi et al., 'Financialised capitalism'.

154. On the latter point, see J. Rabinovich, 'The financialization of the non-financial corporation: A critique of the *financial turn of accumulation* hypothesis', *Metroeconomica* 70, no. 4 (2019), 738–75; G. Liagouras, 'Beyond corporate financialization: From global value chains to the conundrum of intangible investments', *Competition and Change* 27, no. 5 (2023), 685–706.

CHAPTER 4

1. Futures can serve as means for producers or buyers to hedge against fluctuations in price. If you're planning to plant, say, a field of wheat, and know that you will have wheat to sell in six months' time, it can be useful to lock in a price now. Especially if you need to take out a loan to buy seeds, fertilizer, and the like before planting. Prices fluctuate, and from the farmer's perspective, a lower than expected price can be every bit as devastating as a crop failure. But futures are also potentially mechanisms for speculation – that is, you can also buy wheat futures as a way to bet that prices will be higher or lower than the contract specifies, and potentially profit from the difference between actual spot prices for wheat in six months and the futures price. But it's important to underline that, although futures contracts allow for purely speculative gains, the possibility of speculation on futures markets is intimately linked to the spatial and temporal disjunctures of the production process for underlying commodities.
2. S. Martin and J. Clapp, 'Finance for agriculture or agriculture for finance?', *Journal of Agrarian Change* 15, no. 4 (2015), 549–59.
3. Quoted in N. Averett, 'Yes, people are now trading and investing in water as a commodity', *Discover Magazine*, 23 October 2021, available at: www.discovermagazine.com/environment/yes-people-are-now-trading-and-investing-in-water-as-a-commodity.
4. UNHCR (2020), *Press Release – Water: Futures market invites speculators, challenges basic human rights – UN Expert*, available at: www.ohchr.org/en/press-releases/2020/12/water-futures-market-invites-speculators-challenges-basic-human-rights-un?LangID=E&NewsID=26595.
5. UNHCR (2021), *Joint statement by independent UN human rights experts warning of the threat that financial speculation poses to the enjoyment of a range of human rights*, available at: www.ohchr.org/en/statements/2021/10/joint-statement-independent-united-nations-human-rights-experts-warning-threat.

6. Quoted in C. Hodgson, 'Water futures meet cool reception', *Financial Times*, 15 October 2020, available at: www.ft.com/content/016174d0-54ed-4806-9538-acbdf073df61.

7. See J.B. Foster, 'The defense of nature: Resisting the financialization of the earth', *Monthly Review* 73, no. 11 (2022); FoEI, *Friends of the Earth International's position paper on the financialization of nature* (Amsterdam: FoEI, 2014).

8. K. McAfee, 'Selling nature to save it? Biodiversity and green developmentalism', *Environment and Planning D: Society and Space* 17, no. 2 (1999), 133–54.

9. J. Dempsey and D.C. Suarez, 'Arrested development? The promises and paradoxes of "selling nature to save it"', *Annals of the American Association of Geographers* 106, no. 3 (2016), 653–71, p. 654.

10. J. Moore, *Capitalism in the web of life: Ecology and the accumulation of capital* (London: Verso, 2015), p. 2.

11. For major statements on the 'metabolic rift' concept, see J.B. Foster, *Marx's ecology: Materialism and nature* (New York: Monthly Review Press, 2000); A. Malm, *The progress of this storm: Nature and society in a warming world* (London: Verso, 2018); K. Saito, *Marx in the Anthropocene: Towards the idea of degrowth communism* (Cambridge: Cambridge University Press, 2023).

12. K. Marx, *Capital, Vol. 1* (London: Penguin, 1990), pp. 637–8.

13. Foster, *Marx's ecology*, 163.

14. Ibid., 163.

15. Ibid., 174.

16. Saito, *Marx*, 24.

17. Ibid., 28.

18. Most notably in Moore, *Capitalism*. The point about a capital-nature dialectic is expanded in J. Moore, 'Metabolic rift or metabolic shift? Dialectics, nature, and the world historical method', *Theory and Society* 46 (2017), 285–318.

19. A. Malm, 'Against hybridism: Why we need to distinguish between nature and society now more than ever', *Historical Materialism* 27, no. 2 (2019), 156–87, p. 176, emphasis in original; cf. Malm, *Progress*.

20. Saito insists on much the same, see *Marx*, 122–5.

21. Nor, to be fair, is a facile insistence on monism really the main focus of Moore's critiques of the metabolic rift thesis. Which, we ought to note, have also generally been much more conciliatory than the replies – see notably Moore, 'Metabolic rift'.

22. Kai Heron, in a related critique, notes the 'insufficiently materialist' conception of 'nature' underlying the metabolic rift, insisting on

the necessarily 'incomplete' character of nature itself. See K. Heron, 'Dialectical materialisms, metabolic rifts and the climate crisis: A Lacanian/Hegelian perspective', *Science and Society* 85, no. 4 (2021), 501–26.

23. J. Moore, 'Transcending the metabolic rift: A theory of crises in the capitalist world-ecology', *Journal of Peasant Studies* 38, no. 1 (2011), 1–46, p. 8.
24. Ibid., 12, emphasis in original.
25. Foster, 'The defence of nature'.
26. H. Magdoff and P. Sweezy, *Stagnation and the financial explosion* (New York: Monthly Review Press, 1987).
27. Foster, 'The defence of nature'.
28. J.B. Foster, 'Nature as a mode of accumulation: Capitalism and the financialization of the earth', *Monthly Review* 73, no. 10 (2022).
29. Foster, 'Defence of nature'. Foster introduces the concept of the 'metabolic rift' elsewhere in the article, emphasizing the growing displacement under capitalism of production for use values by production for exchange value. He doesn't make the connection explicit in the quoted passage, but it seems a fair inference to make.
30. C. Lapavitsas, 'Financialised capitalism: Crisis and financial expropriation', *Historical Materialism* 17, no. 1 (2009), 114–48, p. 126.
31. Foster, 'Nature as a mode of accumulation'.
32. J. Knox-Hayes, "The spatial and temporal dynamics of value in financialization: Analysis of the infrastructure of carbon markets', *Geoforum* 50 (2013) 117–28, p. 121.
33. S. Bracking, 'Financialisation, climate finance, and the calculative challenges of managing environmental change', *Antipode* 51, no. 3 (2019), 709–29.
34. M. Arboleda and T. Purcell, 'The rentierization of food: Regimes of property and the making of Chile's global agriculture', *Journal of Peasant Studies* 50, no. 5 (2023), 1924–44.
35. J. Clapp, 'Financialization, distance, and global food politics', *Journal of Peasant Studies* 41, no. 5 (2014), 797–814, p. 800.
36. Bracking, 'Financialisation', 723.
37. Though, arguably again a case where the analytic value of the argument comes despite rather than because of its articulation in terms of 'financialization'.
38. K. Marx, *Capital, Vol. 3* (London: Penguin, 1991), p. 516.
39. See P. McMichael, 'Value chain agriculture and debt relations: Contradictory outcomes', *Third World Quarterly* 34, no. 4 (2013), 671–90.

40. On this point, see S. Ouma, L. Johnson and P. Bigger, 'Rethinking the financialization of "nature"', *Environment and Planning A: Economy and Space* 50, no. 3 (2018), 500–11.
41. See K. Bakker, 'A political ecology of water privatization', *Studies in Political Ecology* 70 (2003), 35–58, pp. 46–8.
42. S. Ouma, 'Getting between M and M' or: How farmland further debunks financialization', *Dialogues in Human Geography* 5, no. 2 (2015), 225–8, p. 226; see also S. Ouma, 'From financialization to operations of capital: Historicizing and disentangling the finance-farmland nexus', *Geoforum* 72 (2014), 82–93 and *Farming as financial asset: Global finance and the making of institutional landscapes* (Newcastle: Agenda, 2020).
43. P. Woodhouse, 'New investment, old challenges: Land deals and the water constraint in African agriculture', *Journal of Peasant Studies* 39, no. 3–4 (2012), 777–94.
44. Quoted in C. Hodgson, 'Water futures'.
45. McAfee, 'Selling nature'.
46. CME Group, *Understanding the water futures market* (Chicago: Chicago Mercantile Exchange Group, 2021), p. 3.
47. J. Mount, E. Hanak and C. Peterson, *Water use in California* (San Francisco: Public Policy Institute of California, 2018).
48. Ibid.
49. C. Peterson, A. Escriva-Bou, J. Medellin-Azuara and S. Cole, *Water use in California's agriculture* (San Francisco: Public Policy Institute of California, 2023).
50. CME Group, *Water futures market*, 6.
51. PPIC, *California's water* (San Francisco: Public Policy Institute of California, 2018), p. 44.
52. I. James, 'California says $2.6 billion pact can protect delta amidst drought. Critics disagree', *Los Angeles Times*, 1 April 2022, available at: www.latimes.com/california/story/2022-04-01/a-2-6-billion-drought-deal-is-drawing-fire-in-california.
53. J. Sizek, 'Regulatory alchemy: How the water cycle becomes capital in the California desert', *Antipode* 55, no. 6 (2023), 1898-1918.
54. T. Claire and K. Surprise, 'Moving the rain: Settler colonialism, the capitalist state, and the hydrological rift in California's Central Valley', *Antipode* 54, no. 1 (2022), 153–73, p. 169.
55. G. Henderson, 'Nature and fictitious capital: The historical geography of an agrarian question', *Antipode* 30, no. 2 (1998), 73–118, pp. 95–6.
56. Moore, *Capital*.

57. Ibid., 63.
58. Marx, *Capital, Vol. 3*, 754.
59. Ibid., 756.
60. Ibid., 944–5.
61. K. Marx, *Capital, Vol. 1* (London: Penguin, 1990), p. 1019.
62. Ibid., 1021.
63. Ibid., 1021, emphasis in original.
64. This argument is developed especially clearly in J. Banaji, 'Capitalist domination and the small peasantry: Deccan districts in the late nineteenth century', *Economic and Political Weekly* 12 no. 33–4 (1977): 1375–404.
65. H. Bernstein, 'Notes on Capital and Peasantry' *Review of African Political Economy* 4, no. 10 (1977), 60–73, p. 61.
66. W. Boyd, W.S. Prudham, R.A. Schurman, 'Industrial dynamics and the problem of nature', *Society and Natural Resources* 14, no. 7 (2001), 555–70.
67. Ibid., 563.
68. On this point, see also D. Banoub, G. Bridge, B. Bustos, I. Ertör, M. González-Hidalgo and J.A. de los Reyes, 'Industrial dynamics on the commodity frontier: Managing time, space and form in mining, tree plantations and intensive aquaculture', *Environment and Planning E: Nature and Space* 4, no. 4 (2021), 1533–59.
69. On this point see J.F. Gerber, 'The Role of Rural Indebtedness in the Evolution of Capitalism', *Journal of Peasant Studies* 41, no. 5 (2014): 729–47; W.N. Green, 'Financing agrarian change: Geographies of credit and debt in the global south', *Progress in Human Geography* 46, no. 3 (2022), 849–69.
70. Henderson, 'Nature and fictitious capital', 76.
71. M. Fairbarn, *Fields of gold: Financing the global land rush* (Ithaca: Cornell University Press, 2020), p. 2, emphasis in original.
72. T.M. Li, 'What is land? Assembling a resource for global investment', *Transactions of the Institute of British Geographers* 39, no. 4 (2014), 589–602, p. 589.
73. S. Ouma, 'Defetishizing the asset form', *Dialogues in Human Geography* 14, no. 1 (2024), 30-33.
74. R.S. Dieng, 'Adversely incorporated yet moving up the social ladder? Labour migrants shifting the gaze from agricultural investment chains to "care chains" in capitalist social reproduction in Senegal', *Africa Development* XLVII, no. 3 (2022), 133–66.

75. B. Bhandar, *Colonial lives of property: Law, land, and racial regimes of ownership* (Durham, NC: Duke University Press, 2018), see esp. Chapter 2.
76. Ouma, *Farming as financial asset*, 29.
77. K.S. Park, 'Money, mortgages, and the conquest of America', *Law & Social Inquiry* 41, no. 4 (2016), 1006–35, pp. 1007–8.
78. C. Cumming, 'How finance colonized Aotearoa: A concise counter-history', *Counterfutures* 7 (2019), 40–72, p. 42; cf. C. Comyn, 'Te Peeke o Aotearoa: Colonial and decolonial finance in Aotearoa New Zealand, 1860s–1890s', in P. Gilbert, C. Bourne, M. Haiven and J. Montgomerie, eds., *The entangled legacies of empire: Race, finance and inequality* (Manchester: Manchester University Press, 2023), 73–88; C. Comyn, *The financial colonization of Aotearoa* (Auckland: Economic and Social Research Aotearoa, 2022).
79. Ouma, *Farming*, 30.
80. The following paragraphs are adapted from N. Bernards, 'Colonial financial infrastructures and Kenya's uneven fintech boom', *Antipode* 54, no. 3 (2022), 708–28.
81. P. Van Zwanenberg, 'Kenya's primitive colonial capitalism: The economic weakness of Kenya's settlers up to 1940', *Canadian Journal of African Studies* 9, no. 2 (1975), 277–92.
82. A. Manji, *The struggle for land and justice in Kenya* (London: James Currey, 2020), p. 32.
83. S. Coldham, 'Colonial policy and the highlands of Kenya, 1934–1944', *Journal of African Law* 23, no. 1 (1979), 65–83.
84. Government of India, *Correspondence regarding the position of Indians in East Africa (Kenya and Uganda)* (London: HM Stationery Office, 1920).
85. K. Kanyinga, 'The legacy of the White Highlands: Land rights, ethnicity and the post-2007 election violence in Kenya', *Journal of Contemporary African Studies* 27, no. 3 (2009), 325–44, p. 328.
86. W.T.W. Morgan, 'The "White Highlands" of Kenya', *The Geographical Journal* 129, no. 2 (1963), 140–55, pp. 146–7.
87. M.C. Coray, 'The Kenya Land Commission and the Kikuyu of Kiambu', *Agricultural History* 52, no. 1 (1978), 178–93.
88. East African Protectorate, *Correspondence related to the tenure of land in the East African Protectorate* (London: HM Stationery Office, 1930).
89. J. Lonsdale and B. Berman, 'Coping with the contradictions: the development of the colonial state in Kenya, 1895-1914', *Journal of African History* 20, no. 4 (1979), 487–505, p. 499.

90. Van Zwanenberg, 'Primitive colonial capitalism', 280.
91. B.J. Berman and J.M. Lonsdale, 'Crises of accumulation, coercion, and the colonial state: The development of the labour control system in Kenya, 1919–1929', *Canadian Journal of African Studies* 14, no. 1 (1981), 55–81, p. 62.
92. M. Cowen, 'Before and after Mau Mau in Kenya', *Journal of Peasant Studies* 16, no. 2 (1989), 260–75, p. 264.
93. See J.J. Jørgensen, 'Multinational corporations and the indigenization of the Kenyan economy', in C. Widsrand, ed., *Multinational firms in Africa* (Uppsala: Scandinavian Institute for African Studies, 1975), p. 150.
94. S. Aaronovitch and K. Aaronovitch, *Crisis in Kenya* (London: Camelot Press, 1947), 178.
95. D. Anderson and D. Throup, 'Africans and agricultural production in colonial Kenya: The myth of the war as a watershed', *The Journal of African History* 26, no. 4 (1985), 327–45.
96. D. Anderson, *Histories of the hanged: Britain's dirty war in Kenya and the end of empire* (London: Weidenfeld and Nicholson, 2005).
97. See Manji, *The struggle for land and justice*; B. Van Arkadie, 'Reflections on land policy and the independence settlement in Kenya', *Review of African Political Economy* 43, no. s1 (2016), 60–8; S.B.O. Gutto, 'Law, rangelands, the peasantry and social classes in Kenya', *Review of African Political Economy* 8, no. 20 (1981), 41–56; A. Njonjo, 'The Kenya peasantry: A re-assessment', *Review of African Political Economy* 8, no. 20 (1981), 27–40, for detailed discussions of land policy and political independence. On the connections between the historic privatization and commodification of land and water with intersecting conflicts over land and water access, see K. Mkutu Agade, D. Anderson, K. Lugusa and E. Atieno Owino, 'Water governance, institutions and conflicts in the Masaii rangelands', *Journal of Environment and Development* 31, no. 4 (2022), 395–420; K. Kanyinga, O. Lumumba and K. Amanor, 'The struggle for sustainable land management and democratic development in Kenya: A history of greed and grievances', in K. Amanor and S. Moyo, eds., *Land and sustainable development in Africa* (London: Zed Books, 2010), pp. 100–26.

CHAPTER 5

1. E.g., S. Clarke, ed., *The state debate* (New York: Palgrave Macmillan, 1991); or more recently, R. Hunter, R. Khatucharian and E. Nanop-

oulos, eds., *Marxism and the capitalist state: Towards a new debate* (New York: Palgrave Macmillan, 2023).

2. See also J. Dempsey and D.C. Suarez, 'Arrested development? The promises and paradoxes of "selling nature to save it"', *Annals of the American Association of Geographers* 106, no. 3 (2016), 653–71.

3. A. Gramsci, *Selections from the prison notebooks*, Q. Hoare and G. Nowell Smith, eds. and trans. (New York: International Publishers, 1971).

4. H. Magdoff and P. Sweezy, *Stagnation and the financial explosion* (New York: Monthly Review Press, 1987).

5. This is a recurrent theme in R. Brenner, *The boom and the bubble: The US in the world economy* (London: Verso, 2003) in particular.

6. See R. Brenner, 'Escalating plunder', *New Left Review* 123 (2020), 5–22, discussed in Chapter 3.

7. G. Arrighi, *The long twentieth century: Money, power, and the origins of our times* (London: Verso, 1994), p. 319.

8. J. Copley, *Governing financialization: The tangled politics of financial liberalization in Britain* (Oxford: Oxford University Press, 2022), pp. 9–13 outlines a similar critique.

9. E. Helleiner, *States and the re-emergence of global finance* (Ithaca: Cornell University Press, 1994).

10. G. Krippner, *Capitalizing on crisis: The political origins of the rise of finance* (Cambridge, MA: Harvard University Press, 2011); Copley, *Governing financialization*.

11. Krippner, *Capitalizing*, 16–23.

12. Ibid., 59.

13. Ibid., 2.

14. Ibid., 22–3.

15. Copley, *Governing financialization*, 13.

16. Ibid., 24.

17. G. Mann, 'State of confusion: Money and the space of civil society in Hegel and Gramsci', in M. Ekers, G. Hart, S. Kipfer and A. Loftus, eds., *Gramsci: Space, nature, politics* (Sussex: Wiley, 2014), pp. 104–19, p. 118.

18. See E. Helleiner, 'Historicizing territorial currencies: Monetary space and the nation-state in North America', *Political Geography* 18, no. 3 (1999), 309–39; E. Gilbert, 'Common cents: Situating money in time and place', *Economy and Society* 34, no. 3 (2005), 357–88.

19. M. Mann, 'The autonomous power of the state: Its origins, mechanisms, and results', *European Journal of Sociology* 25, no. 2 (1984), 185–213, p. 192.

20. D. Gabor, 'The impossible repo trinity: The political economy of repo markets', *Review of International Political Economy* 23, no. 6 (2016), 967–1000.

21. C. Alves, 'Fictitious capital, the credit system, and the particular case of government bonds in Marx', *New Political Economy* 28, no. 3, 398–415, p. 410.

22. J. Copley and A. Moraitis, 'Beyond the mutual constitution of states and markets: The governance of alienation', *New Political Economy* 26, no. 3 (2021), 490–508.

23. Copley, *Governing financialization*, 24.

24. S. Clarke, *Kenynesianism, monetarism, and the crisis of the state* (Aldershot: Edward Elgar, 1988), p. 143.

25. K. Marx, *Capital, Vol. 1* (London: Penguin, 1990), p. 241.

26. M. Ivanova 'The dollar as world money', *Science and Society* 77, no. 1 (2013), 51–2.

27. Marx, *Capital, Vol. 1*, 244. Marx saw gold and silver as serving the function of 'world money' in practice in the nineteenth century; but, as Ivanova notes, 'the fundamental feature of Marx's theory of money is not its commodity-based character, but its conception of money as the social expression of value'; Ivanova, 'The dollar', 45.

28. See Copley and Moraitis, 'Mutual constitution'.

29. I. Alami, *Money power and financial capital in emerging markets: Facing the liquidity* tsunami (London: Routledge, 2020), p. 70.

30. Ibid., 73.

31. See Ivanova, 'The dollar'; Alami, *Money power*; 'On the terrorism of money and national policy-making in emerging capitalist economies', *Geoforum* 96 (2018), 21–31; and 'Money power of capital and the production of "new state spaces": A view from the global south', *New Political Economy* 23, no. 4 (2018), 512–29; K. Koddenbrock, 'Hierarchical multiplicity in the international monetary system: From the slave trade to the CFA franc in West Africa', *Globalizations* 17, no. 3 (2020), 516–31; D. McNally, 'The blood of the Commonwealth: War, the state and the making of world money', *Historical Materialism* 22, no. 2 (2014), 3–32.

32. Ivanova, 'The dollar'.

33. E. Helleiner, 'Political determinants of international currencies: What future for the US dollar?', *Review of International Political Economy* 15, no. 3 (2008), 354–78.

34. A. Kaltenbrunner and J.P. Paincera, 'Subordinated financial integration and financialization in emerging capitalist economies:

The Brazilian experience', *New Political Economy* 23, no. 3 (2018), 290–313. p. 294.

35. Koddenbrock, 'Hierarchical multiplicity', 522.

36. See Koddenbrock, 'Hierarchical multiplicity'; N. Bernards, 'States, money, and the persistence of colonial financial hierarchies in British West Africa', *Development and Change* 54, no. 1 (2023), 64–86.

37. P. Burnham, 'Capital, crisis and the international state system', in W. Bonefeld and J. Holloway, eds., *Global capital, national state, and the politics of money* (London: Macmillan, 1995), p. 93.

38. Clarke, *Kenynesianism, monetarism, and the crisis of the state*, 122.

39. Ibid., 122.

40. Ibid., 123.

41. Ibid., 128.

42. J. O'Connor, 'Capitalism, nature, socialism: A theoretical introduction', *Capitalism, Nature, Socialism*, 1, no. 1 (1988), 11–38.

43. Burnham, 'International state system'.

44. K. Tienhaara and J. Walker, 'Fossil capital, "unquantifiable risks" and neoliberal nationalizations: The case of the Trans Mountain Pipeline in Canada', *Geoforum* 124 (2021), 120–31.

45. See N. Bernards and S. Soederberg, "Relative surplus populations and the crises of contemporary capitalism: Reviving, revisiting, recasting', *Geoforum* 126 (2021), 412–19.

46. S. de Brunhoff, *States, capital and economic policy* (Pluto Press, 1978), p. 13.

47. Ibid., 19.

48. See S. Hall, C. Critcher, T. Jefferson, J. Clarke and B. Robert, *Policing the crisis: Mugging, the state, and law and order* (London: Springer, 1978/2013); see also I. Danewid, 'Policing the (migrant) crisis: Stuart Hall and the defence of whiteness', *Security Dialogue* 53, no. 1 (2022), 21–37; R. Shilliam, 'Enoch Powell: Britain's first neoliberal politician', *New Political Economy* 26, no. 2 (2021), 239–49.

49. R.W. Gilmore, 'Globalisation and US prison growth: From military Keynesianism to post-Keynesian militarism', *Race and Class* 40, no. 2–3 (1998), 171–88; 'Fatal couplings of power and difference: Notes on racism and geography', *The Professional Geographer* 54, no. 1 (2002), 15–24; *Golden gulag: Prisons, surplus, crisis and opposition in globalizing California* (Berkeley: University of California Press, 2007).

50. M. Burowoy, 'The functions and reproduction of migrant labor: Comparative material from Southern Africa and the United States', *American Journal of Sociology* 81, no. 5 (1976), 1050–87.

51. R. Ziadah and A. Hanieh, 'Misperceptions of the border: Migration, race and class today', *Historical Materialism* 32, no. 3 (2023), 33–68, p. 49, emphasis in original.

52. S. Soederberg, *Debtfare states and the poverty industry: Money, discipline, and the surplus population* (London: Routledge, 2014).

53. A. Bhagat and R. Phillips, 'The techfare state: Debt, discipline and accelerated neoliberalism', *New Political Economy* 28, no. 4 (2023), 526–38.

54. Burnham, 'Capital, crisis and the international state system', 103.

55. See S. Piccioto, 'International transformations of the capitalist state', *Antipode* 43, no. 1 (2011), 87–107.

56. Burnham, 'International state system', 105.

57. See G. Hart, 'Development critiques in the 1990s: *Culs de sac* and promising paths', *Progress in Human Geography* 25, no. 4 (2001), 649–58.

58. Ibid., 650.

59. See N. Bernards, 'The World Bank, agricultural credit and the rise of neoliberalism in global development', *New Political Economy* 27, no. 1 (2022), 116–31; *A critical history of poverty finance: Colonial roots and neoliberal failures* (London: Pluto Press, 2022).

60. See N. Woods, *The globalizers: The IMF, the World Bank, and their borrowers* (Ithaca: Cornell University Press, 2006).

61. C. Quentin, 'Global production and the crisis of the tax state', *Environment and Planning A: Economy and Space* (2022), doi:10.1177/0308518X221105083.

62. I'll say a bit more about the concept of 'relations of force' in the next chapter.

63. Gramsci, *Prison notebooks*, 184–5.

64. See I. Bruff, 'The rise of authoritarian neoliberalism', *Rethinking Marxism* 26, no. 1 (2014), 113–29; I. Bruff and C.B. Tansel, 'Authoritarian neoliberalism: Trajectories of knowledge production and praxis', *Globalizations* 16, no. 3 (2019), 233–44; S. Axter, I. Danewid, A. Goldstein, M. Mahmoudi, C.B. Tansel and L. Wilcox, 'Colonial lives in the carceral archipelago: Rethinking the neoliberal security state', *International Political Sociology* 15, no. 3 (2021), 415–39.

65. K. Heron, 'Capitalist catastrophism and eco-apartheid', *Geoforum* 153 (2024), 103874.

66. I. Alami, J. Copley and A. Moraitis, 'The "wicked trinity" of late capitalism: Governing in an era of stagnation, surplus humanity, and environmental breakdown', *Geoforum* 153 (2024), 103691.

67. J. Wainwright and G. Mann, *Climate leviathan: A political theory of our planetary future* (London: Verso, 2017).
68. Gramsci, *Prison notebooks*, 109.
69. I. Alami and A. Dixon, 'Uneven and combined state capitalism', *Environment and Planning A: Economy and Space* 55, no. 1 (2023), 72–99.
70. The term 'private turn' is Elisa Van Waeyenberge's, see E. Van Waeyenberge, 'The private turn in development finance', *FESSUD Working Paper Series no. 140* (Leeds: Financialisation, Economy, Society and Sustainable Development Project, 2015).
71. G. Hart, 'D/developments after the meltdown', *Antipode* 41, no. s1 (2009), 117–41, p. 120.
72. The following discussion draws from N. Bernards, 'Where is finance in the financialization of development?', *Globalizations*, 21, no. 1 (2024), 88–102.
73. United Nations, *Financing for Sustainable Development Report 2021* (New York: United Nations, 2021), p. iii.
74. Ibid., 59.
75. United Nations, *Zero Draft – Addis Ababa Accord* (New York: United Nations, 2015), p. 1.
76. World Bank, *From billions to trillions: MDB contributions to financing for development* (Washington: World Bank, 2015), p. 1.
77. World Bank, *From billions to trillions: Transforming development finance* (Washington: World Bank, 2015), p. 12.
78. Ibid., 14–15.
79. G20, *Principles of MDBs' strategy for crowding-in private sector finance for growth and sustainable development* (Hamburg: G20 International Financial Architecture Working Group, 2017), p. 2.
80. World Bank, *Maximizing finance for development: Leveraging the private sector for growth and development* (Washington: World Bank, 2017); *Evolving the World Bank Group's mission, operations and resources: A roadmap* (Washington: World Bank Group, 2022).
81. A. Banga, 'The World Bank reflects our ambition', *Project Syndicate*, 13 July 2023, available at: www.project-syndicate.org/commentary/new-vision-for-world-bank-by-ajay-banga-2023-07. My emphasis.
82. See, e.g.: G. Banks and J. Overton, 'Grounding financialization: Development, inclusion, and agency', *Area* 54, no. 2 (2022), 168–75; D. Gabor, 'The Wall Street Consensus', *Development and Change* 52, no. 3 (2021): 429–52; E. Mawdsley, 'Development geography II: Financialization', *Progress in Human Geography* 42, no. 2 (2018), 264–74; Y. Dafermos, D. Gabor and J. Mitchell, 'The Wall Street Con-

sensus in pandemic times: What does it mean for climate-aligned development?', *Canadian Journal of Development Studies* 42, no. 1–2 (2021), 238–51; E. Karwowski, 'Commercial finance for development: A backdoor for globalization', *Review of African Political Economy* 49, no. 171 (2022), 161–72; F. Musthaq, 'Development finance or financial accumulation for asset managers? The perils of the global shadow banking system in developing countries', *New Political Economy* 26, no. 4 (2021), 554–73.

83. Gabor, 'Wall Street Consensus', 430.
84. Dafermos et al., 'Wall Street Consensus', 239.
85. Ibid., 239.
86. Gabor, 'Wall Street Consensus', 436.
87. See, e.g., Musthaq, 'Development finance'; T. Carroll and D. Jarvis, 'Financialisation and development in Asia under late capitalism', *Asian Studies Review* 38, no. 4 (2014), 533–43.
88. In addition to the pieces in the previous note, see J. Jafri, 'When billions meet trillions: Impact investing and shadow banking in Pakistan', *Review of International Political Economy* 26, no. 3 (2019), 520–44; K. Perry, 'The new "bond-age", climate crisis and the case for climate reparations: Unpicking the old/new colonialities of finance for development within the SDGs', *Geoforum* 126 (2021), 361–71; C. Tan, 'Audit as accountability: Technical authority and expertise in the governance of private financing for development', *Social and Legal Studies* 31, no. 1 (2022), 3–26.
89. See especially Gabor, 'Wall Street Consensus'; Defermos et al., 'Wall Street Consensus'.
90. Mawdsley, 'Development geography II', 271.
91. Dempsey and Suarez, 'Arrested development?', 655. See also J. Dempsey, *Enterprising nature: Economics, markets, and finance in global biodiversity politics* (London: Wiley, 2016).
92. S. Schindler, I. Alami and N. Jepson, 'Goodbye *Washington Confusion*, hello *Wall Street Consensus*: Contemporary state capitalism and the spatialisation of development strategy', *New Political Economy* 23, no. 2 (2023), 223–40.
93. I. Alami, A.D. Dixon and E. Mawdsley, 'State capitalism and the new d/Development regime', *Antipode* 53, no. 5 (2021), 1294–318.
94. I. Alami, C. Alves, B. Bonizzi, A. Kaltenbrunner, K. Koddenbrock, I. Kvangraven and J. Powell 'International financial subordination: A critical research agenda', *Review of International Political Economy* 30, no. 4 (2023), 1360–86.

95. See Alami, *Money power*; B. Bonizzi, C. Laskaridis and J. Griffiths, *Private lending and debt risks of low-income developing countries* (London: Overseas Development Institute, 2022); C. Bassett, 'Africa's next debt crisis: Regulatory dilemmas and radical insights', *Review of African Political Economy* 44, no. 154 (2018), 523–40.

96. See A. Kentikelenis, T.H. Stubbs and L.P. King, 'IMF conditionality and development policy space, 1985–2014', *Review of International Political Economy* 23, no. 4 (2016), 543–82.

97. K. Bayliss and E. Van Waeyenberge, 'Unpacking the public-private partnership revival', *Journal of Development Studies* 54, no. 4 (2018), 577–93, p. 581.

98. A. Edgecliffe-Johnson, 'Business can stop the ESG backlash by proving it's making a difference', *Financial Times*, 23 August 2021, available at: www.ft.com/content/2e77a83b-bf88-4efb-8294-31db74db03c5.

99. USAID, *Mobilizing finance for development: A comprehensive introduction* (Washington: USAID, 2019), p. 5.

100. World Bank, *Investing in urban resilience: Protecting and promoting development in a changing world* (Washington: World Bank, 2015), p. 57; discussed in P. Bigger and S. Webber, 'Green structural adjustment in the World Bank's resilient city', *Annals of the American Association of Geographers* 111, no. 1 (2021), 36–51.

101. OECD, *Sector financing in the SDG era: The development dimension* (Paris: OECD, 2018), 27.

102. Bigger and Webber, 'Green structural adjustment', 37, emphasis added.

103. Ibid., 47–8.

104. Alami, *Money power*.

105. OECD, *Climate finance provided and mobilized by developed countries – aggregate trends updated with 2019 data* (Paris: OECD, 2021).

106. J. Fichtner and E. Heemskerk, 'The new permanent universal owners: Index funds, patient capital, and the distinction between feeble and forceful stewardship', *Economy and Society* 49, no. 4 (2021), 493–515.

107. A. Buller and B. Braun, *Under new management: Share ownership and the rise of UK asset manager capitalism* (London: Common Wealth, 2021). The figure for BlackRock is now over US$10 trillion, see Table 5.2.

108. See Alami et al., 'State capitalism'.

109. W. Louch, 'BlackRock's new climate finance vehicle draws $673 million', *Bloomberg*, 2 November 2021, available at: www.

bloomberg.com/news/articles/2021-11-02/blackrock-says-new-climate-finance-vehicle-draws-673-million.

110. BlackRock, *Investing with purpose: BlackRock 2021 Annual Report* (New York: Blackrock, Inc., 2022), p. 9.

111. Based on information available from BlackRock here, as of September 2022: www.blackrock.com/uk/products/product-list.

112. See L. Adkins, M. Cooper and M. Konings, 'Class in the twenty-first century: Asset inflation and the new logic of inequality', *Environment and Planning A: Economy and Space* 53, no. 3 (2021), 548–72; P. Langley, 'Assets and assetization in financialized capitalism', *Review of International Political Economy* 28, no. 3 (2021), 382–93.

113. BlackRock, *2021 Annual Report*, 2.

CHAPTER 6

1. A. Gramsci, *Selections from the prison notebooks*, Q. Hoare and G. Nowell Smith, eds. and trans. (New York: International Publishers, 1971), p. 235.

2. R. Hilferding, *Finance capital: A study of the latest phase of capitalist development* (London: Routledge, 1981), p. 367.

3. Ibid., 367.

4. Ibid., 367.

5. C. Harman, 'On William Smaldone's *Rudolf Hilferding: The tragedy of a German Social Democrat* and F. Peter Wagner's *Rudolf Hilferding: The theory and politics of democratic socialism*', *Historical Materialism* 12, no. 3 (2004), 315–31, p. 322.

6. Ibid., 331.

7. K. Marx, *The class struggles in France: 1848 to 1850* (Moscow: Progress Publishers, 1960).

8. Stefan Eich, *The currency of politics: The political theory of money from Aristotle to Keynes* (Princeton: Princeton University Press, 2022).

9. C. Lapavitsas, *Profiting without producing: How finance exploits us all* (London: Verso, 2013), p. 307.

10. This latter argument is forcefully made in T. Marois, 'A dynamic theory of public banks (and why it matters)', *Review of Political Economy* 34, no. 2 (2022), 356–71.

11. Lapavitsas, *Profiting*, 307.

12. Ibid., 327.

13. Robert J. Shiller, *The new financial order: Risk in the 21st Century* (Princeton: Princeton University Press, 2003), p. 2.

14. Robert J. Shiller, *Finance and the good society* (Princeton: Princeton University Press, 2012).

15. Ibid., 5.

16. Karl Marx, quoted in ibid., 5. See also Karl Marx, *Capital, Vol. 1* (New York: Penguin, 1990), pp. 874–6.

17. Shiller, *Finance and the good society*, 5.

18. Ibid., 5.

19. For a critique, see N. Bernards, 'Can technology democratize finance?', *Ethics and International Affairs* 37, no. 1 (2023), 81–95.

20. Fred Block, 'The meaning of financial democracy', introduction to Fred Block and Robert Hockett, eds., *Democratizing Finance: Restructuring Credit to Transform Society* (London: Verso), pp. 1–20.

21. Ibid., 14.

22. Michael A. McCarthy, 'Three modes of democratic participation in finance', in Fred Block and Robert Hockett, eds., *Democratizing finance: Restructuring credit to transform society* (London: Verso), pp. 159–86.

23. Ibid., 179.

24. Eich, *The currency of politics*, 219.

25. Debt Collective, *Can't pay won't pay: The case for economic disobedience and debt abolition* (Chicago: Haymarket Books, 2020), pp. 133–4.

26. D. Bryan and M. Rafferty, *Risking together: How finance is dominating everyday life in Australia* (Sydney: Sydney University Press, 2018).

27. J. Montgomerie and D. Tepe-Belfrage, 'Caring for debts: How the household economy exposes the limits of financialization', *Critical Sociology* 43, no. 4–5 (2017), 653–68.

28. K. Marx, *Capital, Vol. 3* (London: Penguin, 1991), p. 516.

29. C. Durand, *Fictitious capital: How finance is appropriating our future* (London: Verso, 2018), p. 62.

30. See M.A. McCarthy and M.H. Desan, 'The problem of class abstractionism', *Sociological Theory* 41, no. 4 (2023), 3–26.

31. Gramsci, *Prison notebooks*, 180–5.

32. S. Hall, 'Race, articulation, and societies structured in domination', in *Sociological Theories: Race and Colonialism* (Paris: UNESCO, 1980), pp. 305–43.

33. See N. Bernards, *The global governance of precarity: The politics of irregular work* (London: Routledge, 2018).

34. A. Mezzadri, 'A value theory of inclusion: Informal labour, the homeworker, and the social reproduction of value', *Antipode* 53, no. 4 (2021), 1186–205, p. 1194.
35. Marx, *Capital, Vol. 1*, 818.
36. S. Mau, *Mute compulsion: A Marxist theory of the economic power of capital* (London: Verso, 2023).
37. D. Bryan and M. Rafferty, 'Deriving capital's (and labour's) future', *Socialist Register* 47 (2011), 198–223, p. 218.

Index

Thanks to our Patreon subscriber:

Ciaran Kane

Who has shown generosity and comradeship in support of our publishing.

The Pluto Press Newsletter

Hello friend of Pluto!

Want to stay on top of the best radical books
we publish?

Then sign up to be the first to hear about our
new books, as well as special events,
podcasts and videos.

You'll also get 50% off your first order with us
when you sign up.

Come and join us!

Go to bit.ly/PlutoNewsletter